the small tigers of shergarh

Ranjit Lal was born in Kolkata in 1955, and educated in Mumbai, graduating in Economics and Sociology. As a freelance writer and columnist, he has over a thousand articles, short stories, features and photo-features published in over fifty newspapers and magazines in India and abroad. He has special interest in areas like natural history, photography, humour, satire and automobiles, on which he writes for both adults and children. He is one of the few Indian journalists to write satire and humour on a sustained basis.

He has authored several books including *The Crow Chronicles, The Life and Times of Altu Faltu, That Summer at Kalagarh, The Bossman Adventures, Enjoying Birds, Birds of Delhi, Birds from My Window, The Caterpillar Who Went on a Diet and Other Stories* and *When Banshee Kissed Bimbo.* Ranjit Lal lives in Delhi.

OTHER INDIAINK TITLES :

A.N.D. Haksar	*Madhav & Kama: A Love Story from Ancient India*
Boman Desai	*Servant, Master, Mistress*
C.P. Surendran	*An Iron Harvest*
I. Allan Sealy	*The Everest Hotel*
I. Allan Sealy	*Trotternama*
Indrajit Hazra	*The Garden of Earthly Delights*
Jaspreet Singh	*17 Tomatoes: Tales from Kashmir*
Kalpana Swaminathan	*The Page 3 Murders*
Madhavan Kutty	*The Village Before Time*
Pankaj Mishra	*The Romantics*
Paro Anand	*I'm Not Butter Chicken*
Paro Anand	*Wingless*
Paro Anand	*No Guns at My Son's Funeral*
Ramchandra Gandhi	*Muniya's Light: A Narrative of Truth and Myth*
Ranjit Lal	*The Life &Times of Altu-Faltu*
Rashme Sehgal	*Hacks and Headlines*
Raza Mir & Ali Husain Mir	*Anthems of Resistance: A Celebration of Progressive Urdu Poetry*
Sharmistha Mohanty	*New Life*
Shree Ghatage	*Brahma's Dream*
Susan Visvanathan	*Something Barely Remembered*
Susan Visvanathan	*The Visiting Moon*
Tom Alter	*The Longest Race*

FORTHCOMING TITLES :

Anjana Basu	*Black Tongue*
Jawahara Saidullah	*The Burden of Foreknowledge*
Selina Sen	*A Mirror Greens in Spring*

the small tigers of shergarh

RANJIT LAL

IndiaInk

First published in 2006
IndiaInk
An imprint of
Roli Books Pvt. Ltd.
M-75, G.K. II Market
New Delhi 110 048
Phones: ++91 (011) 2921 2271, 2921 2782
2921 0886, Fax: ++91 (011) 2921 7185
E-mail: roli@vsnl.com; Website: rolibooks.com
Also at
Bangalore, Mumbai, Varanasi, Agra, Jaipur

Cover Design: Arati Subramanyam
Page Layout: Kulvinder Singh

ISBN: 81-86939-28-8

Typeset in Fairfield LH Light by Roli Books Pvt. Ltd. and
Printed at Anubha Printers, Noida

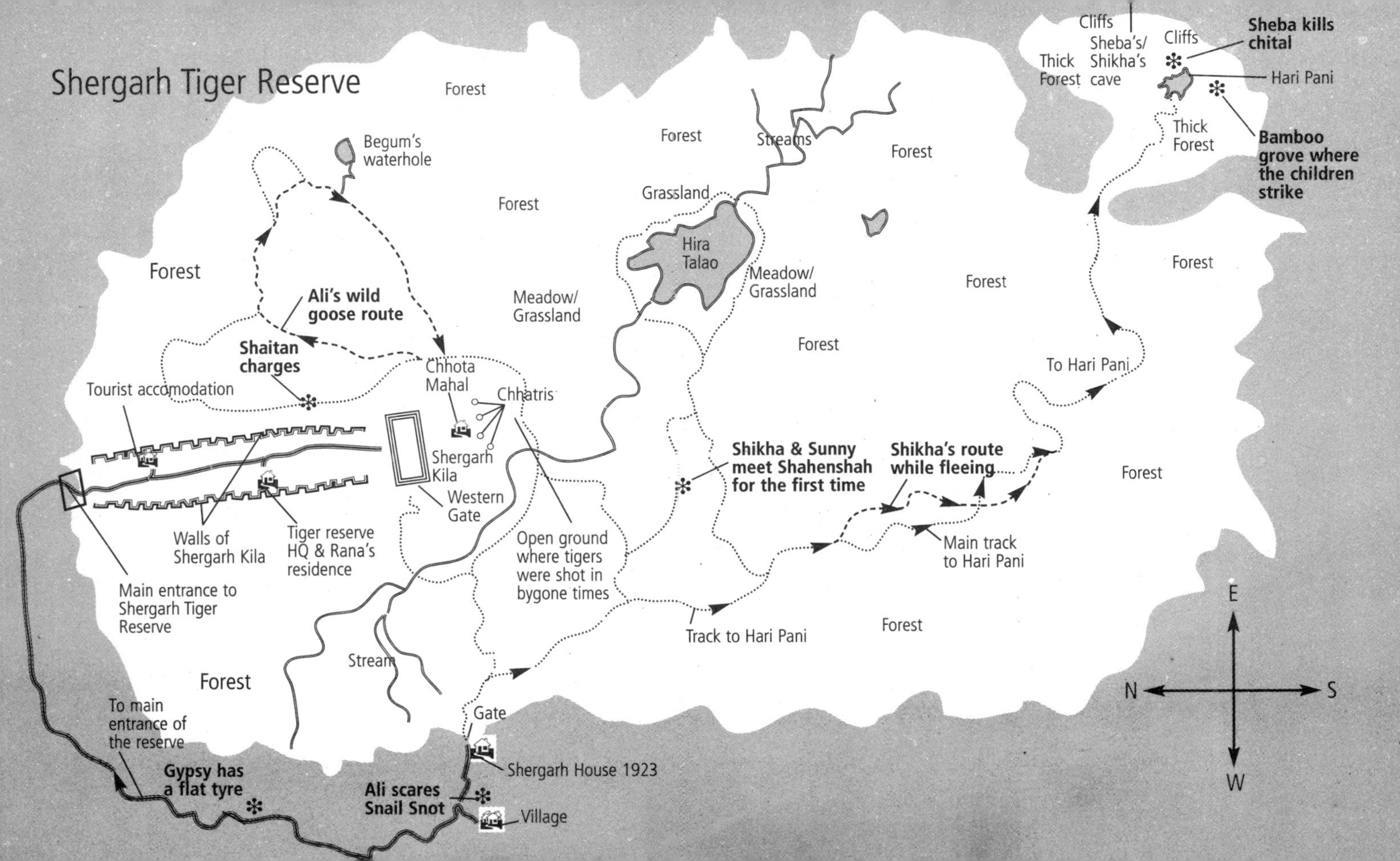

Shergarh Tiger Reserve
Forest
Begum's waterhole
Forest
Forest
Ali's wild goose route
Shaitan charges
Tourist accomodation
Meadow/ Grassland
Chhota Mahal
Chhatris
Shergarh Kila
Western Gate
Walls of Shergarh Kila
Tiger reserve HQ & Rana's residence
Main entrance to Shergarh Tiger Reserve
Open ground where tigers were shot in bygone times
Forest
Stream
To main entrance of the reserve
Gypsy has a flat tyre
Gate
Shergarh House 1923
Ali scares Snail Snot
Village
Forest
Streams
Grassland
Hira Talao
Meadow/ Grassland
Forest
Shikha & Sunny meet Shahenshah for the first time
Track to Hari Pani
Forest
Shikha's route while fleeing
Main track to Hari Pani
Forest
To Hari Pani
Forest
Forest
Cliffs
Thick Forest
Sheba's/ Shikha's cave
Cliffs
Sheba kills chital
Hari Pani
Thick Forest
Bamboo grove where the children strike
Forest
E
N
S
W

1

IF ONLY THE TERRIBLE SCREECHING AND WHANGING WOULD stop echoing inside her head, Shikha thought, she might have some peace. Sometimes, it did disappear, but then always returned like some hideous and malicious banshee, especially when she lay down to sleep. At least now, the rhythmic clickety-clack of the train's wheels drowned the sound, which was some relief. At her side, curled tightly like a pangolin, her small dark brother, Sunny slept, his long curving eyelashes fluttering slightly. On the berth across, Binoy chacha too had just woken up, his beard and hair all awry, making him look like a wild man from the woods. He glanced at her out of his intense hooded eyes and nodded, before feeling around in his kurta pocket for the first of the day's filthy beedis that he smoked all the time.

'Did you sleep well?' he asked briefly, puffing with deep contentment, filling the compartment with the sharp reek of beedi. Shikha nodded.

'Yes, chacha,' she replied, giving him a small smile.

It wasn't returned. Binoy chacha had put on his rimless spectacles and was getting to his feet.

'Is the sound bothering you?' he asked.

'It comes and goes,' Shikha admitted, shrugging as if it were no big deal.

'Don't worry about it,' he said briefly. 'You know what the doctor said … it will gradually disappear.'

'Yes, chacha,' she said, and glanced at her little brother.

Her uncle slid the door open and disappeared into the corridor, carrying his toilet bag with him. Shikha sighed, and looked out of the window. The sun was just lifting itself over the rim of the flat horizon, turning the scrubby desert-like countryside to gold. There were no proper trees, just thorn bushes and scrub, and sometimes a defiant acacia, all crooked and twisted by the harsh environment, being attacked by rangy looking goats. Occasionally, a few straight-backed women in flower bright ghagras – scarlet, pink, flame orange, yellow and magenta – filed past on a dusty path, carrying brass water pots, four storeys high, and never spilling a drop. A chocolate brown baby camel gambolled after its snooty looking mother, kicking its legs out this way and that, and Shikha wished Sunny could see that. The little boy stirred restlessly in his sleep, and then opened his eyes. At once, his hand reached out and he gripped his sister's hand tightly, looking up at her, his big black eyes fixed on her face, but still frighteningly blank.

'Hi, Sunny!' Shikha said, wriggling an eyebrow. No smile, no sign of recognition, except that the grip on her hand tightened. 'Come on now get up. We'll go to the bathroom and get washed up. We should be arriving soon.' He nodded seriously and sat up, his dark curly hair all tousled around his head but said nothing.

'Hiya there babydolldimplechick, how're you doin?' That had been his appalling way of greeting her delivered in a ghastly Yankee drawl that he had picked up thanks to a recent passion for old American gangster movies. To be called

'babydolldimplechick' in front of all your friends by a precocious baby brother who barely reached your belly button while on tiptoe had not been amusing. But now ... now he hadn't said that for a whole month, what a relief, in fact he hadn't said a single word at all, and that was just beginning to bother Shikha a little bit now. From incessant chatterbox to gupchup frightened rabbit – it was too much really.

'He is in total shock,' the doctors had said, wondering by what miracle these children had emerged outwardly virtually unscathed from the mangled wreck that had been their parents' car. In order to avoid a headlong crash with a bus, their father had swerved to the left, the wheels on that side had hit a pile of earth and the car had flipped over, travelling and spinning a considerable distance on its roof emitting a shower of sparks as it swivelled and slid crazily all over the road at 70 kmph, shrieking protestingly before finally coming to a rest in a ditch. In the back, Shikha and Sunny had been asleep. Sunny was thrown squarely into Shikha's lap as the car went over, and instinctively her arms had locked tightly around him, holding on to him for dear life. When there was silence and stillness once again, she opened her eyes and found herself staring at the big gaping hole where the rear windshield had been. Clutching Sunny, she wriggled out on her back, got shakily to her feet, hoisted him on to her shoulder and staggered out on the road. Already, her father's colleagues who had been travelling with them in their car were racing towards the wreckage. She had thrust Sunny at them and collapsed – into a frightening coma that had lasted several weeks. She had awoken at last in a hospital bed to find herself staring at the gaunt, somewhat scary (and very hairy!) face of Binoy chacha, who told her that mama and papa had gone off on a journey and would return after a long, long time.

'You mean they are dead?' she whispered, her face going white, and feeling dizzy and faint, her heart feeling as though it had jumped off Mount Everest straight into the Marianas Trench, the deepest, darkest abyss in the world.

He nodded.

'Where's Sunny?' she asked in panic sitting up, suddenly remembering carrying him out of the car, as the screeching rose up inside her head again like a shrieking banshee.

'He's all right,' her uncle said. 'The nurses are looking after him well!'

'Is he hurt? Can I see him?'

'Um … he's not hurt. But he's not well either. He hasn't spoken since the accident.'

When they had taken her to see him, the little five year old had been tossing and turning restlessly in a cot. They had had to tie his small chubby arms and legs to the bed with soft cloth for several weeks, because he banged them about so hard he hurt himself. He saw her and leapt at her, and ever since had clung to her like a limpet. In two seconds she knew that something was dreadfully wrong with him.

Because two seconds stretched to five, to a minute, to two minutes, to ten – and Sunny had not said a word to her. He just clung to her like a baby orangutan.

'What's wrong with him?' she asked. 'Why doesn't he say something?'

'He's got some sort of amnesia,' Binoy chacha said. 'You know when you forget who you are … he hasn't forgotten that because he's recognized you, but he's forgotten how to talk.'

'It's best the children remain together,' the doctors had told Binoy chacha, 'until at least they get over the shock. You see now they only have each other.'

'How long will that take?' Binoy chacha asked, wondering

what the hell was he to do with the two orphaned children who had suddenly been thrust upon him. He was their only living relative, so he just had to take them.

'There's no way of saying for sure,' the doctor had replied. 'The girl may be all right in a few months, once she finds her feet again. But the little boy has had a very bad fright and shock. Some sort of switch in his brain has tripped, and turned off his power of speech. Probably due to fear … And both have suffered some concussion. It might take him a year or more to become normal …' The doctor shrugged. 'Hopefully I'm wrong,' he added, 'and it should be sooner. Otherwise nothing seems to be wrong with them.'

'Is there any treatment?' Binoy chacha asked, getting increasingly alarmed. Really, the last thing he wanted was to be saddled with two in-shock kids to look after. How would he deal with their tantrums and moods?

The doctor smiled. 'For really specialized treatment you'll have to take them abroad and be there for a very long time,' he said. 'The best thing that I can suggest is to take them home, give them as normal a life as possible and let time do the healing. They're children and so very resilient. Give them six months at least, if you see no change then we'll take it from there.'

'Very well, doctor,' said Binoy chacha heavily. 'I really don't know though. I live in the back of beyond you know, and hardly meet anyone at all.'

'You have no children of your own?' the doctor inquired.

'Never married, no kids,' replied the children's uncle shortly. 'I paint,' he explained as if that were a good enough reason.

In the hospital, Shikha had tried to remember what papa had said about Binoy chacha. How he had been the rebel in the family and had more or less broken away years and years ago, and had stormed off to wild places to paint. He hadn't become very famous (or rich) either, papa had said rather unkindly, and only just managed to make a living. Well, soon they would find out what sort of a living, she thought, not knowing that there would be plenty of money because she and Sunny had inherited the fortune their father had made in his business.

'Come on, Sunny,' Shikha now said, leading the way through the narrow rocking corridor to the tiny bathroom. Thankfully, the train was slowing down as it approached a station. The noise in the bathroom would lessen and maybe, just maybe Sunny would agree to sit on the potty.

A little later (Sunny had sat on the potty successfully!) well-spruced up, the children returned to their compartment just as the attendant brought them steaming hot flasks of tea and grinned at them.

'Milk for him please,' Shikha requested primly.

'Yes, missy,' the attendant said and went off to fetch some.

Binoy chacha was staring out of the window and slurping his tea noisily and clutching on to yet another beedi. Shikha stared at him for a moment, and missed her parents terribly. Had they been here now, there would have been shrieks and screams and gales of laughter, for papa had been a great one for horsing around first thing in the morning, and mama would have been brushing out the tangles in her thick brown hair. And here, all Binoy chacha could do was smoke his stinky beedis one after the other and stare out of the window. She felt the tears prick her eyes and gulped hard. Briskly she opened her little overnight bag and took out her mother's pink enamel hairbrush and began combing out her thick brown hair. She was tall for a fourteen year old, made slim and dusky by swimming and now with sad heavy almond brown eyes in a face that always appeared to be smiling, even when it was not, her cheeks dented with two great dimples.

'How much longer to go, Binoy chacha?' Shikha asked at last, hurriedly wiping a tear that had scuttled down her cheek. He glanced at her, startled, as if aware of the children's presence for the first time.

'Another hour or so before we reach Shergarh station,' he said, glancing at his watch. 'And then we drive for two hours before we reach the house.'

Shergarh station was a tiny faded pink structure with a corrugated iron roof to protect travellers from the blistering desert heat. As the train drew up, Shikha saw that there was hardly anyone on the platform, and the few people she did see didn't appear very friendly. Why did their uncle have to live in this godforsaken little place, she thought bitterly, thinking again of her parents and the friends she had left behind in Delhi. And why did they have to come here and live with him? (But it had been very difficult going back to the house in Delhi too, she knew, now that mama and papa were no longer there. It no longer felt like home.)

A brace of fierce-looking coolies leapt on board like wolves and pounced on their luggage even before the train had halted. Sunny shrank back and clutched Shikha tightly.

Binoy chacha ignored them completely and followed them out into the blazing sunlight. Shikha jumped down on to the platform and looked around. A few tall swarthy men in white, orange or bright yellow turbans squatted in secretive groups on the platform, staring at them out of curious eyes, one or two bubbling over a hookah. Some had guns slung casually over their shoulders. Binoy chacha strode ahead nodding briefly, towards the taxi stand outside, where a gaggle of taxi drivers waited, ready to pounce and drag them to their tinpot vehicles. But a dusty green Gypsy was already waiting for them, with their luggage installed. A small gnome-like man in a faded khaki kurta-pyjama jumped from the driver's seat and greeted Binoy chacha.

'Salaam sahib,' he said, his wispy beard wagging on his chin like a sunbird's nest in the breeze, and touching his forehead with his fingers. He looked keenly at the two children, and smiled at them. His teeth, pan-stained and crooked, made him look even more gnome-like, as did his slightly hunched back.

Binoy chacha climbed into the front seat, indicating that the children get into the back.

'This is Aslambhai,' he said by way of introduction. 'He drives, and er ... looks after things, and his wife, Sharifa, cleans and cooks. She will take care of you.'

'Salaam baby, salaam sahib,' Aslambhai said, twisting around in his seat and giving them a wide happy grin and brisk salute.

'Salaam,' mumbled Shikha shyly, but thinking at least he seemed more friendly than Binoy chacha.

They drove through the same arid countryside that the train had passed through, over bumpy, dusty roads, passing through dun-coloured hamlets and flocks of ragged looking sheep and camels and goats. Then, to the left hills appeared, and the bushes and trees began looking bigger and happier and greener, though most of them had been horribly lopped and disfigured. (Like people whose arms and legs had been cut off, Shikha thought with a shudder.) Soon they were driving alongside a chain of ragged looking hills, red and raw in places, and covered with dusky scrub jungle in others. Large birds of prey wheeled and screamed against a blue sky, shimmering in the heat, and occasionally the Gypsy sped past the horribly laughing skeleton of some poor cow or buffalo that had just lain down there and died. Then, a military green Gypsy approaching from the other side flashed its headlights and drew up alongside. It had

'Shergarh Tiger Reserve' painted on the door, and a burly moustachioed man leaned out from the passenger seat greeted Binoy chacha with a jovial shout.

'Oye Binoy! Welcome back!' he yelled, doffing his hat. 'You have brought the children back with you?'

'Hello Rana, yes, they're here,' said Binoy chacha a little sourly, shrugging his shoulders.

'Hello kids!' Rana boomed, sticking his head through the window. 'Welcome to Shergarh! I'm sure you must be looking forward to living next to a tiger reserve and national park, eh?'

Shikha just nodded blankly and smiled, as poor Sunny shrank back and put his head into her lap. But her heart sank, and sank deep! A tiger reserve? Was that where they were going to live? Rana was looking at little Sunny, a little puzzled.

'He can't talk,' Binoy chacha explained. 'He's been silent ever since the crash.'

Even Rana's natural bounciness seemed to be a little deflated.

'Oh,' he said, taken aback and removed his face from the window. Then, regaining a bit of his boom, 'Well, as long as you have Aslambhai with you, you have permission to drive about anywhere in Shergarh,' he said to Shikha genially, and got into his own vehicle and roared off.

Soon after they left the 'main' road and got on to an even more bumpy and dusty one that led towards the rugged hills. Gradually they entered thin thorn forest, which became thicker and denser as the car began climbing. Flights of screaming parakeets streaked past and the air became cooler.

'Langur!' exclaimed Aslambhai, slowing the Gypsy down and pointing out of his window, at the edge of the road. Shikha peered and at first couldn't see anything, but then spotted the lanky silver-haired black-faced monkeys as they sat (just like the men at the station, she thought) and stared at the Gypsy.

'Look! There they are,' she said pointing them out for Sunny, who just stared wordlessly out of the window. Binoy chacha merely grunted.

'Bahut badmash hai! Baksheesh mangta hai! They're very mischievous! They want baksheesh!' said Aslambhai grinning at the children. Actually they looked as if they were waiting for a bus, thought Shikha.

'Binoy chacha, where exactly is your house? Will we be staying inside the tiger reserve?' Shikha asked.

'It's illegal to live inside a national park,' Binoy chacha said in a tone that implied she should have known that. 'I live just on the border of the park. Shergarh lies just over these hills in a large valley, which has a ridge running through it. We get a beautiful view of the park. You'll see when we get there.'

'Er … do tigers and leopards come near the house?' Shikha asked tentatively.

'Tigers prefer staying inside, but leopards do roam nearby sometimes looking for dogs. So you can't walk about wherever you like alone, especially in the evening.'

'Oh!' Poor Shikha didn't like the sound of that one bit.

The Gypsy was climbing seriously now, going up steep hairpin bends, a cloud of white dust ballooning behind it, and lurching over the rutted road. At last they seemed to have reached the top, for the road levelled out.

'How much further, chacha?' Shikha asked, her eyes on Sunny who had a rather fixed look on his face. She hoped he was not about to be sick; it would be just too embarrassing.

'Nearly there,' grunted her uncle, looking straight ahead.

Five minutes later, Aslambhai turned right, into the gates of 'Shergarh House 1923' and pulled up in the porch of a whitewashed flat-roofed house with dark green bordered windows. A verandah ran around the perimeter of the house, groaning under the weight of massive magenta bougainvillea that grew up alongside the supporting pillars. A small, bird-like woman with sharp darting eyes and spiderweb grey hair scuttled out of the front door as the Gypsy drew up.

'Salaam sahib,' she said to Binoy chacha. 'Baba, baby theek hai?' She peered inside the car, a wide toothy smile on her face. Her face has so many lines and wrinkles, Shikha thought as she got down, it is like a walnut. Sunny followed close behind her, clutching at her again. But the little woman's eyes crinkled up pleasantly when she smiled.

'Sharifa will look after you,' Binoy chacha said, striding inside, as Aslambhai struggled to get the luggage out of the jeep.

'Arre, abhi to heart attack se theek hua, aur bhari samaan utha raha hai, pagal hai kya? – You've just recovered from a heart attack and are now lifting heavy luggage, are you mad?' Sharifa shrilled at her husband, her eyes flashing, and making a grab for the bags.

Inside it was dim and cool, the walls washed pink by the light filtering through the magenta bougainvillea. Shikha and Sunny stood in the lobby of their new home and looked around. As you entered, there was a wrought iron spiral staircase to the left, probably going up to the terrace, and also the door to a room into which Binoy chacha had disappeared. To the right was the dining room, where on a table three stainless steel glasses and a jug of cold nimbu-pani stood. Sharifa poured the cool refreshing drink out, which Shikha gulped gratefully, suddenly realizing how dry her lips and mouth were. Sunny clutched at his glass and sipped it suspiciously. In front another open door led to the sitting room, which was lined from top to bottom with bookshelves. Shikha was relieved to see a TV set crouching in one dark corner. At least they would be able to watch TV here!

'The TV transmission is out of order most of the time,' Binoy chacha said, as if reading her mind. 'Also the electricity here is pretty erratic.'

Sharifa had scuttled mouse-like into the kitchen, which lay beyond the dining room and emerged with a bowl of fruit.

'Er ... Binoy chacha where do we sleep?' Shikha asked tentatively, looking around.

'In the patio at the back,' her uncle replied. 'I've had it converted into a bedroom. I'm afraid it is a little rough and ready at the moment, but there was no time to make proper arrangements. I had to rush out after hearing about what had happened.'

As if it were our fault, Shikha thought, the tears quick to prick her eyes. She followed her uncle through the living room, which led into the patio beyond. Shikha gasped. The room was huge! It ran right across the entire breadth of the house.

'Theek hai sahib, hum baby ko dikhayega – it's all right, sir, I'll show the baby around,' Sharifa said, bustling past them and taking Shikha by the hand. 'Aao – come!' she said perkily.

There was a huge wooden four-poster bed on one side of the room with a mosquito net, a small bedside table and a tall slightly lopsided cupboard in one corner. There was also a large old tea planter's chair – the kind you could almost lie down in and rest your legs on the arms that swung out of its sides. But what caught Shikha's attention immediately was the view. It appeared that the house was built at the edge of a slope; beyond the verandah a rather scraggly garden banked steeply downward to the edge of a cliff. And far away in the middle distance, another rugged rocky ridge ran across the horizon. A ridge guarded with massive crenellated walls that ended in a formidable looking fort that squatted proudly at its very spur.

'Wow!' Shikha whispered in awe. 'Just look at that fort, Sunny!' She walked out into the verandah for a better look.

'Shergarh Kila!' announced Sharifa proudly, as if it were hers. 'Aur uske niche, Chhota Mahal – and just below it, the Chhota Mahal.' Sure enough, halfway down the almost sheer cliff face on a broad ledge, a graceful pale cream-coloured palace with umbrella-like roofs sprawled elegantly in the sun.

'Pehle raja, rani rehte the, ab vaha sher ghoomte hai – earlier kings and queens used to stay there, now tigers roam there!' she explained. 'I will tell you a lot of stories about that place!' she promised, as a soft cool breeze fanned Shikha's cheek. Suddenly she wished so much that mama and papa could have been here to share the view with her. But Sharifa's sharp eyes were on Sunny.

'Bathroom idhar hai – the bathroom is here,' she said shrewdly, going back into the room and opening a door. It was also huge, and a truly gigantic cream-coloured enamel bathtub squatted regally in one corner. Fresh towels had been hung on the towel rail, and there was soap in the soap dishes. Well at least someone had made them feel welcome, Shikha thought, gulping hard at the lump in her throat.

After a refreshing wash up, they went out into the steep garden, to the very edge. The sun was pleasantly warm, but the breeze was springwater cool and refreshing. And once again, Shikha gasped in awe. The view was stunning.

Below them, the thickly forested hillside fell away steeply in a tangle of bush, scrub, scraggy date palms and a series of ravines, tawny, amber and beige, into the valley below. The ridge on which Shergarh Kila stood ran about halfway across their view, from north to south. To the south of the spur, the valley floor was wide and covered with more jungle, dark green in places, brown in others. In the distance, the blue waters of a lake shimmered in the midday sun, surrounded by blue-green grasslands in which Shikha could see a small herd of animals moving around. Beyond that, blue smoky hills rose up in the vanishing distance.

'That's Shergarh Tiger Reserve and National Park,' Binoy chacha said, joining them, now smelling of linseed oil and turpentine in addition to his usual beedi smell.

'It's beautiful,' Shikha said. 'This house has a beautiful view!'

'I hope your room is all right,' her uncle said. 'It may not be as luxurious as your home in Delhi was, but it's the best I can do here.'

'It's fine, chacha.' Perhaps now was the time to try and make friends with him again, she thought. 'Chacha, where do you do your painting?' she asked.

'In my studio,' he replied shortly. 'It's down there.' He pointed towards one end of the garden where steps led down the cliff. Shikha leaned forward to look. A long shed-like structure clung to the steep cliff side, huge glass windows facing the park, and with skylights in its roof.

'Oh,' she said. 'It looks like an exciting place!'

'You're not to go down there! The steps are steep and dangerous, and I don't want any accidents!'

That was a bad word to choose. Shikha paled, and clutched Sunny's warm hand tightly. If only they could rewind time like a cassette, she thought and play it again differently … and if only they had decided to stop at that dhaba instead of pressing on, they would not have met that bus …

But why did Binoy chacha always have to sound as if he blamed her for whatever had happened? She had been dozing in the back seat of the car, for heaven's sake! One thing was certain. She would go down to the studio at the first chance she got. Binoy chacha could say what he liked!

'Aslambhai will take you for a drive in the tiger reserve this evening,' Binoy chacha said, turning back to return to the house. 'There are a pair of binoculars hanging from the hatstand in the lobby. You might want to take those with you,' he added unexpectedly. 'If you're lucky you might see a tiger.'

'Thank you, Binoy chacha,' Shikha said. Inwardly she hoped they would not. It would scare the daylights out of her and Sunny was already so petrified of everything. He'd probably jump into her lap and stay there forever and where would that leave her?

'Be careful that you don't drop them,' Binoy chacha barked suddenly.

'What?'

'The binoculars! Be careful with them!'

'Yes, Binoy chacha,' she said quietly. 'I will.'

She spent the afternoon unpacking, with Sharifa's help. They had had to leave a lot of their things behind in Delhi, packed in cartons in some warehouse, to be sent for later, once they had settled down properly. Sadly she placed the photograph of her parents – smiling happily at the camera while on their Shimla holiday – on the bedside table, while on the great bed, Sunny slept curled up in his pangolin manner. Uneasily, she wondered again how he would react if they did indeed see a wild and roaring tiger in the park that evening. How she would react, for that matter; the tigers at the zoo had always seemed so menacing, as if they were biding their time and plotting about what they would do to the visitors who stared and hooted at them, once they got out. At Shergarh Tiger Reserve, the tigers were probably roaming about everywhere!

'Now rest!' commanded Sharifa firmly, as she helped Shikha put the last of her clothes into the creaking cupboard. 'You must be tired!'

Shikha lay down on the huge bed and looked out through the verandah. She could see Shergarh Fort squatting grimly on its spur, hiding its secrets behind its thick walls, and far in the distance, the reddish hills veiled in a bluish haze. It would be a lovely view to wake up to every morning, she hoped. In the room, it was greeny, dim and quiet and cool. Somewhere nearby a collared dove crooned languidly. Shikha shut her eyes. At once the horrible screeching and clanging began echoing inside her head. She tried to get it out of her mind, and drifted off to sleep. At the foot of the bed, Sharifa hunkered down, and dozed off. These poor children, she thought, they needed a lot of looking after. And Binoy sahib was completely useless – bekar as far as that was concerned!

2

SHIKHA GOT A SHOCK WHEN ASLAMBHAI REPORTED AT SHARP 4 p.m. to take them for their first drive into the reserve. For one, he had changed into camouflage drill trousers and shirt (complete with epaulettes and cap), and had slung a rifle over his shoulder. He was accompanied by an impish looking little boy in a jungle green pyjama-kurta, who seemed about twelve, and who stared at her and Sunny curiously, a shy smile lighting up his face when he caught her eye. But what really shocked her was the Gypsy. Aslambhai had removed the top completely, it was open to the sky, and all a tiger had to do was take a languid leap to join them inside it!

'Arre … are we going in that?' she asked faintly, her heart sinking.

'Hahn, ji – yes, of course!' Aslambhai said grinning. 'Chalo – come on!'

'But … but won't it be dangerous in that?' Shikha asked, clutching Sunny's hand.

Aslambhai's grin grew wider. 'Nahin baby, nothing will happen. You will be able to see much more like this.'

'Er … okay. I'll just tell chacha that we're going.'

She went inside and knocked hesitantly on her uncle's door.

'What is it?' he asked irritably.

'Binoy chacha, we're going into the reserve. But Aslambhai has removed the top off the jeep. Will it be safe?'

The door opened and her uncle stood there, yawning hugely, his hair wild about his face. In spite of herself, Shikha found a giggle bubbling up inside her, in this state Binoy chacha was probably scarier than any tiger, she thought. Honestly, he would scare away a tiger!

'Eh?' he said. 'Of course, it will be safe!' (And she could have sworn he muttered 'you silly girl!' after that under his breath.) 'Don't you know Aslambhai is the best tracker and guide in the reserve? He's worked there all his life and now is honorary wildlife warden. He only had to retire when he developed a heart problem. But he knows the jungle inside out. As for the open Gypsy, you will see much more that way – the sky, the birds, the animals, everything. You will feel much closer to the animals!' By Binoy chacha's standards, that was a very long and passionate speech indeed. 'Now, go,' he commanded and shut the door.

'Come on Sunny, let's go!' Shikha sighed resignedly. 'If we're going to be eaten by a tiger, might as well get it over with!' She turned towards the shut bedroom door, and made a face. 'And it'll serve him right if we do!' she said fiercely, and led her silent little brother out into the sunlight where their Gypsy waited.

They turned right just outside the gate and continued down the road towards the edge of the steep cliff face. Shikha sat in front, with Sunny squeezed next to her, while the impish little boy bounced about in the rear.

'What's your name?' Shikha asked, turning around. She was a naturally friendly girl and liked to know everyone around her.

'Ali,' said the boy, smiling, and looking away.

'Bahut badmash hai – he's very mischievous!' Aslambhai said affectionately. 'He's my grandson and he thinks he knows the ways of the jungle better than I do. And he likes to catch birds and animals!'

A cement gatepost stood at the edge of the slope going down into the reserve proper, with a padlocked gate barring the way. A pitted, faded signboard said, 'Shergarh Tiger Reserve: No Unauthorized Entry'. Aslambhai stopped the Gypsy, unlocked the padlock (with a key from the Gypsy's key ring), drove through, stopped again and locked the gate again. Then he put the vehicle in first gear and began descending the steep path. Alongside, scrubby trees and bushes clung to the slope at precarious angles.

Suddenly he stopped the Gypsy and pointed to the top of a scraggy looking tree, not very far away.

'Wahan dekho – look there, crested serpent eagle!' A large dark brown bird sat on the top of the tree. Shikha raised her binoculars, but couldn't find the big bird in them. She lowered them and spotted it straightaway.

'Look,' she said, pointing out the bird to Sunny. 'There! Can't you see it?' Her little brother stared in the direction of her finger, but made no sign that he had spotted the bird.

They soon reached the bottom of the valley, and were driving alongside a cool jungle stream surrounded by leafy green trees. In places, the stream slowed down in great dark rock pools and here, Aslambhai always stopped the Gypsy and looked around. At the very second such spot, there came a sudden commotion from the undergrowth. Something quite large and very determined was bulldozing itself through the undergrowth, grunting ferociously.

'Oh my God, what's that?' Shikha looked around frantically,

her face pale, as Sunny grabbed hold of her. It sounded like half a dozen charging tigers! Behind her, Ali laughed.

'Jangli sooer – wild boar!' said Aslambhai, pointing to where the bushes were being agitated. A stocky bristly gorgeously ugly creature, with small wicked eyes and curving yellowish brown tusks, emerged and looked around suspiciously. It was dark brown, almost black with a ridge of spiky hair along its back and a small tail that whisked briskly from side to side.

'Are they dangerous?' Shikha asked, and then watched with horrified fascination as the wild boar first scratched its huge bottom on a rock up and down, up and down grunting with bliss, and then, carefully lowered itself into the muddy edges of the rock pool, before collapsing on to its side. It wriggled a bit as if to find a comfortable position, then shut its little eyes in bliss.

'Hut! Hut-hut-hut!' shouted Ali from behind, and collapsed with glee as the poor boar scrambled panic-stricken to its feet, its hooves scrabbling wildly, and charged out of the pool in a welter of muddy spray to disappear into the forest.

'Badmash!' Aslambhai turned around and lightly cuffed the grinning Ali. 'Rana sahib dekhega to bandh ke yahan chor dega – if Mr Rana catches you doing this, he'll tie you up and leave you here! Now sit down quietly!'

'Uff Sunny, it's gone, you can get your head out of my lap now!' Shikha said. 'You should have seen him! That poor fellow got out so fast! Like papa when he saw the jellyfish in Goa!'

They moved on, going deeper into the jungle. It was chilly in the shade and, when Aslambhai stopped the Gypsy, quiet.

'Dekho – look,' he whispered pointing to a pond not too far off the road.

A huge brown, bristly looking deer was waist deep in the water, his chin just cleaving the surface, an expression of disdain on his face. He was stocky and muscular and had a magnificent spread of horns, which he carried with pride. (Actually he was looking a bit silly because he was so enjoying himself, and when you look magnificent and blissful at the same time, well you sometimes end up looking pretty silly!) Around him were three or four smaller deer, without horns but with huge dark eyes and cauliflower ears that kept flicking about back and forth.

'Kya hai – what are they?' whispered Shikha.

'Sambhar!' replied Aslambhai, shooting a warning look at Ali, who was fidgeting in the back seat. 'Aur wahan dekho – chital – and look there, chital!'

At the edge of the pond, six or seven smaller deer had appeared. They were a beautiful golden brown, with white spots all over their shiny coats.

'They are spotted deer, aren't they?' she asked, vaguely remembering seeing similar deer at the zoo. Aslambhai nodded.

'They really are beautiful! They look as though they've been dusted with icing sugar!'

Step by step, and looking warily all around them, the deer came to the pond, splayed their legs and began to drink. Every now and then, they would look around uneasily, and even the sambhar in the water seemed to catch their tension.

'Why are they so scared?' Shikha asked, puzzled.

'They might have caught our scent. Or there may be a tiger or leopard around. In the jungle, it pays to be cautious all the time.'

The sambhar had raised one hoof out of the water and stood poised, its tail up. The chital looked increasingly nervous. Somewhere nearby, a peacock suddenly honked like an out-of-control lorry hurtling downhill without brakes.

'Dhonk! Donk!' the sambhar let off loud bell-like sounds and splashed its hoof sharply into the water.

'My God!' squealed Shikha, her heart suddenly taking off

like a racehorse. The sambhar had splashed out of the pond in a scatter of spray, and the chital had fled, rolling their eyes in panic.

The pond was quite deserted.

'Something scared them,' said Aslambhai, darting a suspicious look at Ali, radiating innocence in the back seat.

'Don't look at me. I didn't do anything,' he protested in an injured tone.

Aslambhai grunted, and looked around. They drove on, with Aslambhai occasionally leaning out of the Gypsy to stare closely at the road.

'What are you doing?' Shikha asked. 'Have we got a puncture?'

'Nahin baby, tiger pugmark ke liye dekh raha tha! I'm looking for tiger pugmarks. Like us, they too like using the road!'

'Oh,' said Shikha.

Another Gypsy, with five prawn-pink foreign tourists in floppy hats, loaded down with cameras, trundled down the road towards them.

'Salaam Aslambhai!' the driver said, 'kuchch mila – found anything?'

'Khas nahin – nothing special.'

They drove on for a bit, and came to a broad lazy stream that ran over a bed of smooth pebbles and rocks. The Gypsy splashed through and climbed out on the other side. Ahead, the land had begun to slope upwards again, getting steeper as the ridge on which Shergarh Kila was located approached. They rounded a bend, and there, framed by a gap in the trees, it stood, now beautifully gilded by the evening sun.

'Can we drive up to the fort?' Shikha asked, looking at its thick walls and forbidding façade.

'Hahnji, bilkul – yes, of course!' said Aslambhai. 'You will get a good view of the park from the top.' He put the Gypsy in gear and they began the climb.

They entered in a very dramatic fashion through the western gate of the fort. The road passed over an ancient stone bridge that spanned a deep tangled gorge.

'Look,' Shikha told Sunny, 'this must have been where the moat once was.' Normally he would have been so excited by all this, it would have been difficult to make him sit still. Well, she thought wryly, certainly he was a bit easier to manage like this, but it would have been nicer if he had been well and sat still!

Actually, not much remained of Shergarh Kila, except its massive walls. Inside, most of it had been reduced to rubble, rooms torn asunder by massive peepul and banyan trees, whose python-like roots had split the very granite apart. But there were many mossy niches and nooks, and steps leading down into mysterious depths, through which greenery exploded upwards. And several rooms and galleries and hallways still stood intact, at various levels on the ridge face, built into the hill.

Aslambhai parked the Gypsy and got down, shouldering his gun. 'We can walk here a little bit,' he said. 'But don't wander about.' Again, he looked keenly at the ground, looking for tiger pugmarks. They walked to the south facing wall, and looked down at the park. Below them stood the lovely Chhota Mahal, with its graceful roofs and chhatris and in the distance at the bottom of the valley, the lake sparkled blue and spangled.

'Can we go down to the Chhota Mahal?' Shikha asked, glancing with a shudder at the huge rusty cannon that still threatened all comers from the walls of the fort. She glanced at Sunny again, but the little boy just stood by her side, his little hand clutching hers. By now he should have been swarming all over the cannon, making a hideous amount of noise.

'Hahn – yes,' Aslambhai replied, 'but we'll have to be careful. It is a favourite spot of tigers to roam in!'

'Oh, then maybe we shouldn't go there!' Shikha said, not liking the cheeky grin Ali was giving her. He knew she was scared and was enjoying it! Well, she'd show him. 'Maybe we shouldn't disturb them,' she added.

Aslambhai snorted and jerked his chin at Ali. 'Isko laye hain, poora jungle disturb to ho gaya – we've brought him, so the whole jungle is already disturbed!' he said. Ali just grinned and leapt down the steep path like a mountain goat. Fortunately steep rock steps led down to the Chhota Mahal, and Sunny was soon jumping down these as if his life depended on it.

'Hey, be careful!' Shikha warned, but a little relieved that at least he had let go of her hand.

The Chhota Mahal too had an abandoned and derelict air about it, its open-sided rooms filled with leaf litter and twigs, its walls zigzagged with cracks. It was in a much better condition than the fort, because for some time it had actually been used as a forest resthouse, before being surrendered again to the jungle. Shikha walked up into one of the chhatris and sat down, her thoughts wandering.

How many princes and princesses had sat here, she wondered, and what had become of them? Had they all become kings and queens? How many battles had been fought here and who had won and who had lost?

'Yahan se tiger hunt dekha jaya karta tha – they used to watch tiger hunts from here,' Aslambhai said quietly, squatting on his heels beside her. He pointed to a relatively clear patch of land at the bottom of the hill, which was surrounded by forest on three sides. 'Beaters would drive the tigers through the jungle on three sides into the clearing. The elephants with the hunters on the machans would be waiting on the fourth side. The tigers would be driven towards the elephants, through the open ground and shot. Or they would tie a bait in the clearing and wait for the tiger to come.'

'How horrible,' Shikha said and shuddered.

'Dekho, dekho – see, see!' cried Ali suddenly pointing to the dust on a path nearby. 'Tiger ka pugmark!'

'Oh my God, should we get back to the Gypsy?' Shikha said, looking around, rather like the spotted deer had back at the pond. But Aslambhai had jumped down and was examining the ground where Ali was pointing.

'Badmash!' he roared suddenly. 'Khud banaya hai aur kehta hai tiger ka hai – you've made them yourself and say they are a tiger's!' But Ali, grinning gleefully, had skipped out of reach again.

The sun was just above the rim of the western ridge they had driven down, and in a few moments, it would sink behind it, plunging Shergarh Tiger Reserve into the shadows of evening, dark as a moth's wing. Now, the day's last rays lit up Shikha, sitting in the chhatri turning her hair afire and encasing her in gold from head to toe.

Glancing up at her, Aslambhai muttered in awe, 'Bilkul rajkumari lagti hai – she looks an absolute princess!' and sighed tragically. So beautiful, but orphaned! Such was life! Leaning against one of the pillars of the chhatri, with Sunny resting his head against her, Shikha gazed at the forest, a sense of peace seeping into her, like sap in a tree bark. This world was so different from the one she had known. For a brief instant, it even made her forget what had happened to mama and papa and Sunny. She gulped as she remembered and wished they could have been here. And then she gave a start and a stifled squeak. About forty metres away, stood another sandstone chhatri, quite like the one she was in. A small slight figure, in a richly embroidered cream and gold tunic, was reclining against one of the pillars, rather like she was, staring at the clearing where the hunts of the past had taken place. He wore a tasselled turban and a long sword hung from one side. One hand was gently stroking the head of an enormous tiger that was lying calmly beside him. Slowly Shikha raised her binoculars and focused them on the figure.

A pale sensitive looking face leapt into view. It was a young boy – a rajkumar, no doubt. He just sat there, gently stroking the head of his tiger. And then to her amazement, Shikha saw that there were tears running down his cheek. He was weeping. For one bizarre moment she wondered whether he too had just lost his parents in some horrible accident. She lowered the binoculars, her mouth open. Aslambhai stared at her in concern.

'Baby – theek hai – baby are you all right?' he asked anxiously. She blinked and raised her glasses again.

The chhatri was empty. The rajkumar and his tiger had gone! She swallowed and blinked. Was she going nuts?

'Chalo,' Aslambhai said decisively, 'let's go back. Bahut ho gaya – we've had enough.' She nodded. In her lap, Sunny was asleep. Shikha picked up her little brother, hitched him on her hip, and staggered towards the Gypsy.

They had been driving back in silence for about ten minutes, with Aslambhai still leaning out to look for tiger's pugmarks, when he grunted and stopped the vehicle suddenly.

'Pugmark!' he grunted.

'What?' said Shikha, waking up with a start. 'But … but we drove up that way and there was nothing!'

'Look,' said Aslambhai pointing. On the top of their tyre marks was the clear imprint of a tiger's pugmark. It was the size of a dinner plate. With a stick, Aslambhai drew a circle around it, and then again on another just down the road. 'He followed us,' he said, looking around.

'What?' Shikha squeaked, wishing they could just roar off at top speed from the spot. 'Then let's get out of here.'

'Nothing to worry about,' Aslambhai said, starting the engine and engaging gear. 'But I wish you had seen the fellow. His name is Shahenshah and he is the ruler of all Shergarh! The most magnificent tiger in the park!'

'And that chhatri you were sitting in,' piped up Ali from the backseat. Shikha could feel him grinning at her. 'That was the favourite resting spot of Sheba.'

'Sheba? Who's Sheba?' she asked turning back to see the whites of his eyes and teeth gleaming maliciously at her in the twilight.

'She's the fiercest tigress in the park. Usne to Shahenshah ko bhi kar ke dikha deya – she's even shown Shahenshah where he gets off!'

'Oh,' Shikha said, turning back to face the road.

'Ab to Sheba aap ke peeche par hi jayegee – now Sheba will definitely come after you,' the wicked little boy added gleefully. 'After all, you have claimed her throne!'

'Oye, bakwas mat kar – don't talk rubbish!' Aslambhai said warningly as they bumped along.

It was quite dark by the time they reached Shergarh House. As the Gypsy's headlights raked the driveway, a few long-winged birds darted past, swerving deftly from side to side, and emitting a strange 'chuck-chuck' sound.

'What are those?' Shikha asked, hoping they were not bats. Imagine one in your bedroom!

'They are nightjars,' explained Aslambhai, 'they keep their mouths open and fly and catch insects that way.'

Sharifa was waiting anxiously for them on the porch, and quickly carried a fast-asleep Sunny inside.

'Would you like to come for a drive tomorrow morning?'

Aslambhai asked. 'The jungle is beautiful in the early morning. We could drive to the talao. It is Shahenshah's favourite place.'

'Okay,' Shikha shrugged. 'I'll ask chacha.' Not that it seemed necessary, for there was no sign of him. He didn't seem to care when or where they came or went, she thought, gulping.

'Can you be ready by six o'clock?' Aslambhai asked.

'That early?' That devil of an Ali was grinning at her again. She shrugged. 'I suppose so. But I hope Sunny wakes up. Otherwise he'll make a fuss and tug and pull and refuse to budge!'

Normally, Sunny was the first to rise in the family (so that he could gleefully wake everyone else up at some unearthly hour) but since the accident, he'd been dropping off and waking up at all sorts of odd hours.

'Aao baby, ab naha lo – come baby, take a bath now!' Sharifa reappeared, and took her by the hand. In the dim patio-cum-bedroom Sunny slept on the great bed in his pangolin position.

'Where is Binoy chacha? Does he know that we are back?' Shikha asked, as Sharifa handed her a glass of milk.

'Pata nahin baby – painting kar raha hoga – I don't know, baby, maybe he's painting,' Sharifa replied, frowning in disapproval. She wished so much she could tell the bewakoof (idiot) that ignoring two recently orphaned children who were going to live with you was no way of making them feel at home, but felt it was not her position to do so. Maybe she could tell Joginder memsahib (Mrs Rana) that – she would not hesitate to haul Binoy sahib over the coals, serve him right. In the meanwhile at least she could make them feel at home, as much as possible.

'So how was your trip in the big bad jungle?' asked Binoy chacha, after having been hauled out of his studio by an indignant Sharifa, for dinner. He had wanted to eat in his studio but she had put her foot down.

'Sahib, baby baba table par hai! Sahib, the children are at the dining table. At least eat dinner with them,' Sharifa had told him, her beady eyes flashing.

He glanced at his niece. 'I see no tiger has eaten you,' he added a little sarcastically. (As though he were sorry it hadn't Shikha thought.)

'It was quite exciting,' Shikha said her spirits rising, nonetheless. She was dying to talk of their trip, it had been her very first jungle safari after all, and what's the fun if you can't talk to anyone about it afterwards? 'We saw a wild boar and deer and the pugmarks of … what was his name … Shahenshah. The greatest tiger in the park! And chacha, the Chhota Mahal is so beautiful. Aslambhai said they used to watch tiger hunts from there. Imagine they were so cruel they cornered the poor tiger and then shot it!' She wanted to talk so much about what she had seen, and was so happy that her uncle at last seemed ready to listen.

'People are much more cruel nowadays!' he grunted, barely glancing at her, and then going back to his food. 'They are much worse now!' And again, poor Shikha got the awful feeling as though he were blaming her for that!

'Oh,' she said quietly. She looked at Sunny, who was playing listlessly with his peas. 'Come on toodledumps, eat up your peas, now!'

It felt strange lying on that huge four-poster bed, in the huge bedroom-cum-patio that night. The windows were shut, and the curtains were drawn, so it was quite snug. It was also sharply chilly, and Shikha drew the sheet and quilt up to her chin, and tried to sleep. She could see the dim figure of Sharifa wander in and out as she settled their clothes and things. Restless, Shikha tossed and turned in her bed, unable to sleep. The whanging and clanging was back in her head, like some horrible banshee. Speaking of which, was that really a rajkumar she had seen standing in the chhatri stroking a tiger and weeping? Maybe he was there again. Perhaps she should take a look? She got out of bed and fetched the binoculars from the drawing room. Sharifa had disappeared somewhere, probably to the kitchen to eat her dinner. Carefully, Shikha unbolted the patio doors and stepped out into the icy verandah. She shivered and dragged her quilt out with her. It took a while for her eyes to get accustomed to the dark, but even in the bright starlight, she could hardly make out the burly outline of Shergarh Kila on the distant ridge. She walked into the dew-drenched garden, feeling the hem of her nightie get freezing wet in the frosty grass. From the edge of the garden, you could just make out a ghostly white shimmer of the Chhota Mahal. But even with the binoculars it was too far away and dark to make out anything else. You'd need a powerful telescope for that. Shikha sighed, and glanced upwards. And stared, frozen with wonder.

Never in her wildest dreams had she imagined that there could be so many stars. The black velvet sky shimmered with them, crammed and jampacked; sparkling, winking and twinkling everywhere, and somehow making her feel calm and secure. There must be millions and billions and trillions and zillions of them, Shikha thought. Did anyone live on them, she wondered? Even on some of them? Or maybe all the people who died and went to heaven became stars. She gave a small wry smile, after all the stars were in the heaven, so it made sense! And they seemed to be so alive, winking and twinkling all the time as though talking to each other in some strange silent language. Were mama and papa there, winking and twinkling at her from somewhere up there, even now?

'Aaooom-aaoooom-aarooom-aaargh!' From somewhere in the tiger reserve below, the call of the tiger floated up and drifted up

to Shikha. *'Aaaooom-aaaooom-aaao!'* She stood still and listened, her heart racing. Somewhere in the jungle laid out before her, Shahenshah, or was it Sheba, was calling. Like her, they sounded desperate as if they wanted someone (a tiger, of course) to talk to! But imagine being alone in the jungle in the middle of the night! Even if you were a tiger, it was sure to be scary. Yet, this was where they lived, hunted and brought up their cubs. Worse, imagine if you were a deer, and had just heard the tiger in the dark! Even just a terribly lonely tiger or tigress who just wanted to say hello and maybe talk a bit, and a little bit more!

'Chalo, baby, andar aao – come on, baby, come inside! It's very cold! You'll catch a chill!' Sharifa had appeared beside her, and gently took her elbow. And like the little rajkumar in the chhatri, Shikha found herself weeping quietly as she was led off to bed. But this time, she drifted off to sleep almost as soon as her thick brown hair bloomed out on thc pillow.

3

'SUNNY, WAKE UP! IT'S TIME FOR OUR DRIVE IN THE JUNGLE!' Shikha leaned over her sleeping little brother and shook him gently. Fingers crossed he wouldn't throw a tantrum or be cranky. Sunny opened his huge black eyes and Shikha smiled. 'Hi,' she said, 'come on, we've got to get ready. Aslambhai will be waiting for us in the Gypsy.' Sunny nodded solemnly, and yawned. Then he got out of bed and trundled off towards the huge echoing bathroom, pulling Shikha with him. In the bathroom of course, Shikha had to stand in the farthest corner, facing the wall, with her hands in front of her eyes (and occasionally holding her nose!) while Sunny went about his business. When he was all done he would simply walk up to her and solemnly take her hand. Occasionally he would forget to wash his hands, and Shikha, very particular about this, would snatch her hand away and say, 'I don't think you washed your hands, Sunny!' They had been following this routine ever since the accident, and often Shikha wondered if Sunny would ever go to the bathroom by himself again. It was tiresome but it was better than him refusing to go at all and what happened when he didn't! At any rate, he was ready very quickly this morning, and they emerged from the bathroom just as Sharifa scuttled in with two glasses of milk and some glucose biscuits. Over one shoulder, she had slung a water bottle and carried another packet of biscuits.

'Come on, have this. And take the water bottle and biscuits. It will get warm in the jungle later on, and you will get hungry.'

'Sharifa, are you coming with us?' Shikha asked, dipping her biscuit in the milk till it was soft and gooey and almost broke away and fell into the glass.

'Nahin baby, I have to give sahib his bed tea and then breakfast.'

'Oh! Er ... doesn't sahib ever go into the jungle?'

'Yes he does. Sometimes he goes for the whole day and even spends the night inside, though he is not supposed to do that.'

Sharifa accompanied them to the porch, where Aslambhai and Ali were already waiting in the Gypsy. He grinned at the children and beckoned them in.

'Salaam baby, salaam chhota sahib!' he greeted them his wispy beard wagging, and Ali as usual grinned slyly. 'Chalo, let's go. We'll go to Hira Talao today.'

'Aslambhai, I heard two tigers roaring last night,' Shikha said as they drove into the jungle.

'Hahn, baby, zaroor! Yes, miss, definitely.' The ex-tracker's eyes sparkled. 'After all there are more than twenty-five tigers in the park! You didn't get scared did you?'

'No, actually they sounded lonely. As if they wanted to talk to each other. Do tigers talk to each other, Aslambhai?'

'Hahnji, kyo nahin – yes, why not? They call out to each other, to tell each other where they are and what they've been doing, and to guard their territory.'

'Bahut baate karte hai – they talk a lot!' piped in Ali from the back seat. 'They talk about all the delicious wild boar and deer they have eaten, and about what Rana sahib ate for his dinner, and what he would taste like if they ate him and how much they should charge from the firangi tourists who come here to take their photographs. Do you know, they eat one firangi every week, and only then let them take pictures and make videos?'

Shikha laughed.

'Phir bakwas kar raha hai! Again he's talking rubbish!' Aslambhai was once again leaning out of the Gypsy and staring at the path, looking for tracks. Suddenly he stopped the Gypsy and switched off the engine.

'What is it?' Shikha whispered, looking around.

'Nothing. Just listen to the sounds of the jungle waking up.'

The chilly morning air was full of birdsong. The loudest was a cheerful musical call made by small brown birds with black heads and red bums that zipped about everywhere.

'What are those?' Shikha asked, trying in vain to catch one with her binoculars.

'Bulbul. Red-vented bulbul! Bahut hai – there are plenty here.'

'Bobo-link! Bobo-link!' Another hoarse but musical call came from nearby and two lovely cocoa brown, grey and white birds flew past, their long grey tails glittering in the sun. They perched on a bare branch near the Gypsy and looked inquisitively at them. Luckily Shikha managed to zero in on them immediately.

'They're lovely!' she exclaimed. 'But they look like crows. And as if they've put their heads in a coal bin!'

'They are tree pies. And yes, they belong to the crow family.'

'Vahan dekho! Look there! Scarlet minivets!' Ali pointed

excitedly at a branch some distance away, where at the very top, several vivid red and black birds flitted restlessly. Shikha caught them with the binoculars and gasped.

'Oh, wow! I've never seen such beautiful birds in my life!' Sunny reached for the binoculars from her, and she handed them over to him.

'Pateela! Pateela! Pateela!' The shrill metallic call made her jump. Aslambhai laughed and pointed to a rock nearby.

'Teetar! Partridge!' he explained. A rusty brown bird with a basket weave pattern on its breast, and about the size of a chicken, was standing on tiptoe and hollering away.

'Look, down the road!' Again, Ali pointed down the track. A small herd of chital was crossing it daintily, with one or two fawns, bucking and kicking in sheer high spirits.

'Look at them, Sunny!' Shikha whispered, pointing them out. 'Aren't they beautiful?'

They stared as the deer crossed the road and began to graze by the side, quite unconcerned and relaxed.

Then, from behind them and seemingly very close by, Shikha heard the low moaning call. *'Aaaon! Aaaon! Arrgh!'* She felt the hair at the back of her neck prickle and rise, and the blood rushed to her face. There was no doubt about it: the call was just like the one she had heard last night from the house. The call of a lonely (at least she thought) or worse, hungry tiger! She clutched Sunny and slowly turned around. In the back seat Ali too had turned around and was staring over the Gypsy's spare wheel at the path they had driven down. Then again, that low moaning call ... only Shikha's attention was momentarily distracted by Ali. His shoulders seemed to be trembling! Perhaps he had seen the tiger, and it had seen him and even now, was preparing to spring ...

'Aslambhai!' Shikha whispered urgently. 'Sher! Tiger!' She

fully expected the tracker to take up his gun and get ready to shoot. Ali's shoulders were now shaking real bad. And he was making strange stifled sounds as if he were crying. Aslambhai raised his eyebrows and turned around.

'Badmash!' he roared. 'Phir kar raha hai! Ek din tiger sachee kha jayega! Rascal! You're doing it again! One day a tiger will really eat you up. And then what will I tell your grandmother?' He turned Ali around. The little boy was giggling fit to bust.

'He … he made those noises?' Shikha squeaked weakly. Gleefully Ali nodded. Then he tried to look serious and made the sound again, only his giggles got in the way this time.

'Bahut log ko budhoo banaya hai – he's made a fool out of a lot of people!' Aslambhai said. 'But one day, he'll be made a fool out of!'

'Oh,' said Shikha, not knowing whether to be annoyed or to laugh. She glared at him, as he grinned cheekily back at her. Then she glanced at Sunny. He was staring fixedly through the windshield at the golden deer at the side of the road.

Aslambhai started the Gypsy and they drove on. And gradually, Shikha found herself feeling less upset and sad than she had ever since the accident and its terrible aftermath. That strange empty hollow feeling in her stomach didn't feel quite so big and hollow anymore, there was a sense of peace there in its place, as if from now on, everything would be all right.

'How much farther to the lake?' she asked Aslambhai, enjoying the feeling of the breeze in her hair.

'About half an hour, now!'

They had driven down the same road as they had the previous evening, but after crossing the stream had turned right and were now driving more or less alongside the massive ridge at the top of which Shergarh Kila stood. Shikha watched as Aslambhai's eyes darted from side to side, and occasionally heavenwards, looking for signs of wildlife. They saw plenty of sambhar and chital and some nilgai, as well as langurs whooping up in the trees, and peafowl, drifting like princes on the path and vanishing uncannily into the jungle.

Then Shikha felt Sunny tug at her arm. He fixed his big black eyes on her, and fidgeted in his seat.

'Oh God, do you want to go to the bathroom?' Shikha asked, recognizing the signs all too well. Her little brother simply nodded.

'Can we stop here a bit?' Shikha asked Aslambhai. 'Sunny wants to do susu!'

'Achcha! Okay!' Aslambhai stopped the Gypsy and got off, taking his gun. 'Chalo!' They had stopped at a point where rocks and great fountains of golden grass crowded the sides of the road. Shikha got off, and helped Sunny down.

'Okay, Sunny, fire away!' she said. 'Hurry up!'

The little boy grabbed her wrist and led her off the track between two huge fountains of golden grass. Aslambhai followed close behind, with Ali still in the Gypsy, thinking that he should have saved his tiger imitation prank for now. How they would have scampered back to the Gypsy! Sunny led the little procession through the grass and rocks out to a small path obviously used by a lot of animals, for hoof marks were everywhere. Then he turned around and stared fixedly at Aslambhai.

'Er ... Aslambhai, he wants you to go where you can't see him!' Shikha explained apologetically. Really this kid could be so embarrassing!

'Sahib sharamaa raha hai – the sahib is shy?' The old forest guard's eyes twinkled. 'Okay, I will go away! But first I will check the area.' He walked up and down the path a little way, peered into the lovely golden grass and nodded. 'Theek hai! It's okay! Then he took a step back and more or less disappeared from view of the children. But through the waving golden grass he could still see them of course – he wasn't going to let them out of his sight in the jungle! And Sunny, with those big black eyes of his, could certainly see the glint of Aslambhai's rifle barrel. The little boy ducked, and still clutching his sister's hand ran across the animal path on to the other side, and slipped behind a rock. He looked at her earnestly, his fingers on his lips.

'Okay! Okay! Now hurry up! He can't see you! He'll get worried!' she whispered conspiratorially, helping him undo his overalls. 'Okay, so I'll stand there and turn around and won't peek, I promise! Now get on with it!'

Aslambhai would surely have got worried, except that he had got hopelessly distracted. Some insect had crawled up his trouser leg and had stung him badly behind the knee and it was itching like hell. He rolled up his trouser leg and bent down to examine the spot and to see if he could remove the sting, which now had begun to burn and swell.

Shikha grinned as she heard Sunny pee into the dust, and looked through her fingers down the jungle path. The dust was fine, and silvery gold, the great plumes of grass leaping upwards on either side, bending over in great fountains, some gold, others silvery green. Bright yellow butterflies (and one gorgeous dark blue one with orange eyespots) flitted about and glittering dragonflies, in midnight blue, fire engine red and golden orange patrolled the sky like miniature First World War fighters. But mostly, there was that lovely sense of peace and tranquility and restfulness.

She felt a bump behind her. Sunny had finished his business. She turned around and glanced down at him, a little surprised. He had backed straight into her, and was staring fixedly at something on the animal track, just as it breasted a rise, a little ahead.

An absolutely huge tiger was padding down the path, his great paws puffing up little clouds of pale blonde dust as he walked towards them framed beautifully by the whispering golden-green grass fronds bending over him from either side. His fiery rufous coat, with its beautiful black flames, shone in the early morning sunlight. His great golden amber eyes stared at them gravely, and just for a second, his ears cocked interrogatively forward, like a dog whose name has been called.

'I am here, alone in this jungle, with Sunny, and there's this enormous tiger walking towards me,' Shikha thought disbelievingly, both arms clutched around her little brother. *'Is this really happening or am I dreaming? I should be screaming … mama and papa where are you?'*

Soundlessly, the tiger drew closer, his moustache of sharp white whiskers glittering in the sun, his great head steady. Slowly Shikha moved Sunny behind her, covering him with her body. (Of course, he peeped from around the side though!)

'He seems so immersed in his own thoughts,' Shikha thought unexpectedly, and surprising herself. 'Perhaps he hasn't seen us at all.'

No hope at all of that! She flinched and looked down as she saw those great amber eyes rest full on her face, as the tiger stared straight at her, but continued unperturbed down the path, his paws still puffing up small clouds of gold dust. He took care to place his rear paws exactly where his front paws had been, as he walked.

'One smack from those paws, and we'll be history!' Shikha thought, *'I just hope if he does swipe us, he'll keep his claws retracted! Mama and papa are you watching this?'*

But the great animal didn't seem to be very troubled by what he saw. (A little flattered perhaps, but that we shall never really know …) A slim, pretty girl of fourteen with dimples in her cheeks and a mane of thick brown hair, beautifully lit up by the sun, and a small curly haired boy with huge black eyes, peeping out at him …

Afraid. Well, petrified really! Also entranced. Enchanted. Spellbound. Too spellbound to scream and run. In too much awe to even panic, thank God!

When the tiger drew abreast, he was perhaps ten metres away from them, about the distance from the back of a classroom to the blackboard. They heard his rasping, woofing breath, and watched the muscles flex and ripple under his gorgeous coat, the tail swinging in time with his lordly gait. For a moment, he turned and glanced at the opposite side, where behind a clump of grass poor Aslambhai was still trying to remove the nasty black sting from the back of his knee. Then he was past them, and walking away. Just before he disappeared round a bend, he glanced briefly back towards the children, raised his tail and squirted the grass with a jet, like from a fire hose. And then he was gone.

'Oh my God!' whispered Shikha weakly, sinking to her knees, as Sunny hugged her tight. 'Sunny, did you see that! First you did susu! Then the tiger did susu! And now I have to go to the bathroom very badly too!' she giggled. 'I can hardly stand up, he's turned my knees to water!'

He was still staring in the direction the tiger had disappeared, wonderstruck.

'Baba, baby! Shikha baby!' Aslambhai had gotten rid of his sting and had appeared at the other side of the path, looking around anxiously for the children. Then he spotted them, still huddled together. He bounded over.

'Theek hai, na? You are all right? I was just here!' He thought the children had got scared, when they couldn't see him.

'Sher!' mumbled Shikha weakly, now beginning to tremble uncontrollably.

'Kya – what?' Aslambhai looked at her sharply. Something had given the girl a big fright.

'He was here. He came from over the rise and just walked past us.' She indicated the path. And added incredulously, more to herself, 'As if he were walking in Lodi Gardens.'

Aslambhai examined the track. Then he raised his head and sniffed the air, his beard jogging up and down. And now it was his turn to go pale and tremble. He looked around quickly, slipping the gun off his shoulder.

'He went that way,' Shikha said. 'But he minded his own business.'

Aslambhai squatted on his heels, breathing deeply. He lit a beedi – even though it was against the rules of the park and his doctor had forbidden it. He felt he needed it badly. The children had had a mighty narrow escape.

'You saw a tiger walk past you?' he asked, just to be sure and to give himself time to get used to the idea. There was little doubt that they had: the sharp, hot animal reek was still hanging in the air, reconfirmed by those massive fresh paw prints on the path.

'Yes. He was huge! With a massive head! But he was very polite. He didn't show us his teeth! Or growl or snarl! I would have died if he had!' Relief was pouring into Shikha. Along with it, came another strange and new feeling. That beautiful tiger had just walked past them, minding its own business. It could have easily eaten them both for breakfast. But it had just wished them good morning – in a manner of speaking of course (that interrogative look with cocked ears) and had gone on its way. As if it were on its way for its morning swim or, like papa, on his way to the golf course. Why then did people have to get after this poor animal? How could anyone point a gun at such a beautiful creature? If you left it alone, it left you alone. And how could people feel brave or great by stuffing its body, or using its skin as a rug? Surely no one could feel greater than what she was feeling at the moment: to have been able to share a private moment with a wild tiger in the jungle! It was like being alone on the road while the president or prime minister or king passed by, only the tiger was much more handsome than any of them! If only mama and papa had been here to see it. She looked up at the huge blue sky, tears on her cheek. Well, if they were up there somewhere, hopefully they had seen it.

'Come on,' said Aslambhai recovering somewhat from the shock and taking her hand. 'Let's see if we can spot the fellow,' he set off down the path the tiger had taken. They went around the bend, where the path sloped downwards, towards the road they had driven up and then across it to the other side.

'There!' exclaimed Aslambhai, whose sharp jungle eyes had caught a glimpse of fiery orange, way down in the distance just before it disappeared behind some thick grass. He looked gravely at Shikha.

'Baby, aap ne to Shahenshah se mulakaat ki – baby, you have met Shahenshah!' he said, and for a second, Shikha thought he might bow before her!

'Shahenshah? That was Shahenshah!' Just to think! The greatest tiger in the park had just walked past them. She felt honoured. She looked at Sunny. 'Hells bells Sunny bunny what do you think of that? We just met Shahenshah, the greatest tiger in the park. Just wait till we tell ma … er Binoy chacha!'

Her little brother just looked up solemnly at her, and did not say a word. But there was a faint sparkle in those coal black eyes of his that had been missing all these months.

'Bahut achcha kiya chilaya nahin – you did very well by not

screaming!' Aslambhai said, wiping his brow at the thought of what might have happened if the children had screamed and panicked. This little girl had really kept her cool. And silently he thanked Shahenshah for being the great gentleman that he was. There were other tigers in the park that were not so even-tempered or tolerant. They had been hugely lucky.

'Come on,' said Shikha, still a little wobbly in the knees. 'Let's tell that silly Ali! Making tiger noises to fool us! Hahn!'

In the Gypsy, after Ali had been duly humbled, Aslambhai turned to Shikha.

'Should we turn back, or do you want to go ahead?' he asked, thinking that the children had probably had enough for one morning.

'Let's go to the lake!' Shikha said determinedly suddenly aware of a strange feeling rising up inside her. She wanted to see more tigers, she wanted to see tigers all day, she wanted to see what they did, how they lived and hunted and brought up their cubs! And somehow she felt she had Shahenshah's permission and blessings to do so which, of course, was absolutely not the case! But then, when the greatest tiger in the place has graciously given you 'darshan' and walked past you just ten metres away, you do feel specially privileged and Shikha was right to feel that way.

They drove along the lake, where the great grinning crocodiles, or muggers, sprawled at the edges and slipped into the blue waters with barely a ripple. Her cheeks tinged with pink from the excitement of the morning, Shikha turned to Ali with a grin.

'You know,' she said. 'You smile just like them!'

And Ali grinned happily back at her.

Suddenly the mischievous little boy became all serious and

sat down low in the back seat of the Gypsy. Another Gypsy was approaching them.

'Rana sahib round le raha hain – Rana sahib is taking his rounds,' said Aslambhai, indicating the tiger reserve Gypsy that drew up beside them. Mr Rana greeted them cheerily.

'Hello children! Salaam Aslambhai, theek ho? Are you enjoying yourselves? Have you seen anything?' A trim short-haired lady (maybe thirty years old Shikha guessed) with a chubby round face and friendly eyes sat in the back seat, with three cameras slung around her neck. A huge telescope-like lens stood fixed on a tripod, pointing out of the jeep like a massive short-barrelled cannon.

'This is Dipti, my daughter,' Rana said by way of introduction. 'She takes tiger pictures in her spare time!' He turned to her. 'Dear, these are Binoy's niece and nephew.' He frowned and then turned to Shikha. 'My dear, your uncle didn't even introduce you to me yesterday,' he said.

'Trust Binoy!' the lady called Dipti snorted and then smiled kindly at the children.

'Er ... this is Sunny. He's five. And I'm Shikha!'

'Hi Sunny! Hello Shikha! So have you seen anything today?'

'Shahenshah bade ghass me ghoom raha tha! Shahenshah was roaming about in the big grass,' said Aslambhai, jabbing a finger in the direction.

'We saw him from real close!' Shikha said, unable to keep the excitement from her voice.

'Oh, yes that fellow's a big show-off. He knows there's no tiger as handsome as he is!' Rana laughed. 'But you were very lucky. Sometimes you can spend a month and not see even the tail of a tiger!'

'Lucky kids!' agreed Dipti wistfully, fiddling with her cameras. 'He's been giving me the royal runaround!'

'Okay children! Will you tell your uncle to bring you to my house this evening for tea? We haven't even welcomed you properly. And Joginder aunty wants to meet you very much!'

'Okay, uncle, I will. And thank you.'

The Gypsy drove off, and from the back seat, Ali sat up again, perkily as a bird that has just found a worm, and pulled a face at the departing vehicle.

'He and Rana sahib don't get along very well,' explained Aslambhai grinning. 'He's always making a fool out of Rana sahib's guests and the tourists. Isleye chup ho kar baith gaya – that's why he sat down quietly.'

Back home at Shergarh House an hour later, Shikha raced excitedly to her uncle's room. She had so much to tell him. What a trip it had been! But his room was empty.

'Sahib studio mein hai – sahib is in the studio,' said Sharifa laconically. Gently she took Sunny by the arm. 'Chalo, time for a bath,' she said, but the little boy dug in his heels until Shikha, with a shake of her head and sigh of resignation, accompanied him.

'Binoy chacha! Guess what we saw today?' Shikha said at the lunch table to which her uncle, smelling strongly of oil paint and turpentine, had finally been hauled by a firm Sharifa.

'What?' he asked, disinterestedly.

'Shahenshah! The tiger!'

'Very nice,' her uncle said, attacking his food.

'He was so huge and beautiful! We were so scared, but he didn't do anything to us. He just walked past us. Like he was big boss.' She wanted to talk and talk and talk about what they had seen and felt that morning.

'Hmm … very nice,' her uncle repeated, seemingly more interested in his sukhe aloo than in their encounter with Shahenshah.

He doesn't care, Shikha thought, appalled, the tears again quick to rise. He doesn't care about us, about what we see or don't, about how we might feel or not. He just doesn't care. He's all shut up. I wish mama and papa were here! She lowered her eyes to hide the tears.

'And chacha, Rana uncle has asked us for tea this evening at his house. We met him and his daughter Dipti by the lake,' she added in as matter-of-fact a voice as she could.

'I don't know whether I can come,' he said shortly, looking up. 'But Aslambhai will take you anyway.' He pushed away his plate and stood up. 'Get some rest in the afternoon. I don't want you falling sick.'

'Okay, chacha.'

What a beast he was, Shikha thought, bitterly. Any day Shahenshah had better manners than he had. She thought again of the great tiger they had seen that morning, padding down that golden jungle path and felt her heart lift inside her.

4

THAT AFTERNOON SHIKHA WORE HER LOVELY BLACK SKIRT WITH the scarlet lorikeet embroidery and thick cream cardigan, which her mother had given her for her last birthday, and carefully brushed her hair until it shone. Sunny, in his best dark blue and red overalls, and smart windcheater, his unruly hair temporarily tamed by water, sat on the edge of the bed and watched her solemnly, swinging his feet. She slipped a scarlet hairband over her hair and her favourite parakeet pendant round her neck and examined herself closely in the cupboard's crooked mirror.

'All polished and scrubbed,' she sang, stifling a giggle, because the mirror was so distorted it made her waist look three times its size, and sort of elongated her head. She loved dressing up and going out, and this would be the first time she would be doing so after the accident.

'Wah baby, wah!' Sharifa was stunned. She had just come in to wake up the children, and here they were spick and span and ready to go! And Shikha was looking so lovely even if the sadness was still there in her almond brown eyes when she smiled.

'Is chacha ready?' asked Shikha, slipping on her matching cream sandals, and unconsciously imitating her mother. Sharifa screwed up her face.

'Voh to studio mein hai! He's in the studio,' she replied, with a snort.

'Come on Sunny, let's go and call him. Mr Rana said four o'clock, and it's already three thirty.'

Gingerly they walked down the steep stone steps to the studio. It really was perched right at the edge of the cliff, and there was only a rickety wooden railing to hold on to. The rough wooden door was firmly shut. Tentatively Shikha knocked.

'Chacha?' she called. 'Binoy chacha?'

She heard an impatient exclamation, and then footsteps. The door opened, and her uncle, in a paint spattered crushed shirt and vile green muffler, glared at her, his hair all over his face.

'Yes?' he asked. 'What is it? I thought I told you not to come down here. The steps are dangerous!'

'Oh, sorry,' poor Shikha was taken aback. 'We have to go to Mr Rana's house ...,' she said falteringly, feeling Sunny shrink back against her.

'Oh,' he said. 'You go on ahead in the Gypsy. Aslambhai will take you. I'll follow later on the motorcycle.' And with that he shut the door in their faces.

For a moment Shikha felt the tears well up again, but then suddenly she felt angry instead. She made a rude face at the door.

'Rude fellow!' she said to Sunny. 'What a rude fellow he is. Like some wild man, with hair all over his face! Well, he doesn't scare me! And one day we are going inside that studio and will see what he paints and keeps so secret! Big, fancy artist he thinks he is! Come on, let's go!'

Aslambhai and Ali were waiting for them in the kitchen.

'Sahib will come later,' Shikha said, with an impatient toss of her head. 'We can go.'

'Chalo, baby,' agreed Aslambhai.

'Will we be going into the reserve again?' Shikha asked, as the Gypsy started up. Imagine if they did, and if Shahenshah saw her and Sunny like this, all dressed up! This time he might just eat them up – they really did look that delicious!

'Nahin, baby! No, baby. We will take the road that goes around the park from the outside, and then enter again from the main gate. We can go from inside also, but it will take much longer and there will be too much dust and your nice clothes will get spoilt.'

They climbed partially down the outside of the ridge surrounding Shergarh Tiger Reserve, and then drove along the slope northwards. To the west, the flat arid plains stretched, patchworked with farmers' fields, but now most were brown and barren. On the slopes of the ridge, groups of village women cut fodder from the trees, or gathered firewood. Goats swarmed up, with baleful eyes, devouring everything in their path, thorny or not. Then the road turned eastwards and they were climbing up to the rim of the ridge again.

Suddenly, in front of them stood the main gate of Shergarh Tiger Reserve, a massive granite arch with an impressive barrier (like they have in front of some railway crossings) across it. The guards at the checkpost just grinned and lifted the barrier when they saw the Gypsy and they drove through. The smooth gravel road ran down the middle of the ridge, the park lay sprawled a thousand feet beneath it on both sides, protected by the burly fort walls.

'Is this the central ridge on which the kila is built?' Shikha asked, enjoying the view.

'Hahn, baby. We are already inside the walls of the fort. The main gate to the fort itself is up ahead some distance away. The offices and staff houses are built on one side of this road, and there are resthouses and rooms for tourists on the other.' Aslambhai explained. They drove past some buildings and then entered a fenced in compound.

'Here we are,' he said, stopping the vehicle in the driveway. The field director's house seemed quite like Shergarh House, but was painted a faded sandstone pink. In the garden (much neater than their own, thought Shikha), a table had been laid out for tea. A fat, fair lady with three wobbling chins was bossing around a couple of the staff, and surged towards them when she saw them. A huge smile lit up her face, displaying nearly all her thirty-two teeth. A nose ring glittered dangerously in her small nose.

'Helloo bachche! Helloo children!' she shrilled surging up like a beaching walrus, and promptly enveloped both of them in a giant soft scented bear hug. 'Welcome to Shergarh! I am Joginder aunty!'

Shikha and Sunny disentangled themselves from the great scented embrace and took a breathless step back. There were tears in Joginder aunty's eyes, Shikha noted with surprise, and then realized with a frog in her own throat that this was the first time anyone had really hugged them properly since they had come to Shergarh. Joginder aunty also wore the most humungous bindi Shikha had ever seen and a sari patterned with vivid hummingbirds and hibiscus.

'Rana sahib!' she bellowed now, turning to the house. 'Your little guests have come!'

'Er ... I am Shikha Saini, and this is Sunny,' Shikha said, ever correct. It was something mama had taught her; always introduce yourself properly when meeting new people.

'My, my!' gushed Joginder aunty, taking a step back and

looking at Shikha approvingly. 'But you are so lovely!' She took out a scrap of a hankie and dabbed her eyes.

'Hello Shikha! Hello Sunny! That's a lovely skirt you are wearing!' Dipti, in blue jeans and an olive green cardigan, had come out on to the lawn and Shikha smiled at her in relief.

'Hi Dipti,' she said shyly. 'Thanks.'

'Come on, sit down, sit down. Make yourself at home.' Joginder aunty gazed at them and shook her head tragically. It was so terrible that these lovely children were orphans! And in such a terrible way! And to be looked after now only by that irresponsible, bad tempered Binoy! She leaned forward earnestly. 'Bachche, children, remember! This is now your home as much as Shergarh House. You can come here any time you want and spend as much time as you wish.' She sniffed and turned away.

'Mama,' said Dipti reprovingly.

'Thank you,' said Shikha. She looked around. 'Er ... Chachaji will be following later, he told us,' she added. Joginder aunty snorted.

'I hope he is looking after you properly,' she said. 'And not forgetting all about you. Does he speak to you at all?'

'Er ... we're fine, thank you ma'am,' Shikha said politely.

'Ah, there you are! Good God what a beautiful young lady you are! And what a smart little man!' Mr Rana strode out of the house with a big smile on his face. He turned to his wife. 'Do you know she has already met Shahenshah in the jungle! This morning only!'

'Bachche, what will you have? Something cold? Nimbu-pani? Coca-cola?'

'I'll have a nimbu-pani, thanks. Sunny likes Coke.'

There was a commotion at the gate. A large man in a gaudy T-shirt strode belligerently up the lawn, along with two others. He was bristling with anger.

'Mr Rana?' he inquired throatily. 'You are the field director?'

'Yes, sir! And you are?'

'Myself Goldie Singh, NRI! I have a complaint. I have spent four days in the park and haven't seen a single tiger! Not so much as the tail of a tiger! Your staff says there are more than twenty-five tigers in the park. You charge hefty fees every time we go inside, but we don't see a tiger. This is a rip-off! There are no tigers in this park!'

'Mr Goldie, you must have seen tiger pugmarks?'

'How do I know they are genuine tiger pugmarks? Your guards say, dekho, tiger has gone from here, tiger has followed us, but I am suspecting they are making tiger footmarks themselves! I want a refund! Back in the USA I would have got a refund and an apology already!'

'Mr Goldie, I'm sorry but no refund is possible. If you think there are no tigers in the park, you may ask this young lady what she saw this morning.'

Mr Goldie jerked his head towards Shikha.

'She saw a tiger?' he said incredulously. 'I bet you are just making it up!'

Shikha shook her head. 'No, sir,' she said shyly. 'We didn't just see any old tiger. We saw Shahenshah!'

And Sunny nodded, his black eyes wide as he remembered.

Mr Rana soothed the seething visitor and saw him off politely.

'I am staying another three days!' Mr Goldie Singh warned, firing a parting shot. 'If I do not see a tiger in that time, you will have to answer!' Mr Rana merely smiled and waved him off. 'All they want is to be able to tell their friends back in the States that they saw the tiger! They miss out the whole jungle experience. Stupid people!'

Dipti took Shikha's arm. 'Come,' she said. 'Let's go inside. I'll show you some of the pictures of the tigers of Shergarh!'

She showed them four hefty albums full of pictures (not only of tigers, but also other animals and birds), pointing out the tigers as though they were members of the family.

'That's Sheba,' she said, pointing to a lean looking tigress, snarling at the camera. 'She's dangerous! Especially when she has cubs!'

'Do you have pictures of Shahenshah?' Shikha asked.

'Yes, here he is! He's magnificent, isn't he?'

The picture was beautiful; it showed the great tiger stalking along the lake, looking intently at a chital some distance away. But it was nowhere near as beautiful as the image that Shikha had of him in her head, striding down the path towards her, framed by the golden-green grass, clouds of gold dust puffing up at his feet. And those glinting amber eyes …

'I'll never forget what I saw this morning,' she told Dipti, who smiled at her.

'You were very lucky, child! Ah, and this fellow – he's Shaitan, and the very devil. He loves mock charging tourists, but he can be dangerous. I think at the moment he's trying to muscle in on Shahenshah's territory.' She grinned. 'I hope that Goldie Singh fellow meets him!'

'But how can you tell one tiger from another?' Shikha asked puzzled. 'They all look the same to me!'

'The markings on their faces are different. You can identify them by those. You have to study them closely.' Dipti looked up. 'You know what, I've got a lot of slides too. We can have a slide show one of these days. They look much better that way.'

'That will be nice,' Shikha agreed.

'Bachche!' shrilled Joginder aunty from the garden. 'Come and have tea!'

They went back outside, and Shikha was relieved to see that Binoy chacha (in a fresh khadi kurta, thank God) had arrived and was staring into the distance. Sunny fixed his eyes on the huge pile of samosas and sandwiches and rather violently coloured pastries that had been placed on the table. 'Come on children, help yourselves!' Joginder aunty gushed, flashing her dazzling smile. After she had piled their plates high, she turned to Shikha.

'So my dear, when will you be going to school?' she asked. Shikha looked blank.

'Er … I don't know ma'am,' she said. 'I missed my exams.' She glanced at Sunny. 'I suppose when Sunny gets well and starts talking again, when things get back to normal. But I don't know … You see he won't leave me!' She smiled wanly at her little brother who was seriously digging into his pastry.

'Binoy?' said Joginder aunty in a voice that rang of steel. 'Have you thought about their school and all that?'

Binoy chacha ran his fingers through his beard and cleared his throat. 'Of course,' he said, sounding sheepish. 'The girl has already lost a year, though, if not more. That couldn't be helped. Once the little boy is okay, we'll think about their school. Shikha can go to that convent in Shergarh town. Or maybe we will think of some boarding school.'

Shikha winced. Why did Binoy chacha have to refer to them as 'girl' and 'boy'? They had names! They were real life people, whether he liked it or not. Again, she felt the hot tears prick her eyes, but blinked them away.

'And how long will that take?' Joginder aunty was frowning. 'For Sunny to get well?'

'The doctors can't say. They think he will get over the shock gradually. At the moment he doesn't leave his sister even for a minute. The doctor said that the best treatment is to give them a normal home life.'

Joginder aunty snorted. 'So you mean to say that until that

happens they just stay at Shergarh House and do nothing?' She sounded quite formidable, and Shikha looked at her alarmed.

'They have the whole of Shergarh Tiger Reserve to explore!' Binoy chacha said. 'Many children would give anything for that! I have told Aslambhai to take them inside whenever they want.'

'True, mama,' said Dipti pitching in unexpectedly. 'There is so much to see and learn. Missing a year or two of school isn't such a big deal. Besides, I can help Shikha with her studies if she wants.'

Joginder aunty looked at her daughter doubtfully.

'You have your job to go back to, and only come here during holidays. Besides she will miss having friends and classmates,' she pointed out.

'She'll make new friends here!' Dipti said, smiling.

'Here?' Joginder aunty snorted. 'Bah! What is over here except those tigers you keep running after? No children to play with, no raunaq, nothing! Not for a young girl like her!'

'I'll be fine,' Shikha said, blushing. 'My school books and other stuff should be coming soon, so I can get down to study.' But suddenly she felt a pang; she would miss her school terribly, she knew. So far she had been taking each day as it had come. She hadn't thought of what would happen next week, or next month, or next year, because that was frightening.

'Er ... Joginder,' said Binoy chacha diffidently. 'I will have to go to Delhi again, to settle my brother's affairs. I'll appreciate it if you could keep an eye on the children when I'm gone.'

Joginder aunty gave him a look that would have vaporized steel. Or, had she been a witch, turned him from an artist into cockroach poop.

'I will be keeping an eye on them whether you are here or not,' she said coldly. 'That you can be sure of! Now beta, have another pastry no?'

It was dark when they returned to Shergarh House, and Binoy chacha disappeared again into his studio, saying he wasn't going to have dinner. After their baths and a snack (because they had eaten a lot for tea), Sunny fell asleep (pangolin style as usual) quickly and Shikha took out her writing pad and pen. She looked out into the starlit night and wondered, again, where her parents were at that moment, and what they were doing and thinking. What happened when people died, she wondered. Maybe they went to the same place they had been before they were born … She gave a tiny gasp as she saw a star fall, streaking through the black velvet sky. Did that happen when someone was born? A star fell out of the sky. But people were being born every second. Well maybe there were stars falling every second too. And a comet … that would mean someone truly great was being born! Like Gandhiji. Or maybe even a tiger like Shahenshah! But comets came and went – oh hell, she was getting confused!

She sighed and picked up her pen and began a letter to her best friend Rini back in Delhi. Rini had spent so much time with her, both in the hospital and when they had returned home. Both Rini and Miss Nikita, her class teacher actually, had soothed and consoled her so much during those horrible days.

Dear Rini,

Hi, and how are you? Guess what? This morning Sunny and I saw an absolutely huge tiger from just a few feet away! He just walked past us. You won't believe it. He didn't even growl or snarl. There are twenty-five tigers in the Shergarh Tiger Reserve, which is next to where my uncle lives. We get a lovely view of the park – you must come here. I'm just dying to see more tigers now. And yesterday, I saw this rajkumar (at least I think I did!) sitting on the porch of his palace, with a huge tiger lying beside him! He must have been a ghost because there are no rajkumars here anymore! Sunny is fine, well not like he used to be, but okay. He still clings to me and won't let go of me; it can get a bit tiresome really but what to do! And he still doesn't say anything – not even when Shahenshah (that's the tiger's name) walked past us, but thank God for that maybe! Dipti, who is the field director's daughter, has promised to take me around. She's really cool and I like her a lot. Aslambhai, my uncle's driver and his grandson Ali have been driving us around in the park, and he carries a gun with him. My uncle is a strange fellow; he hardly talks to us and tries to ignore us. He locks himself up in his studio (where we are not supposed to go, but I am going to have a look one day definitely!) all day, painting away and mutters rudely if we interrupt him. Miss you.

Lots of love,
Shikha

She yawned. It had been a tiring day. Still, she better write to Miss Nikita at least a short note. Otherwise she would worry.

Dear Miss Nikita,

We reached Shergarh House safe and sound, yesterday morning. It is a beautiful place, right at the edge of Shergarh Tiger Reserve. I have already seen a tiger: this morning both Sunny and I saw a huge fellow called Shahenshah from just a few feet away. But I do miss you all, and mama and papa, a great deal. Binoy chacha just doesn't like to talk. Sunny has still not said a word, but I am better. The screeching noises in my head only bother me at night now when I want to sleep, but I haven't heard them during the day at all. My uncle says I'll be missing a year or more of school: I think it will be more because I could not give last year's exam and now will not be going to school for another year at least, or until Sunny gets all right. He still doesn't let me out of his reach. I have met Dipti here, the daughter of Mr Rana who is the field director, and she's very nice. She showed me some great pictures of the tigers and other animals here. I am quite sleepy now so will end here.

Love and regards,
Shikha (Saini)

Carefully she folded her letters and put them into envelopes and wrote the addresses. Tomorrow she would have to ask Binoy chacha for stamps. She wondered where the post office was.

'Baby, so jao – baby go to sleep.' Sharifa had been keeping a watch over her quietly, squatting at the bottom of the bed and watching her as she wrote. She got up and began brushing Shikha's hair, bringing the tears back into the girl's eyes, because she did it the same way as her mother had. With firm and brisk strokes.

A little later, Sharifa watched as Shikha tossed and turned trying to sleep. The noises in her head were back full blast; those ghastly banshee screechings and shriekings, and the horrible bang clang of the car's roof skating crazily on the road …

'Let me tell you a story,' Sharifa said softly, squatting down by her bedside and smiling. 'About a rajkumar who lived here many years ago …'

5

'IT HAPPENED A LONG, LONG TIME AGO, WHEN THE MAHARAJA of Shergarh ruled over this whole area. He and his queen lived in the fort and ruled wisely and well. For many, many years, they had no children and this bothered them a lot, for they needed an heir to the throne. But then at last, the queen gave birth to a little boy and there was much rejoicing throughout!'

Shikha smiled faintly in the darkness. Here she was, a fourteen-year-old girl, being told a bedtime fairy tale by this sweet little woman. Mama would have shaken her head disapprovingly and murmured, 'You never do grow up, Shikha dear,' knowing her fondness for fairy stories. Still it was comforting to hear Sharifa's soft sing-song voice in the darkness.

Sharifa went on with her story. 'They were so happy that the king ordered celebrations for two whole years. Big hunts were organized and many hundreds of tigers were killed. So many animals died that the forests started themselves to die of grief. The trees began to wither, the waterholes and lakes were parched because the streams simply flowed out or dried up, there were flash floods or drought. And then, when the young rajkumar was about ten years old, he fell very ill. For many days he lay sick and pale on his bed, looking down at the cracked up talao bed, too weak almost to talk. It was a bad time too otherwise, for the rains had failed yet again and droughtstalked the kingdom, starving many thousands of cattle and people. The maharaja and maharani were beside themselves with worry, because it seemed like the rajkumar would die. One day, the maharaja rode out into the forest, and swore to keep riding until he discovered some way of saving his son. He soon came across a holy man living in a cave on the banks of a stream at the far end of his realm, and asked him what he should do to save his son. He was ready to make any sacrifice to save his son's life.

'You must bring the child a tiger cub,' the sadhu said, firmly. "A small tiger cub for the boy to look after and raise! It will make him well again!"

'Well, the king rode back to the palace and immediately organized a massive tiger hunt. No time was to be lost because the rajkumar seemed to be sinking fast. After great difficulty, and scouring the forests for many days and nights, the hunting parties came across a tiger cub that was starving, because its mother had just died. They caught the little weakling, and brought it to the palace. It howled and screamed and scratched and bit, but they brought it up to the young rajkumar nevertheless. The maharani didn't like the idea one bit, she was afraid the prince would be scratched and bitten by the little cub. But amazingly, the cub became quiet when it was put in the rajkumar's arms. A buffalo was milked. The maharaja and maharani knew that if the little tiger cub died, then so would their precious rajkumar; the sadhu had not said that would happen, but in their heart, they knew that that was what he had meant. And then, to everyone's amazement and relief, the little cub drank hungrily. And for the first time in months, they saw the rajkumar smile again …'

'Oh,' Shikha said, waking up from the cozy dreamy state the story had put her into. 'Sharifa, do you think Sunny will start talking if we get him a tiger cub?' she sighed. 'But he didn't say a word even when Shahenshah walked past us … Anyway, what happened next, Sharifa?'

'Well, as the sadhu said, the rajkumar recovered swiftly. But he and the tiger cub grew to be inseparable. They went everywhere together. They played together in the forest, they swam together in the royal pools and talaos, they wrestled each other and chased deer together. It worried the maharani a lot, because tiger cubs grow very fast, and grow very big and strong; within a year or so, her lovely rajkumar was running around everywhere with a full grown tiger at his heels, scaring all the palace officials senseless. And he didn't seem to mind in the least all the bruises and scratches he received from his tiger, though it must be said that the big animal was extremely gentle with him. But as I said, it scared everyone senseless!'

'I can well imagine that!' Shikha said, wondering what her uncle's reaction would be if, for example, she walked into Shergarh House with Shahenshah at her heels!

'And because the young prince was so fond of his tiger, he made his father decree that there would be no more tiger hunts in the length and breadth of Shergarh! And you must remember that in those days, maharajas went on tiger hunts nearly all the time, so this was a big thing. Well, the maharaja and maharani had to agree, and so a law was passed banning the hunting of tigers throughout the kingdom. And now, Shergarh really did become the "fort of the tiger", the realm of the tiger! And to his amazement, in a few years the maharaja found that his kingdom had begun prospering again as never before. There were no droughts, no famines, and food and water was plentiful. You see, the tigers had started looking after the jungles again and you couldn't have better caretakers of the jungle! The tigers made sure that there were just enough deer and antelope for the forests to support, that they didn't eat up all the bushes and plants and so the trees grew tall and strong. And the trees ensured that the rainwater was caught between the wide and deep net of their roots in the soil, leaking it out bit by bit all the year round in springs and streams, so that there could never be a drought even if the rains were not good.'

'Ummm ...' murmured Shikha, blinking her eyes to stay awake. 'Sharifa, when do the horrible things start happening again? Everything is going a little too well!'

Sharifa smiled sadly in the darkness. 'Hahn baby – yes baby, you are right! Well, the prosperity of Shergarh meant that there were many powerful rulers of neighbouring kingdoms who were jealous of it, and who wanted to conquer it. They cast their evil, greedy eyes on it. They got together and decided to teach the maharaja of Shergarh a lesson. They marched on Shergarh and after a terrible battle, defeated and killed the maharaja. But they were wicked, malicious men; they captured the young prince and the maharani and brought them to the Chhota Mahal. To celebrate their victory they organized a massive tiger hunt, in which scores of tigers were killed. And then they smiled and told the young prince, "If you want your mother to live, you will have to shoot your pet tiger in front of us. Otherwise, we will catch three wild ones and make them fight it to death. Your big pussycat will not stand a chance! And then we will feed your mother to them in front of your eyes, before throwing you in with them!"

'The young rajkumar knew that they would keep their word. "Give me the gun," he said, "and bring me the tiger." So they brought him a gun, and wheeled out the cage in which his great pet tiger had been kept. Without flinching, the young prince shot his beloved pet …'

'Oh,' said Shikha, rather upset that the story had taken such a disastrous turn. Sharifa nodded dolefully.

'Hahn baby, but there is more to come! Immediately after shooting his tiger, the prince turned his gun on the maharani and shot her through the head. Then he surrendered the gun and simply said, "Now do whatever you want!" Of course they killed him but that was their biggest mistake. That night, a huge tiger entered the tent of the leading enemy king and ripped his throat out. The soldiers swore that the young rajkumar had been riding on his back. One by one the great tiger attacked and killed all those who had conspired against the kingdom of Shergarh. The conquerors fled, but ever since, the fort and palace have been deserted, and inhabited only by tigers. It is said that the rajkumar and his tiger will appear in the park again when there is some great danger or threat …'

Shikha sat bolt upright. 'But Sharifa, I saw the rajkumar and his tiger yesterday! He was reclining under one of those chhatris, his arm around the tiger's neck!'

'Oh,' said Sharifa, a little taken aback, and annoyed with herself. Then she smiled. 'Hahn, baby, and it is also said that the rajkumar and his sher will make an appearance whenever a beautiful rajkumari enters the place. To guard her and see that she comes to no harm!'

'Sharifa, now you are teasing me!' In the dark Shikha blushed, but remembered that Shahenshah had not harmed either her or Sunny …

'Sharifa, what was the name of the rajkumar's tiger?'

'He called him Badshah!' said Sharifa. 'Now try and sleep!' In the dark she frowned at herself. She had better be careful of the kind of stories she told Shikha baby. The girl had a vivid imagination, and Binoy sahib had warned her that she might have a head injury, which could affect her thinking. Like she was saying that she had seen the rajkumar and his tiger under the chhatri! Yes, she had better be careful about the stories she told the girl. She and her brother had been through quite enough.

'Now, Shikha baby, go to sleep,' she said softly.

Sleep? How could she sleep? Shikha thought. She had seen the rajkumar and Badshah! Were they her guardian angels or was something terrible going to happen in Shergarh? She didn't really notice that the horrible screeching and clanging in her head had disappeared altogether. Within a few moments, she was fast asleep.

6

'RIGHT, SUNNY NOW I WANT YOU TO STAND HERE!' SHIKHA brushed her hair out of her face, and led Sunny under the huge banyan tree that shrouded the unkempt garden of Shergarh House. 'Now I'm not going anywhere so don't freak, I'm just going to step back slowly, one at a time, until I reach the other end of the garden, okay? You just stay where you are.'

Solemnly Sunny nodded. But he fixed his black eyes firmly on his sister. Step by step, Shikha walked backwards along the length of the garden, one hand held out towards Sunny, like a traffic policeman stopping traffic. She was about halfway across when she noticed her little brother get fidgety.

'Sit, Sunny bunny,' she called out firmly, 'sit and stay.' She backed up some more, until she was at the far end of the house. Now, would come the real test. 'Okay, Sunny, now I'm just going to go round the corner of the house for a second! You won't be able to see me, but I'll be right there and pop back in a jiffy. Okay?' She nodded encouragingly. She had read somewhere that this was how one trained a puppy to sit and stay and not get anxious when you disappeared. 'Good boy!' she encouraged him, remembering that you had to praise your puppy too! 'Okay, now off I go!' Slowly, she slipped behind the side of the house and waited, her heart pounding. Would he stay where he was? He allowed her out of his sight only when she went to the bathroom, but even then she had to call out to him every now and then to reassure him that she was there, or he'd be banging on the door. But sure enough, within seconds she heard his scampering footsteps as he charged down the lawn and round the corner, his eyes anxious. Damn!

'That was great, Sunny! Just great!' She swallowed her disappointment and forced what she hoped was an encouraging smile. Okay, no problem, so they would try it again.

Hand in hand they walked back to the big banyan tree.

'Okay,' Shikha said again, removing her watch. 'Let's do it again, but differently. See the watch? It says the time is 8.25 a.m. – you can read the numbers on the dial. Now I'm going back around the house again, and I want you to come running to me when the watch shows 8.27, okay? Not before! Got it?'

Solemnly, Sunny nodded and strapped on the watch. She backed off, watching him stare at the watch with great earnestness as if willing the numbers to move quickly. She slipped behind the house again, but this time peeked through the bougainvillea trellis overhanging the verandah. Sunny was looking anxiously at the watch, and at the spot he had seen her disappear. Then he looked all around him and she knew he was about to panic; he stuck out his lower lip, trying not to cry, but then his face began to crumple. Those two minutes seemed to be the longest in his life. Should she step back into view and put an end to his misery? Then she saw his expression change. He stared at the watch as if he couldn't believe his eyes and with an exuberant leap came charging down the garden towards her. Beaming, he proudly showed her the time; he had done it!

'Good boy!' she said, unconsciously imitating the dog trainers she had seen on the National Geographic channel. 'Good boy!' She gave the delighted little fellow a hug.

'Two minutes, Sunny bunny! What do you think of that you little sonofagun!' He chortled and giggled back at her, pride and delight lighting up his eyes, but said nothing.

Okay, Shikha thought happily, we've made a start. Two minutes today, three or four tomorrow, and within a week or so, he should be allowing her out of his sight for five to ten minutes if he kept this up! Great! And who knows, soon he might start talking again too. For a second she wondered whether they should try it again, but changed her mind. He had made more progress today than she had thought he would, and she didn't want to spoil things.

'Hi Shikha, what on earth were you two doing, child?'

'Dipti! You startled me! When did you come here?' Dipti, all dressed up for the jungle safari in khaki jeans and jacket and hat, had stepped noiselessly beside her on the lawn, smiling. She had arrived a few minutes earlier, and unseen, had watched the whole performance, wondering what in the world Shikha was doing.

'He follows me around everywhere like a little puppy, so I thought that maybe if I started training him to sit and stay like one, he might eventually let me get out of his sight for a bit,' Shikha explained, blushing, and shrugging her shoulders. 'I just hope it works! He managed two whole minutes by himself!'

'I think he deserves a chocolate,' said Dipti digging deep into her pockets and producing an éclair. 'And you, child, deserve a big hug for being the sweetest big sister there ever was!' Shikha blushed.

'I just wish he'd be normal again,' she said simply. 'I just wish he would *say* something. It's creepy and weird to have a chatterbox brother all gupchup! He used to call me babydolldimplechick, can you imagine! Sheesh!'

Neither of them noticed that there had been yet another witness to the little drama. From the top of the stone steps leading down to the studio, Binoy chacha had watched the whole thing, his face as usual expressionless. (Actually covered by too much hair to show one, if he had one.) Silently he disappeared down the steps into his studio.

'Now,' said Dipti, putting an arm around Shikha. 'I came here to take you guys into the park with me. I've got the Gypsy and the driver waiting and we can spend the whole day there. Mama has packed parathas and wafers and soft drinks in a hamper, so we can have a great picnic.'

'I suppose I'll have to ask Binoy chacha,' said Shikha, frowning.

'Where is he?' Dipti asked.

'In his studio, where else?' Shikha shrugged. 'He spends the whole day there.'

'Well I suppose he is a painter, so he must paint,' Dipti said reasonably. 'I think he's started on a new series of paintings and that always makes him more crabby and short-tempered than usual.'

'I guess artists are funny people,' agreed Shikha. 'But I do wish he would talk to us more!'

'Will you tell him that I'm taking you into the reserve?' Dipti said.

'Er ... Dipti, could you do that? He doesn't like us going down the steps to his studio. He nearly bit my head off the last time I went down!'

'Okay, Shikha, no problem.'

Of course, they took Aslambhai along too, and before

anyone knew it, Ali had slipped into the back of the Gypsy too, grinning in his usual slithery way.

'Let's see if we can find Sheba today,' Dipti said, checking out her cameras. 'We'll go to the fort first, and check out the palace too.'

'You know, Dipti,' Shikha whispered as they drove silently past the great granite walls, ears pricked for the alarm calls that would tell them that the tiger was on the prowl. 'The last time I came here I saw a rajkumar reclining in one of the chhatris, stroking a great tiger. And then, Sharifa told me a story about a rajkumar who lived here and brought up a tiger ...' She giggled. 'Do you think I was dreaming?'

Dipti looked at her curiously. 'Oh,' she said. 'So you saw the legendary Badshah?'

But just then another Gypsy drove up and a loud voice hailed them.

'Oye, madams, have you seen anything interesting? Any tigers?'

It was Mr Goldie Singh, who had made such a scene at the tea party the other evening.

'Oh God, no!' Dipti groaned. 'Now he'll stick to us like a leech and shout like a loudspeaker!'

'Mind if I join you?' Goldie Singh yelled. 'Rana sahib said that that girl had seen a tiger, so maybe if she is having luck again, we will all see it now!'

Without waiting for a response, Goldie Singh and his friends jumped out of their vehicle and joined the girls and Aslambhai. Dipti smiled as politely as she could, making Shikha want to giggle.

'Okay, Mr Singh, now we have to be very quiet! If we shout and make a noise, the tiger will disappear.'

'I am not shouting! I am simply talking normally,'

Goldie Singh bellowed aggrievedly. 'I can't help it if my voice is loud! In America you have to have a loud voice!' His friends laughed uproariously at his wit.

'Shhh!' admonished Dipti, frowning and rolling her eyes in despair. She was the daughter of the field director after all, and couldn't possibly be rude to Goldie Singh and send him packing. He didn't really mean any harm; he just didn't know how to behave in a national park and he was desperately afraid of being 'ripped off' and made a fool of. And if anyone had to tell him that, it was her father, not her.

'Okay, Mr Singh, come along with us! We'll look around for tiger pugmarks here and let's hope we have some luck. They love coming to this area, I know.'

They walked amidst the ruins, between the wavy golden grass, the spiky thornbush and abandoned cannons, Aslambhai looking intently at the dusty tracks that criss-crossed the area.

'I say,' Mr Goldie Singh whispered hoarsely, looking around. 'This seems to be a perfect place for a tiger to ambush us! Is that fellow's gun loaded? And does he know how to use it?'

Actually he was right. There were many nooks and crannies, alcoves and hidden stairwells, turrets and walls, in, on, or behind which a tiger could lurk, waiting to pounce.

Dipti stopped and stared at him with withering scorn, as if implying that no tiger in its right senses would waste its time ambushing Mr Goldie Singh. He may be fat and juicy, but he wouldn't be good for the heart or blood pressure of the animal! Any tiger interested in its health and fitness would tell him that! But then Shikha squeezed her hand, an old forgotten mischief lighting up her brown eyes.

'Actually, uncle, you may be right,' she said solemnly, as Dipti looked at her surprised.

'What?' Mr Goldie Singh looked alarmed. 'You think there is a tiger nearby? Maybe we should get back to the vehicles.'

'I saw a huge tiger reclining in one of those chhatris, the other morning,' Shikha said, perfectly truthfully. 'Let's see if he's there again.'

They had just turned to go towards the edge of the fort wall from where they could look down to the palace and chhatris, when they froze.

'Aaaooom! Aaaooom! Aargh!'

The call appeared to come from right behind them! A peacock honked in alarm and flew off in a great flurry, scaring the daylights out of Mr Goldie Singh and his friends, and making Shikha and Dipti jump with squeals of alarm. A langur caught the panic and whooped hollowly in the trees while somewhere not too far away, down the cliff, a sambhar belled in alarm and clattered away. The forest was on red alert!

'Whatwasthat? Tiger? Right here! Oh, my God, we've had it! Guard, bandook uttaro! – guard, get your gun ready,' Mr Goldie Singh and his friends had gone white as kheer and huddled around each other, their faces pale.

'It seems to be quite close!' Shikha whispered, looking around fearfully and gripping Sunny's hand tight. She caught Dipti's eye and winked faintly. Dipti's eyebrows shot up. Aslambhai was looking exasperated – as well as slyly pleased. A smirk lurked behind his sunbird beard.

'Aaaoom! Arrooom! Arrgh!'

'Oh shit, I think we've disturbed him while he was hunting!' Dipti whispered. 'We'd better get out of here quickly. Before he decides to choose one of us as his next meal.'

'Next meal? What are you talking about, madam? Guard, fire karo! Shoot!'

'Mr Singh, this is a national park and tiger reserve. The

tigers have complete protection here. And if Aslambhai fires, who knows what the tiger will do? Probably attack straightaway! I just hope it is not that Shaitan fellow!' Dipti rolled her eyes, and looked around uneasily. 'Shaitan charges everybody!'

'Shaitan? What Shaitan? Oh bloody hell, there is a charging tiger called Shaitan here?'

'The wickedest tiger in the park!' Dipti agreed with relish. 'He will surely charge!'

'Wait a minute!' Mr Goldie Singh said looking around wildly. 'There was a little boy with us! Where is he?'

'Oh my God! Ali! Where is he?' The girls looked at each other shocked. 'Aslambhai do you think the tiger has eaten Ali? We didn't hear him scream though!'

'Ho sakta hai – quite possible,' Aslambhai agreed, deadpan, and not in the least bothered by the fate of his grandson. 'Par Ali tiger ka peth nahin bhar sakega! But Ali won't fill the tiger's stomach!' He looked pointedly at Goldie Singh. 'Usko bada khana mangta hai! He'd want more substantial food!'

'Madam, why is he looking at me like that?' Goldie Singh stared at Aslambhai, rolling his eyes like a sambhar about to be spooked.

'Sir,' said Dipti in a rather polite official voice. 'I think you better return to your vehicle immediately, along with your friends. The tiger is a very discretionary hunter – he chooses his fare carefully. And amongst us, Aslambhai thinks that you probably look the most suitable and tasty for the tiger.' She swallowed. 'Actually a research study showed that man-eating tigers have a preference for NRIs. They seem to be more tasty, juicy and soft than the locals.' It was a wonder she kept a straight face.

'Tasty? Oh, bloody hell, we are out of here, man!'

Escorted by Aslambhai and their own forest guard,

Mr Goldie Singh and his friends returned to their Gypsy at a hurried trot.

'What about the boy?' Goldie Singh yelled as he slammed the Gypsy door.

'I think he must have got scared of the tiger and hidden somewhere,' Dipti said innocently. 'We'll find him, don't worry! He would have screamed had the tiger pounced on him!'

'Ali! Ali! Where are you?' Shikha called, pretending to be scared and grinning at Sunny, who smiled back and winked.

'Aaaroom! Aarrooom!'

'Oh, hell, driver chalo! Before the tiger makes hamburger of me!'

The Gypsy lurched off in a cloud of dust. Shikha and Dipti collapsed on the ground in hysterics, and even Sunny chortled richly.

'Tiger Ali!' Shikha called, wiping the tears from her eyes. 'You can come out now!'

'I tell you that fellow is going to get me into trouble one of these days! Scaring the tourists away like that!' Dipti said. 'Tiger Ali! Shaitan Tiger Ali more like it!'

But even Aslambhai was grinning.

And in his unobtrusive, sly way Ali joined them as suddenly as he had vanished and looked around, as if surprised.

'Voh log chale gaye – those people have gone?' he asked innocently.

'Come on,' Dipti said, getting to her feet. 'I don't think there are any tigers here. I want to take you to another beautiful spot that is tucked away in one corner of the park. Hey Shikha, child, what's the matter? Are you okay? Why are you crying?'

To her amazement, Dipti saw that Shikha was suddenly weeping quietly. She put her arm around the girl as Sunny looked up anxiously at his sister.

'I don't know, Dipti,' Shikha sobbed. 'That was the first time I really laughed after the accident and it felt good, but I don't feel so nice about it now! I feel kind of guilty! What would mama and papa think? Me laughing my head off like that, with them dead and gone forever?'

'I think they'd be laughing too, wherever they are, Shikha. I think they'd want you to laugh as much as possible. I don't think they'd want to see you being sad all the time! That would make them sad too, don't you think?'

Dolefully Shikha nodded and gulped. 'Yes,' she sniffed. 'I suppose so! I hope you're right!'

'Now come on, let's see if we can find Sheba or some of the other tigers!'

They stopped for about half an hour at the lake and were now heading deeper into the forest, towards the western ridge. At the lake they had watched the crocodiles sunning themselves, and the big shiny purple swamphens stepping over the water hyacinth, balancing clumsily on the shiny green leaves.

'Dekho – look,' said Aslambhai quietly, pointing towards what seemed to be a huge floating log in the water.

'What is it?' asked Shikha, peering through her binoculars.

'That's a crocodile!' said Dipti, peering through the viewfinder of her camera. 'It's waiting for those chital to come down to drink. He's humungous!'

'Oh my God, no! Can't we warn them off?'

'Shikha dear, this is their jungle and their life. We can't interfere. The crocodile has to eat as well. Maybe it has young to look after and bring up.'

'I can't watch!' said Shikha, still glued to her binoculars. 'You silly deer, get away!'

But the silly deer were being sillier still. Looking around warily, they approached the water and bent down to drink.

'Get ready,' muttered Dipti, 'those crocs can move with hellish speed.'

Just then a pond heron (that surely needed spectacles!) landed on the crocodile's snout, thinking it to be part of a log. The reptile reared up with a great whoosh and roar, its huge jaws snapping, its tail thrashing. The bird leapt skywards and flapped to safety, shocked out of its wits, and the deer turned and fled helter skelter, their hooves drumming. Every chital, sambhar and nilgai in the area looked up alarmed by the commotion, but soon many returned to grazing calmly.

'Wow!' Shikha said, lowering her glasses with relief. 'That deer sure had a narrow escape, eh, Sunny bunny?'

The little boy nodded.

'The deer was lucky,' Dipti said. 'The heron saved its life!' She looked pleased. She had got a nice set of photos of the event.

The radio set in the Gypsy crackled. The driver spoke into the microphone and then handed it over to Dipti.

'Sahib wants to talk to you,' he said.

'Papa? What is it? Over!'

'Dipti!' Mr Rana's voice sounded pretty exasperated. 'Dipti what is this about a tiger attacking and eating that Ali fellow at the fort? This Mr Goldie Singh has been jumping up and down shouting how a tiger nearly made him a McGoldie burger after eating up the boy ...'

'Nothing to worry about, papa,' Dipti said, trying to keep a straight face. 'Ali is here with us, sitting quietly in the back of the Gypsy.'

'Aaoon!' called Ali softly. *'Aargh!'*

'I can't make head or tail of what this fellow is shouting about,' Mr Rana complained. 'I hope that Ali fellow has not been up to his pranks!'

'Papa, Ali just helped Mr Goldie Singh experience being near a tiger. He's been complaining so much about not having seen one.'

'Oh, I see!' said Mr Rana, a thoughtful note entering his voice. 'I understand. We shall leave it at that. Okay, now where are you?'

'We're at the talao.'

'Okay. Be careful! Over and out!'

They skirted the lake and lurched through some deeply rutted ravines. Date palms grew in secretive clusters, and the fronds of wild grass leaned over their heads. Suddenly Aslambhai tapped the driver on his shoulder and pointed upwards.

'Kill!' he said softly. 'Tiger kill. Let's go!'

High above, vultures and other birds of prey were circling over an area towards the north. As they watched, some of the birds began losing height, and lowered their legs.

'What is it?' Shikha asked, her heart beginning to thud in excitement.

'Probably a tiger kill!' replied Dipti. 'Now we'll have to be very quiet indeed. Tigers don't like being disturbed while at their meals.'

'Do we go on foot?' Shikha asked, anxiously. True, she and Sunny had stood ten metres away from Shahenshah as he walked past, but he was, well, Shahenshah after all, and not hungry then. This could be a very different sort of tiger in a very different mood.

'We'll try and get as close as we can in the Gypsy,' Dipti whispered. 'The tigers tend to get more annoyed by people on foot.'

'Poor Mr Goldie Singh!' Shikha whispered, as the Gypsy clambered up the steep side of a ravine. A deep thickly forested gully lay on the other side.

'I know. He's missing all this!'

Slowly the driver took the Gypsy along the ridge, towards the clump of bamboo and trees on which the vultures had gathered. The unmistakable stink of rotting meat wafted up to them, making Shikha and Sunny screw up their noses in disgust.

'How do the tigers eat that stuff?' Shikha whispered. 'It's all rotted to hell!'

'They don't mind,' said Dipti. 'Now watch those tree pies. Those ones hovering on that big dhak tree growing up from the bottom of the ravine. I think the tiger is somewhere nearby.'

Three or four rufous tree pies, handsome crow-like birds in cocoa brown, white and grey (and black of course) fluttered about a huge dhak (flame of the forest) tree, intent on something at the bottom of the ravine. Then, one flew down, followed by another, and disappeared from view.

Not for long.

A malevolent, blood-curdling snarl erupted from the bottom of the ravine, and Shikha saw a flame orange flash as the tiger sprang at the birds that had dared to rob its kill. It was a 'I'll rip your throat out, see if I don't', kind of snarl, and Shikha went pale, and Sunny clutched her hand tightly.

'My God!' she whispered. 'He sounds very angry!'

'Yes,' Dipti agreed. 'You wouldn't want to eat at the same table as it, would you?'

Expertly the driver inched the Gypsy forward, till they were virtually looking straight down the ravine at the spot where the kill surely lay.

'Udhar – there!' whispered Aslambhai suddenly. 'Just beside that bush next to the tree! It's a chital that the tiger has killed. There it is – a tigress!'

Through the mesh of branches and grass, Shikha strained her eyes, trying to make out the tigress, superbly camouflaged in its habitat. A sudden movement down below caught her attention, and she realized she was staring at the leg of a chital, sticking out at a weird angle and being waved around violently. It reminded her of someone waving a drumstick while talking and eating at the same time. And then she saw it.

The bloody mouth and bristling whiskers. The lean head and angry baleful stone-coloured eyes looking around – even up at her – uneasy and suspicious. And the graceful body, crouched low, the great front paws gripping the chital firmly.

'Look, Sunny bunny – there!' whispered Shikha, as the little boy stared downwards, fascinated.

'I think she's Begum,' whispered Dipti squinting through her viewfinder, trying to get a clear shot. 'Sheba's sister!'

There came a splintering crack as the tiger bit deeply into the thigh of the chital, followed by a crunching of bone and gristle.

'She's enjoying her meal,' Dipti whispered, letting off a couple of quick shots. The camera's 'shhtuck-shhtuuck' sounded like a cannon going off in the quiet of the forest. The tigress looked up and emitted a low growl.

'I … I really don't think you should take any more pictures,' Shikha whispered nervously. 'Or she is going to get very annoyed with us!'

'As long as we keep our distance, we'll be okay,' Dipti murmured. 'But she does look pretty bad-tempered, doesn't she?'

Another cheeky tree pie landed close by and the tiger was after it in a flash, swiping at it wildly with her paws. It flew off with a rude 't-chak-t-chak' on to the tree.

They watched the tigress eat for a good hour and more, till the chital began looking quite depleted. Apart from the cracking and crunching of the bones, and the odd enraged snarl, the jungle was quiet. Eventually the tigress had had enough. She got up and gripping the chital by its neck began dragging it across the ravine, towards a thicket at the edge.

'She's going to hide it,' Dipti whispered. 'So that she can eat it later.'

'Hells bells Sunny bunny, even tigers have leftovers!' Shikha whispered. 'What d'you know!'

They drove on, at last, digging ravenously into their parathas as they drove. As they approached the western ridge, the jungle became greener and more lush. The breeze was positively chilly here. The Gypsy began labouring up the steep ridge slope, rocking on its springs as it climbed the bumpy path.

'This is a very special place, Shikha,' Dipti said. 'I love coming here. I think it is the most beautiful spot in the tiger reserve. No one really comes here, because well, I've sworn everyone who knows about it to secrecy! It's called Hari Pani.'

'Oh,' said Shikha. 'Then why are you showing it to me?'

'Because I think you need a special secret place you can come to when you want. A place where no one will bother you.' Dipti grinned. 'But, of course, you'll have to watch out for tigers. It is a favourite spot with some of them too!'

'Thanks,' said Shikha grinning. 'I'll try and remember that! But really, thanks.'

'Only these fellows know about the place,' Dipti said. 'And I've warned Ali that if he so much as squeaks about it, I'll personally use him as bait for Shahenshah or Shaitan!'

Great trees – banyan, peepul and figs of other types – soared high and wide above them. There was dampness and chill in the air. The path, strewn with boulders, narrowed as the jungle crowded around it and then petered out altogether.

'Come on,' said Dipti, jumping off. 'We go on foot from here. It's just a little way.' She led the way, followed closely by the forest guard, whose eyes flicked everywhere watchfully. They entered by clambering over the rocks, which led to a sort of cliff top. 'Nearly there!' whispered Dipti.

And then Shikha stared in astonishment. The jungle suddenly gave way at the edge of a small cliff. Below them, reposing peacefully in the gloom of the forest stood a small stone pavilion-like structure, mostly intact, but split asunder here and there by powerful ancient peepul roots. In front of it lay a forest pool, glinting a deep clear emerald green shrouded by a cathedral of great trees. A small chhatri with a beautiful lattice-worked low wall around it stood in the middle of the pool, perfectly reflected by the glinting green waters.

'This is Hari Pani,' whispered Dipti. 'They say that when the enemies of Shergarh attacked, the maharani poured all her emeralds into this pool, and it has remained green ever since. She had a passion for emeralds and one of the largest collections of them in the world. You can see, the water is a clear, clean deep green, not the sort of scummy, mossy mouldy green you get when algae and other stuff grow in it.'

'Sunny bunny, isn't it absolutely beautiful?' Shikha whispered as they clambered down towards the pavilion.

'It gets rather chilly and misty here during winter,' Dipti said. 'But it is beautiful and cool in summer. I've seen tigers bathing in this pool several times.'

'Wow!' Shikha looked around, awestruck. Across the pool, on the opposite side, the rocks reared high and here and there in the rock face she could make out dark openings.

'Dipti, are those caves up there?' she asked.

'Yes,' Dipti nodded. 'And they are inhabited by tigers and sloth bears. So it's better to stay down here, where you can see them!'

Sunny had clutched Shikha's hand and tugged her arm.

'What is it, Sunny?' she looked down. Silently he pointed up the cliff, towards one of the cave-like openings.

'What is it?' Shikha stared in the direction Sunny indicated but could see nothing. Aslambhai grunted.

'See there,' he said. 'Great horned owl at the entrance of that cave! Near where those white droppings are!'

And Sunny gave a wide delighted grin and nodded.

'Oh, wow! Dipti have you seen it! It's huge. And look at those eyes! Like honey!'

Sphinx-like the huge owl stood stolidly at the entrance to its home, occasionally turning its head this side and that, and blinking its great golden eyes.

'Dipti, have you swum in this pool?' Shikha asked. It was far too chilly now to think of swimming, but in summer … In summer this would truly be a princess's swimming pool!

Dipti grinned. 'Yes I have, but don't tell papa!' she said. 'But before you get into this pool you have to make sure there are no tigers in it first!'

They sat in silence at the edge of the pavilion and dangled their feet over the water. The forest guard and Aslambhai squatted patiently, their eyes scanning the area as always.

'Shikha,' said Dipti breaking the silence at last. 'I want to ask you a favour!'

'What?' Shikha was surprised.

'Well, it's like this. I'll have to go back to Delhi in a few days – my leave gets over. And then I won't be able to come here for several months maybe. Now you're going to live here all the time. How would you like to observe and study the tigers for me, in that time?'

'Observe and study the tigers? What do you mean?' Shikha looked puzzled.

'Actually it's not too difficult. You'll have to come into the reserve every day and drive around. Of course, Aslambhai or one of the good forest guards will take you. Well, you'll have to see how and where the tigers live. The male tigers have fairly large territories, which they patrol, and visit the female ones from time to time. You'll have to see what they do and make notes. Just keep a diary of what you see every day when you visit the reserve. And over the next few days I'm going to teach you how to use a camera, so that you can take photographs too. You can use one of mine while I'm away.'

'But ... but ...!' Shikha was astounded by the request.

'No buts, child!' said Dipti firmly, grinning. 'I've already asked papa and he has agreed. Provided you promise you will never enter the reserve without Aslambhai or a forest guard.'

'I won't!' Shikha said fervently. 'You can count on that!'

'Once a week or so, you can write to me about what you've seen,' Dipti went on.

'But I'll have to ask Binoy chacha,' Shikha said. 'He might not like me wandering about in the reserve the whole day.'

'Binoy chacha will not be a problem,' said Dipti, a new steeliness entering her voice. 'You can be sure of that! At any rate it will be better than rattling about alone in Shergarh House while he locks himself up in his studio all day, appearing like a starving madman once in three days to eat!'

Shikha grinned and nodded. Dipti had a point. She looked puzzled.

'But why, Dipti? I'm not a scientist or anything like that who can properly study the tigers. So what is the point of my following them around?'

'It's just that I would like to know that there's someone reliable and sweet watching over my tigers,' Dipti said, ruffling Shikha's hair affectionately. 'And you've already been approved of, by Shahenshah. Need I say more? Now I'm also going to give you my photo albums so that you can study the tigers and get to know them by name.'

What Dipti didn't reveal to Shikha was the battle she had had with her father over the matter the previous evening. He had nearly thrown a fit when she had put the suggestion to him.

'Are you mad?' the field director had said incredulously. 'You want that girl and her gupchup little brother to roam about in the tiger reserve the whole day? Who will look after them? Who will be responsible if anything happens? This is a jungle! Not a playground!'

'Papa, she can take Aslambhai with her. He's been by far the best forest guard, tracker and teacher this place has ever had. And he's going downhill ever since he's retired. He'll love to show her around.'

'But why? Why? You – we – hardly know the girl!' spluttered Mr Rana. He looked around furtively. 'And have you put the suggestion to mama?'

'No,' said Dipti, and added frankly, 'mama will freak out when she hears it, I know! But she's irrelevant to the matter. You are the field director. And papa, I like Shikha – she's an unusual child. Look at the way she takes care of her little brother!'

'But why? You haven't answered my question!'

'It's simple papa. Just think of what that child is going to have to go through in the months ahead. She's just lost her parents, her little brother can't talk, she has been thrust into a completely strange place, and is living with a reclusive half nutcase uncle who perhaps says three words to her in a week. No school, no friends, nothing! She'll go crazy in no time at all. And they're supposed to have a normal life, their doctor said, if they are to recover!'

'And you think she'll be okay if she runs around the jungle all day like some Tarzan girl looking for tigers? I don't think that is a normal life for a fourteen-year-old girl.'

'It will give her something worthwhile and exciting to do! At the moment the poor girl doesn't even realize how much she is missing her parents, she's so desperately trying to be mother, father and big sister to her little brother all at the same time!'

'Do you think that this might help the little boy talk again?'

Dipti shook her head. 'I don't know papa, I really don't know. But I do know that it wouldn't help anyone if poor Shikha went to pieces now. Not in the least the little fellow. And I'd hate to have to feel responsible for letting that happen.'

'How will you be responsible? She is Binoy's responsibility, not yours or mine! Maybe you should just tell him to be more talkative and friendly with the children.'

'You know him and his nature. Just be grateful he hasn't taken off somewhere again for three months just because he feels like it. And now he's doing this new series of paintings and will be virtually impossible to live with. So Shikha and little Sunny do become our responsibility whether we like it or not; they are our neighbours after all. And we know that she's going to be in trouble if we don't help out in whatever way we can!'

Mr Rana got up and strode up and down, staring at the beautiful view out of his office window. To allow a fourteen-year-old girl and her tiny five-year-old brother into the tiger reserve, every day, even with the best forest guard in the world, was not an easy thing to do. Of course he would willingly put his life in Aslambhai's hands – he was that reliable. But that was not the point. The jungle was a strange place, where the most unexpected things happened. Anything could happen. Anything could go wrong. He shook his head aggrieved.

'You should have been with Mother Teresa!' he said half-crossly. 'Always wanting to help others and not thinking about the consequences for yourself!'

'But I am, papa! I'm thinking about what the consequences will be if we do not help Shikha and Sunny now.'

Mr Rana threw up his hands and exhaled noisily. He'd given up. He knew Dipti. She'd be at him and at him and at him till he gave in. Might as well do so gracefully right now and be done with it.

'Okay! But this is how we will do it. Aslambhai will have to inform the office exactly where they will be going every day. The girl must learn to use the radio. In case there is an emergency she can radio for help. She must be told that on no account must she leave the Gypsy to wander about on foot without Aslambhai. I will talk to her myself. And of course, we have to get Binoy's permission. He may object! Besides, it is his Gypsy that is going to be used, not the department's, so he better get it checked thoroughly. I don't want it to break down in the middle of nowhere, with the girl and her brother on board. And of course, she will have to agree. If she doesn't want to go running after the tigers as you think she does, then well there's nothing more to be said!'

'Binoy will not be a problem!' said Dipti, a flinty look in her eyes. 'And I think Shikha will agree. I'll speak to her. And thank you, papa, you're the best father in the world!'

'Now that you've got what you wanted, don't maska (butter) maaro me!' Mr Rana said grumblingly, but he kissed her cheek.

And deep inside her, Dipti hoped that the tigers of Shergarh would protect the children she was putting into their fierce care.

'I'm taking Shikha and Sunny into the reserve tomorrow,' she said. 'We'll spend the whole day there and I'll put the suggestion to her.'

And when she saw young Shikha making her little brother 'sit and stay' in the unkempt garden outside Shergarh House, that morning she knew she had done the right thing.

7

DIPTI STAYED ON FOR DINNER THAT NIGHT, MUCH TO SHIKHA'S delight, after informing her father on the phone. It was so nice to have someone normal to talk to at the dining table, Shikha thought, as she tucked Sunny's napkin under his chin. To her surprise, Binoy chacha also made a brief appearance. He raised his eyebrows sardonically when he saw Dipti, but said nothing. It's almost like a normal family, Shikha thought and then smiled sadly to herself. Not normal, no – not like mama and papa and Sunny and she had once been, but still like a family.

'Hello, Binoy,' Dipti said, 'how's the work coming along?'

Binoy chacha just glared at her and said nothing. He hated talking about his work (and for that matter about anything!) and Dipti knew it. He tackled his food with ferocity.

'Er … Binoy, there is something I want to ask you,' Dipti went on, undaunted.

'What is it?'

'I want Shikha and Sunny to go into the tiger reserve every

day with Aslambhai, to study the tigers for me. You know I'll be leaving for Delhi in a few days. You'll have to give them permission.'

He stared at her as though she were a lunatic.

'Please, Binoy chacha,' Shikha pleaded. 'We saw a tigress at her kill today. It was real great.'

Binoy chacha waved a fork about in the air.

'Let me get this straight,' he said. 'You want Shikha and Sunny to roam about in the tiger reserve every day? For the whole day? Why? Do you want to feed Shahenshah on young children?'

Dipti bristled and her eyes glinted dangerously.

'Binoy, I said they'd go with Aslambhai!'

'In the Gypsy, I presume?'

'Of course! Certainly not on your motorbike!'

'Hmm ... and who will pay for the petrol and other costs? That Gypsy drinks like a fish!'

'You will, Binoy,' said Dipti pleasantly. 'You just told us that Shikha's father has left them more than enough money. Plus, for at least two years you won't have to bother about school fees.'

'But ... but what about her studies? When will she do her studies?'

'I'll ask mama to see if she can help,' Dipti said, nodding. 'Shikha can study during the afternoons. Besides, with summer coming on, she'll only be able to go into the reserve early in the morning and then in the evening maybe. She'll have plenty of time for her studies.'

'I can write to my old class teacher to help,' Shikha said.

'I don't like the idea of the two children roaming about in the tiger reserve the whole day,' Binoy chacha said, as if he had made up his mind and conveniently forgetting what he had told Joginder aunty about the children 'having the whole tiger reserve to explore' just the other evening. 'I won't be able to concentrate on my work, thinking about it. Will they return safely, or has one of those tigers decided on a change in its diet?'

'Binoy,' said Dipti evenly, 'I think it would be more difficult for you to paint if you knew that Shikha and Sunny will be rattling around Shergarh House all day, doing nothing.'

'But what will they do in the reserve the whole day?'

'Binoy, you know there is enough to see and observe in that reserve to keep anyone occupied for a lifetime. You said so yourself, at least they'll be busy.'

'What if the Gypsy breaks down? What if Aslambhai falls ill? No, Dipti, I don't like it. I'll take the kids inside the reserve once a week myself. But going inside all by themselves every day, even with Aslambhai, no! Now if you will excuse me!' He got up and left the room as Shikha stared at him in dismay. Why did he always have to spoil things like this? Sunny was looking at her anxiously, and she squeezed his hand reassuringly.

'Don't worry Sunny, everything will be all right,' she whispered almost automatically, feeling a leaden weight settle inside her and the sobs rising up dangerously.

But Dipti hadn't given up and didn't seem very bothered either.

'Don't worry, Shikha, he'll come round. He always first says no to something he will agree to fifteen minutes later!'

'But why does he have to be like that?' Shikha wailed, not knowing quite why she was breaking down. She gulped down her sobs as Sunny crawled into her lap, whimpering.

'Child, it'll be all right! I promise!'

'Voh Binoy sahib aise hi karta hai! That Binoy sahib is always doing things like that,' Sharifa snorted, her eyes flashing angrily as she cleared the table. 'Can't you put some sense into his head? He listens to you!'

Dipti grinned. 'The hell he does, but this time he will.' She got up determinedly. 'I'll be back!' she said. 'With permission from the monster!'

She was as good as her word. Ten minutes later there came a knock on the children's bedroom door, and Dipti poked her head around it. Shikha, with Sunny in her lap, was sitting in the huge tea planter's chair, staring out at the night sky.

'Permission granted!' Dipti sang. 'The monster of Shergarh House changed his mind!'

'What?' Shikha jumped up. 'Wow, thanks Dipti! How did you make him do it?'

'Well child,' said Dipti her eyes sparkling. 'I told him that if you were to hang about here all day, you would of course be disturbing him in his studio every fifteen minutes or so, no matter what he said about forbidding you to come down. "Binoy chacha can I have a coke? Binoy chacha can Sunny have a coke? Binoy chacha, we'd like Pepsi actually. Are there any chips in the house? Binoy chacha the TV doesn't work! You don't get Cartoon Network! You don't even have cable TV! Don't you have any better videos? Binoy chacha, I'm bored!" All day long, and day after day! Little Sunny here could of course get loose amongst his paints and stuff and make a thorough mess!' She laughed. 'He looked absolutely horrified and believed me!'

'Dipti! I'd never do things like that!' Shikha looked absolutely shocked. She was not one of those cranky whiny spoilt brats – she knew that!

Dipti hugged her. 'Of course you're not, sweetheart, only it won't hurt if that monster believed you were! Considering he hasn't even bothered to try and get to know you!'

'So what did he say?' Shikha asked, her brown eyes shining.

'He said he'll think about it again, and let you know! That means yes!'

'Oh, so he hasn't actually said yes as yet, has he?'

'Patience, child, patience! You'll have to learn to be patient when you follow the tigers in the reserve, and you will have to learn to be patient when dealing with obdurate monsters like Binoy chacha!'

'What's obdurate?'

'Stubborn!'

'Oh!'

They looked up as the door creaked open and Binoy chacha entered the room. It was only the second time he had done so, ever since they had moved in, Shikha realized. He glanced at Dipti, his bushy eyebrows rising.

'You still here? You should be getting back. Your father will be worried!' Then he looked at Shikha. 'I've decided to allow you to go into the reserve with Aslambhai in the Gypsy as Dipti has suggested,' he said. 'But you will have to do exactly what he says, and what the field director says. I don't want to hear any complaints!'

'Thank you, Binoy chacha! Thank you!'

He nodded. 'And how are the noises inside your head?' he asked, as if an afterthought.

'They seem to be better, Binoy chacha. I hear them only at night, and that too, not always.'

'Good,' he said. 'And goodnight!'

'Okay, Shikha, I'll be going too!' Dipti said, getting up. She paused for a second, looking at the photograph of Shikha's parents. 'You know,' she said softly, 'you look a lot like your mother.'

Shikha nodded wordlessly, not trusting herself to speak.

'Okay,' Dipti went on in her usual brisk way. 'I'll see you tomorrow. There's a lot I have to tell you about those tigers. And we can begin the photography lessons too.'

She gave Shikha a quick hug, kissed her on her head and left.

But Dipti, who had dealt so skilfully with both her father and the 'obdurate monster' of Shergarh House, had not accounted for her even more formidable mother! When Mrs Rana heard of the plans that had been made for Shikha, she went off like a pressure cooker doing a banshee act.

'What?' she shrilled. 'You want that motherless fatherless little girl to roam about in a tiger park the whole day, all by herself? What for? So that the tigers can eat her and her little brother up? You wildlife people are mad! Of course the little girl will agree – she doesn't know what she's letting herself in for! Being jolted about all day in that jeep, getting covered from head to toe with dust and such a pretty thing too! And who will be responsible for her safety?'

Mr Rana shrugged and raised his eyebrows. He grinned sardonically at Dipti.

'Your call, my dear,' he said. 'It is your brainwave!'

'Mama, she will be fine! And she wants to go. If she doesn't like it she can always say so. No one is forcing her to do anything.'

'But what will the little bitiya do all day? Who will she talk to? Her own brother is gupchup, poor little fellow. Aslambhai doesn't say very much either!'

'At least she will be occupied.' Dipti eyed her mother shrewdly. 'Or did you have your own little plan for her too?' she asked.

'Of course I did,' her mother said scornfully, her triple chins wobbling like melting triple ice-cream scoops. 'You thought I was going to let that sweet girl rot by herself in that crackpot artist's house all day? I thought she could help in my school! At least she would be meeting other children then. Maybe she can even start giving them lessons in English.'

Mrs Rana ran a small informal nursery school (more a crèche really) for the children of the staff of the forest and wildlife department.

Mr Rana nodded in approval.

'Great idea!' he said. 'It's better than letting her loose in the tiger reserve. At least she will be meeting and talking to other children. Inside, she can hardly talk to the tigers and sambhar and nilgai and langurs! And it will be nice for Sunny too.'

But Dipti shook her head, the old flinty look coming over her face.

'No, papa,' she said. 'I think Shikha needs to go into the reserve every day. It will help her find her bearings. Mixing around with a whole lot of yelling tinytots doing susu all over the place is not what she needs now. The poor child has her hands full with Sunny as it is.'

Mrs Rana looked sulkily at her husband. She knew how stubborn Dipti could be, once she had set her mind on something. (Actually as obdurate as the artist monster!)

'Tell her!' she pouted. 'Tell her it is silly to let a young girl into a wildlife park full of hungry tigers, all by herself!'

'I think,' said Mr Rana, wishing to free himself of the debate once and for all. 'I think we should let Shikha decide. Let her go into the park for a few days and see how she likes it. She might get bored of it within a week. She can also go to your school. I am sure she will find something to her liking one way or the other.'

So Shikha spent the next few days driving around the tiger reserve with Dipti, learning how to make observations, take down notes and to take photographs. She was quite thrilled and quite nervous too, but Dipti was a good and patient teacher.

'It's like preparing for an exam,' she admitted to Dipti. 'The first day will be like flying solo!'

'You'll be fine!' Dipti assured her. 'And you'll love it!'

'You know what I'll miss,' said Shikha, frowning. 'If I see something exciting, I'll miss not having you or anyone else with me to share it with.'

'Shikha, you'll have Aslambhai and Sunny, and if I know him, that little Ali who needs any excuse to bunk school. Besides, if you take pictures, you can always share those with me and papa later on.'

'I guess so!'

'Now, let's check that you are properly kitted out. Make a checklist – then you won't forget! You must take your hat, water bottle, penknife, pen and pad, and of course camera and plenty of film rolls with you. Papa will give you as many as you need. I've given Aslambhai a first-aid kit, which he will keep in the Gypsy. Don't wear bright clothes when you go inside, and make sure your shoes are comfortable! And carry a torch with fresh batteries – always! I've also given you a whistle in case of an emergency. Make sure Sharifa packs a case of emergency food in the Gypsy too.'

'Wow, Dipti, it sounds dangerous! Hey Sunny bunny we're going to feel like real explorers! How do you like that!'

'It's not dangerous, Shikha, but it's just sensible to be well prepared. The jungle can throw quite a few surprises at one!'

'I wish you weren't going away, Dipti!'

'I too wish it child, but what to do! Can't be helped. Don't worry, you'll be fine! And remember, report to papa if you see anything unusual – like a tiger that is looking ill, or people where there shouldn't be any.'

'Dipti, are there poachers in Shergarh?'

'There haven't been any for a long time. But that doesn't mean that there is no danger. But I don't think you need to worry about that. Aslambhai will take care of anything like that. You just follow the tigers and write to me about them.'

Joginder aunty cooked a fabulous farewell dinner on the eve of Dipti's departure which, surprise, surprise, even Binoy chacha attended, and neatly dressed too!

'My, my!' Dipti grinned, nudging Shikha. 'Is the ogre changing his ways? He's actually combed his beard!'

Shikha shook her head. 'I don't think so, Dipti! Look, he's got that broody hooded look in his eyes! Any minute now, he'll snap like a shark!' Bit by bit, she was regaining her old mischievous ways too.

'So how is Sunny baba?' Joginder aunty said, flashing a 500-watt smile at the little boy.

'He's fine!' said Shikha. 'He can now stay all by himself for four whole minutes!' She had been continuing her 'sit and stay' lessons diligently with her little brother and progress was being made. The next thing she had in mind was to make him go into an empty room and fetch something for her ... And, she noticed, he was smiling more. If only he would start talking again

That night, as usual she stared at her parents' photograph, and wondered where they were.

'Don't worry about us mama and papa! We're doing okay,' she whispered. She made a face. 'If only Binoy chacha were not such a kebab mein haddi – always grumpy and glowering! I wonder if he has ever smiled in his life! Miss you!'

'Aaaooom! Aaarroooon! Aaargh!' Somewhere in the reserve, a tiger was announcing its presence. 'Did you hear that, mama?' Shikha whispered. 'I wonder if that were Shahenshah!'

And as she closed her eyes, she didn't notice that for the first time since the accident, the clanging and shrieking of the car roof on the road was completely absent.

8

'OKAY, SHARIFA, OKAY SUNNY, LET'S GO THROUGH THE checklist one last time!' Shikha sang, rubbing her hands in the early morning chill. On the big four-poster bed, she had laid out all the equipment Dipti had suggested they take along for her study of the tigers of Shergarh.

'Camera! Check!' Sunny nodded, pointing it out.

'Film rolls, check! Zoom lens, check! Binoculars, check! Sunny you got yours too?' Just before she had left, Dipti had given a thrilled Sunny a small pair of binoculars for his own use. He nodded, grinning. The pair was already around his neck.

'Notebook, check! Pens, pencils, check! Whistle, check! (Sunny blew a short blast!) Hat, check! Gloves, check! You got your gloves, Sunny?' (A cold wave had brought the winter right back to Shergarh.)

'Isme khane peene ka saaman hain – the food and drink is in this!' Sharifa said, opening a huge wicker hamper that she had pulled out from somewhere, polished and cleaned.

Shikha opened the hamper and peered inside, sniffing

approvingly. Sharifa had made sure they would not go hungry – she had made a heap of aloo and keema parathas (that smelled divine!) and mixed fruit jam sandwiches. There were four bottles of water, and four bottles of orange juice and two packets of biscuits.

'Wow!' said Shikha, thrilled. 'We're going to have a good time, Sunny bunny!' Carefully she put all her equipment into the knapsack, and heaved it on to her shoulders.

'Ready to go?' She jammed on her ochre and olive green woolly hat, and looked at herself in the wobbly mirror.

'God! I look all fluffed up!' she giggled. In khaki windcheater and baggy safari trousers (both belonging to Dipti, who thankfully was not much taller than her, even if slightly plumper), and cap, she looked quite the jungle explorer she thought. 'I wonder what mama would have said,' she thought, tying her laces. Sunny stood in front of the mirror and was examining himself critically.

'You look like quite a roly-poly too!' Shikha said, 'here let me do up your laces now, or you'll fall!'

She shouldered her knapsack and they went out to the porch where Aslambhai and Ali (so wrapped up that he was just a bundle with a pair of glittering eyes!) were already waiting in the warmed up Gypsy.

Aslambhai grinned delightedly. 'Salaam memsahib,' he said, throwing her a brisk salute.

'Sharifa, where is Binoy chacha?' Shikha asked, looking through the open door of her uncle's bedroom.

'Motorcycle le ke gaya – he's taken the motorcycle and gone! I don't know when he will be back!' She snorted. 'It could be in ten minutes, it could be in ten days! Who knows? He doesn't tell anybody anything!'

'Oh! But he knew today was going to be our first day out in

the tiger reserve!' Shikha bit her lip and swallowed. 'After all we are doing this partially to get out of his hair and let him do his stupid painting in peace. At least he could have said bye to us!' She felt her eyes fill up, and brushed the tears away impatiently. What a hateful person he was! Spoiling her first day out, even before it had begun. Well, she wouldn't let him do it! If he didn't want to say goodbye, that was his problem! She and Sunny could manage quite well without his good wishes or anything, thank you. In fact, they had already been doing that! Just to spite him, that evening when they returned, she wouldn't tell him what their first day had been like. Two could play the same game, you know. If he was never there for them, then there was no reason for her and Sunny to be there for him! If he asked them, she would just purse her lips, and say, 'very nice, thank you!' or something like that. Like mama used to when she had had an argument with papa and was upset.

'Come on, Sunny,' she said, 'let's go!'

Aslambhai drove very slowly, because if he put on speed, the wind would bite right into their faces, chilling them to the bone. As they descended the steep ridge, into the tiger reserve, Shikha looked about her in wonder. The valley floor was wreathed in blue-grey fog and mist, the branches of the crooked acacia trees stuck out ghostily at all angles, chocolate dark against the pale blue-mauve of dawn. High up in the distance, Shergarh Kila reared out of the fog, but sometimes disappeared completely, as the fog swirled and rose up above it. Aslambhai suddenly slowed even more, and then stopped. Looming up ahead, in the mist, were mysterious animal shapes, moving about like ghosts in the mist.

'Sambhar!' he whispered. 'Chital!'

'Okay, Aslambhai, where do we go today?' Shikha asked, standing up and taking her first pictures. 'Ooof,' she complained.

'My fingers are so cold and stiff I can hardly press the shutter button!'

'We'll go to the fort and then the talao!' Aslambhai said, accelerating gently. 'If we get any message on the radio about tigers, then we'll follow that up.'

'It's so peaceful here!' she said dreamily. Another thing that had made her cheer up was that Sunny had, on his own, decided to sit in the back of the Gyspy, along with Ali.

'Well, Sunny this beats going to school any day!' Shikha grinned. A mischievous sparkle lit up her eyes. 'I really wonder what mama and papa would think! Us here gallivanting about in a jungle all day, instead of going to school and saying "good morning, Miss Golguppa" at assembly!' (That was what they had called their principal!) She rolled her eyes and her little brother chortled. Ali grinned; he knew exactly what she was talking about, because he was at the moment bunking school too, having told his grandfather that it was closed for a week.

'Dekho! Photo lo! – See, take a photo!' Ali pointed out at something along the burly buttress of the fort wall. A langur, cuddling her brand new (and bald) baby was sitting on the wall, just as the sun's first rays lit them up, outlining them with gold.

'Oh, wow!' Shikha was so excited she could hardly keep the camera steady and focus.

'Udhar dekho, aur langur! And look there, more langurs!'

Suddenly the langurs were everywhere! A big group swarmed up the fort wall and leapt about from place to place, each monkey trying to get a nice place where the sun would warm it. Some jumped out of the peepul trees abutting the great wall, some climbed as high as they could to catch the rays, stuffing their faces with leaves and drupes at the same time.

'Oh no!' Shikha wailed. 'There are so many of them, I don't know which one to photograph!'

'See, look at this one!' Ali said, taking her arm. 'He's come right here so you can take his picture!' She looked down. At the side of the road, not five feet away on a heap of rocks, sat a langur looking at her out of its wise brown eyes.

She trained the camera on him. 'Wow,' she breathed. 'I can see every hair on his face!'

Another one joined the big monkey, and they both stared at the Gypsy, their fur washed a pale silken gold in the early sunlight.

'Ab isko photo kab deyga? Now when will you give them their photos?' Ali asked her, innocently. Shikha grinned.

'Oh Ali, I will, as soon as they're ready. But first I want to take a picture of you with them! Will you go and stand by their side? But we might have a hard time captioning it correctly, I know!'

Ali rolled his eyes. 'Have you seen their teeth?' he asked. 'They're bigger than a tiger's!'

Tigers! Oh hell, she was supposed to be following tigers, not wasting time – and so much film – over langurs!

'Chalo, Aslambhai. Tiger dhoondte hai – come on Aslambhai, let's find some tigers!' she said, slipping back into her seat, and putting the lens cap on her camera.

'Theek hain, memsahib! Okay, memsahib!' Aslambhai grinned, and switched on the wireless. A static-ridden mostly incomprehensible conversation followed, before Aslambhai said 'Over' and switched off.

'We'll go to Hira Talao. Something always happens there.'

The mist was lifting slowly but surely by the time they reached Hira Talao. A whispery breeze shifted and stirred it, till it looked like a tattered gauze coverlet over the great blue-green lake. Herons and blazing white egrets croaked hoarsely as they fished, and overhead, flights of cormorants flew over and then landed, witch black. The tall spear grass was pearled with dew as were a million zillion webs strung like strings of pearls, shooting rainbow lasers in every direction as the sun hit them. Shikha and Sunny were absolutely enthralled.

'Can we get down here, and roam about a bit?' Shikha asked, as Aslambhai stopped the Gypsy in an open area.

'Hahnji, zaroor! Yes, certainly!' he said. Of course he got down too, with his gun on his shoulder.

'I simply must photograph those webs!' Shikha said. 'They look like diamond necklaces strung about everywhere!' She frowned as she adjusted the camera, struggling to remember what Dipti had told her about taking close-up photographs. It was so damn complicated. In the end she just set the camera to 'automatic' and began shooting. Sunny and Ali had begun chasing each other around the Gypsy, though Sunny, of course, made sure that he could see Shikha at all times – even when he went behind the Gypsy. (He simply looked under it, and saw her feet and ankles!)

'Wahan, dekho – look there!' Aslambhai said, pointing out in the distance. Across, at the other side of the lake, a pair of sambhar were butting at each other fiercely, clouds of vapour erupting from their nostrils as they heaved and shoved one another.

'Oh, great!' Shikha set her zoom to its most powerful position and began clicking away furiously.

'Look, Sunny! Look at those guys fight!'

But Sunny and Ali were too occupied with their own games, dodging around the Gypsy.

'Aslambhai, why are they fighting?' Shikha asked.

'They are fighting over those does,' the old forest guard said, pointing to a small herd that was grazing peacefully nearby, not very concerned by the battle.

They could hear the clashing of the horns, and even the harsh grunts and snorts, as the sambhar fought.

'Oh, shoot!' Shikha said, suddenly realizing she had finished her roll. 'I've already shot an entire roll and not a single tiger picture! We haven't even seen a pugmark today!'

'Koi baat nahin, baby – it doesn't matter, baby,' Aslambhai said. 'There will be many days when you won't see any tigers. But you will see the places where the tigers live, and the other animals that share the tigers' habitat. Without these beautiful places and without them, the tiger can't live and without the tiger, they can't live either. That is why we must keep these places beautiful and not destroy them, and that is why you must photograph them as well as the tiger.'

'But I hope we see them all the same!' Shikha said, reaching into her knapsack and taking out a sheaf of photographs that Dipti had given her. How had Dipti managed to take such lovely pictures? She sighed.

'Hey, you guys, Sunny, Ali let's have some breakfast,' she said, and her brother came running up, delighted. He was hungry.

They drove on after breakfast, Aslambhai taking a route they hadn't been on before, that led towards the northern boundary of the park. Sunny fell asleep soon, curling up in the back seat, next to Ali. Shikha was too keyed up to relax in any way, she had to photograph tigers, and she would! It made her feel guilty and impatient with herself that she hadn't managed to so far, even though this was just her first morning out. But there had been so many other distractions – the langurs, the spiders' webs, the fighting sambhars, and now, when they stopped, glittering squadrons of dragonflies landing on the Gypsy's bonnet, soaking up the warmth from the engine! They had met a couple of forest department Gypsys, with tourists that had looked at her curiously, making her feel very proud and important indeed. 'Mama, papa, you should just see me now!' Shikha had thought proudly. But then, her face fell when she realized that she still hadn't seen a tiger (or pugmark) let alone taken its picture. Just what would Dipti think!

'Oh, damn those tigers! I wish they would show up!'

They stopped for lunch next to a natural waterhole, near the northern boundary; but the water was a nasty green colour, and Shikha wondered how the animals actually drank from it. A big bushy looking mongoose had slithered down the bank and drunk, before looking at them in its eye-popping manner and disappearing. A plaintive squeak made her look up, and there, hovering above the waterhole was a black and white bird with a long beak, looking straight down at the water and hovering on blurry wings.

'What is it?' Shikha mumbled, struggling to stuff her sandwich into her mouth and pick up the camera at the same time.

'Pied kingfisher!' said Ali. 'Abhi dive marega! Now it will dive!'

And sure enough the bird plunged straight into the water, like a feathered dart. And Shikha shot off a couple of beautiful shots of an empty sky!

'Oh, damn! Missed it!'

To her delight, the bird climbed up into the sky again, and began hovering. She had just focused on it, when the wireless set in the Gyspy crackled.

'Rana sahib baat karega! Rana sahib wants to talk to you,' Aslambhai informed her, as she clicked a couple of shots of the hovering bird, determined to get it just as it folded its wings and dived.

'Oh, damn!' she said, lowering her camera, just as the bird plunged, with a triumphant squeak.

'Hello, Rana uncle!' she said, brushing her hair out of her face.

'Hello, Shikha! So how is it going? Are you enjoying yourself?'

'Yes, uncle! Very much! But we haven't seen any tigers as yet. Not even a pugmark! Well, one set of pugmarks, but Aslambhai says they are pretty old. The edges were all soft and blurred. But I've got no photographs yet, of tigers …'

'Don't worry about that, beti. How is Sunny doing? Not getting tired?'

'He's having a great time, uncle. He's made friends with Ali and they've been fooling around all morning. He's asleep now!'

'I see. Good!'

'Uncle, have you heard of any tiger reports today?' Shikha asked.

'Umm … yes! I heard that they've all booked appointments with their hairdressers and make-up people, which is why you haven't seen any today!'

'What, uncle? Can you say that again?'

'They've all gone to get make-up and hairstyles done. They know that a very beautiful young photographer has come to photograph them, so they want to look their best for her …!'

'Uncle, really!' Shikha blushed.

Mr Rana laughed. 'But don't worry, Shikha. Tigers can be very exasperating. You won't see one for days and days and days, and then suddenly without warning you'll see something really great. So never lose hope. And there is so much else to see in the park too …'

'Yes, uncle, I know! We saw langurs and their babies, and

sambhar fighting and spider webs like jewellery and kingfishers diving ...'

'Good! Then you will have plenty to write about in your daily report!'

'Yes, uncle!'

'Don't forget to do that! Dipti boss is very particular about things like that!'

'Yes, uncle!'

'Okay! So enjoy yourself. If you need anything you can radio me! Over!'

Oh, shoot, Shikha thought, scrabbling about in her knapsack for her notebook and pencil. She hadn't written a single line of notes till now. She had been so busy looking at things and taking pictures, there had been no time at all. Well, now seemed to be the right time, it was quiet and peaceful, even Aslambhai was dozing by the side of the Gypsy. She opened her notebook on the Gypsy's flat bonnet (still nice and warm!), wrote the date and time and began writing. Fifteen minutes later, she put down her pen and looked around. It was so lovely out here. Ahead, the waterhole reposed peacefully, now looking somewhat less murky in the bright afternoon sunlight. Behind it, clusters of date palms reared high, rustling mysteriously in the breeze, growing out of great tufts of golden grass. The rugged cliffs rose again behind the trees, reddish and looking somewhat raw. It was a dramatic country, harsh in a beautiful sort of way. And who knew, a tiger might just step into the scene at any moment, perhaps for a drink of water ... What was best was that all the things she had seen today seemed to belong to her and her alone (even if the others had seen them too).

'Wonder what Rini and Miss Nikita would think, if they knew where I was now!' Shikha thought. 'Sitting in the middle of a tiger reserve, with Sunny bunny (who was still fast asleep!), trying to observe and take photographs of tigers. And just to think, I'll be doing this tomorrow and day after and day after too, for as long as it takes Sunny bunny to get okay!' It was so strange: if the accident had not happened, or if Sunny had not been struck dumb by the shock of it, she would not probably be here right now, doing this. She would probably be back in school in Delhi. Of course the most horrible part was that mama and papa had died; it would have been perfect if they had been at Shergarh House, awaiting her return in the evening, mama ready with a humungous tea, like she used to be when she returned from school. And it must be awful for Sunny too, not to be able to talk, given the chatterbox he used to be. The whole thing was horrible, but right now, at this moment, she couldn't help feeling just a teeny-weeny bit happy. It made her feel all confused and mixed up inside. It was so peaceful and beautiful here. It made her happy; yet she felt sad at the same time. And it was so unbelievable that she was here, in the first place. 'Just what would Rini and Miss Nikita think!' She grinned. What had Dipti told her to do, to set the timer of the camera, so that she could take a picture of herself? She fiddled with it a bit, and leafed through the manual, which sensibly she had carried, and figured out what she had to do. She set the camera on the Gypsy's bonnet and took a picture of herself, with the waterhole and date palms in the background. Well, she would send Rini and Miss Nikita a copy of the picture. She sighed. It would have been so nice if she could have sent a copy to mama and papa too … wherever they were.

They started the drive back to Shergarh House at around four in the afternoon, Aslambhai steering the Gypsy quietly, his eyes scanning the road for tiger pugmarks as always. Sunny, tired out by the day in the open, had fallen asleep again, curled up next to Ali, who seemed to be practicing making faces for a competition. Shikha too was tired. She packed away her camera, feeling a little guilty about the amount of film she had used, when Aslambhai shook his head.

'Don't put it away,' he said. 'Not yet! Tayaar rakho – keep it ready. You never know when we might come across something interesting.'

'Okay, Aslambhai.' Fat chance of that happening! They had not seen the slightest sign of a tiger, not a fresh pugmark, not a whisker, all day. Her great first day out in the jungle had been a huge flop! Stupid tigers, now even they had started behaving like Binoy chacha!

Not quite. They were bumping along at the base of the west-facing ridge on which Shergarh Kila stood, when a movement high up on the great battlements caught her eye. She gasped, and gripped Aslambhai.

'Stop! Look!' Already she was scrabbling to take the lens cap off the camera. Up there, on the battlements, leaping lithely along the great crenellations was a tiger, its coat set afire by the lowering sun. Occasionally it paused and looked down at the valley below, like an emperor surveying his kingdom.

Well, empress.

'Sheba!' said Aslambhai lowering his glasses. 'That's Sheba.'

'Just look at her!' Shikha breathed. 'Hey, Sunny bunny wake up, dumbo! Look at that tigress!' Impatiently she woke her brother; it would be too awful if he missed seeing this. The tigress had now draped herself along the fort wall, and was looking straight at them far below, her tail twitching behind her like a lariat. She was lean and even at this distance Shikha could see the dangerous glitter in her golden eyes, through her binoculars.

'Oh, shoot! I've run out of film again!' Shikha moaned, and began struggling to reload, one eye on the tigress. Up on the wall, the tigress suddenly looked at something inside the fort, her ears pricked alertly. Lithely she rose to her feet, and even as Shikha rammed shut the camera, leapt off the fort wall and down the steep rocky ravine slope, with the grace of a ballerina, followed by a cacophony of alarm calls from chital, peafowl and langur. Within seconds she had plunged out of sight, into the thickets that swarmed up the ravine slope.

'Oh, damn! Missed it! Why do I keep missing shots!'

'Something disturbed her!' Aslambhai said. 'Most probably some tourists coming to the fort.'

But the sighting perked her up. At least she had seen Sheba – that was something she could write to Dipti about. And after this she would always be prepared with her camera. They reached Shergarh House an hour later, just as dusk had begun to fall, where Sharifa was waiting for them in the porch. She scooped up a dead tired half asleep Sunny into her arms and whisked him inside. Shikha followed, suddenly realizing her shoulders were aching after lugging the camera and stuff all day.

'Thank you, Aslambhai,' Shikha said getting out of the Gypsy, and grinned at Ali. 'We had a great day! See you tomorrow morning same time!' The forest guard nodded, his sunbird's nest wagging.

'We had a great time,' Shikha told Sharifa, glancing at her uncle's bedroom door as she passed it. 'We saw Sheba! She was so beautiful!' She made a face. 'I suppose the big artist sahib is in his studio?' she asked.

'Sahib poora din bahar raha. Sahib has been out the whole day. He still hasn't returned. I don't know where he has gone. But he'll be back. He always does things like this.' Sharifa seemed completely unconcerned.

'Oh,' said Shikha. What a weird uncle he was. Secretly of course, she had been hoping that he would be waiting for them, eager to hear of their day, and apologetic for not being around in the morning to see them off. Fat chance of that! As Sharifa got Sunny ready for his bath, she began telling her about their first day in the jungle. At least Sharifa was a willing listener.

But it was tough, sitting down after tea to write notes, when all she wanted to do was to listen to her CD-player and relax. Also, she would dearly have loved to be able to pick up the phone and chatter with Rini about her day – she could talk for hours on the phone. Here there was nobody to ring! And even if there was, she wondered if the phone worked. It had hardly rung at all.

'Heck, this is like doing homework!' Shikha complained, trying to make sense of the excited scribblings she had made while out in the park. But she knew Dipti would be disappointed (and maybe annoyed too) if she didn't. Then she remembered that Dipti had also told her to clean her camera and binoculars every evening. And also that she had better sort out her rolls of film properly. She got so engrossed in her work that she didn't hear the soft burble of her uncle's motorcycle in the driveway. Sunny now awake after his nap, sat next to her, using the blower brush to clean his own binoculars. He looked at his big sister, but she was busy, frowning at her camera because it had just shot off a couple of frames apparently on its own. Would she ever master the wretched thing?

Sharifa had made a delicious pillau for dinner that night, and wonder of wonders, Binoy chacha actually made an appearance at the dining table. He nodded at the children and attacked his food.

'So, how was your day, Binoy chacha?' Shikha asked him brightly, at last, unable to stand the silence.

'Like any other! You went into the park today?' he asked. As if he hadn't known! Or had he forgotten? With Binoy chacha, you never knew!

'Yes,' Shikha said excitedly. 'We drove around for the whole day and stopped at various places and never saw the faintest signs of a tiger, but then at last just before we got home we saw Sheba on the fort wall. And of course my film had to get over just then. But she was so beautiful, Binoy chacha. Have you painted her?'

He looked up from his plate. 'No,' he said shortly. 'And you will be going in tomorrow as well?'

'Yes, Binoy chacha! We'll be going every day, as Dipti had said. Like going to school, I suppose! If it is all right with you, of course!' Oh God, she prayed, don't let him spoil that now! We've been through all this before!

'Please be careful when you're inside. Those animals may look pretty and cuddly, but they are wild.' He jerked his chin towards Sunny. 'And how did he take it? He looks tired!'

'He is! And so am I. Sunny sleeps when he gets tired and he's been no trouble. And chacha, he's made friends with Ali! Isn't that great?'

'Hmmm ...' Again, Binoy chacha seemed more interested in the contents of his plate than in their brief conversation. Then he looked up.

'Some more of your things from Delhi should be arriving here eventually. I'm arranging for them to be sent,' he said.

'Oh,' Shikha said, surprised. 'What things, Binoy chacha?'

'Some of your furniture and books and clothes! Sunny's toys.'

'Oh! Thank you Binoy chacha!'

She was almost asleep as Sharifa brushed out her shining hair later that night. Sunny had passed out in usual pangolin style, his eyelashes fluttering gently as he dreamt.

'Go to sleep now,' Sharifa said. 'You are very tired! Maybe you should come home at lunchtime tomorrow. A whole day is too tiring.'

'No, Sharifa! I'm fine! We'll be fine!'

And she was asleep the moment her head hit the pillow.

No shrieking. No banging. No clanging. The noises had gone.

And a strange new – and dangerous – life had begun for her and Sunny.

9

WITHIN A WEEK'S TIME SHIKHA HAD GOT SO USED TO HER strange new way of life, it felt like she had been doing it forever. Even Sunny had got used to the daily routine very easily. Every morning, with knapsacks loaded up (Sunny had one of his own now) they would stagger out into the porch rubbing their hands and stamping their feet against the cold, where the ever-faithful Aslambhai would greet her with his cheerful, 'Salaam memsahib!' which made Shikha feel so good. Ali, of course, would grin shyly and help Sunny into the Gypsy. Sunny and he had become thick as thieves and he looked after the still silent little boy more fussily than even Shikha did. With a warning to be careful from Sharifa, who had already packed their lunch, snacks and water, they would set out in the chilly dawn. Shikha would, as a matter of duty, ask Sharifa about Binoy chacha, but mostly he was either in his studio or asleep, or out on his motorbike. She soon got used to his absence, and though it still twinged, like a pinch, she didn't let it get her down.

And so they would drive into the tiger reserve and set out on their search for tigers. On most days, they didn't see any, on others a message would come over the radio about the sighting of a tiger, though inevitably, by the time they reached the spot, the tiger was long gone. Sometimes, however, they caught a glimpse of orange as the animal disappeared into the high grass or undergrowth. At first this bothered Shikha; Dipti had asked her to observe and photograph tigers for her, and the tigers of Shergarh seemed not to want to be observed and photographed. But then, there was so much else to see and photograph that she often didn't know where to start or when to stop. Well, usually she discovered with a gasp of horror that she had used up far more film than she had wanted to! At first, both Aslambhai and Ali were her expert spotters – it astonished her how they could winkle out a beautifully camouflaged owl, or partridge, from a seemingly empty landscape. But then, she found that she was spotting things on her own too, and soon even Sunny was, though often the things he pointed out to her were of the hairy creepy crawly variety that scuttled about on the ground or on leaves and that made her want to scream. At least twice every day, Mr Rana or Joginder aunty would call on the radio to check that all was well, and it always made her feel good and safe. It was nice to know that they knew of their whereabouts in the park. Often, at around midday, Aslambhai would head the Gypsy in the direction of Hari Pani, and they would spend the rest of the day there. Somehow the old forest guard had realized that Shikha had been attracted to the place ever since their first visit there with Dipti. Its deep green waters and dramatic ochre cliff faces, its steep ravines with their rugged date palms and giant bamboo clumps, somehow soothed and calmed her, it brought a serenity to her eyes in which he still saw sadness mixed with laughter when she played with her little brother and made him chortle and giggle.

Shikha would often settle down at the edge of the little

pavilion, take out her increasingly tattered notebook and jot down notes about what she had seen and photographed that morning. Then she would stare out at the deep green waters, watching a pair of dabchicks putter about like a pair of little tugs (they were so cute and they had no tails!) or an egret fish with deadly intent. Kingfishers would flash like sparks low over the water, and usually by about three or four o'clock (by which time Sunny was usually fast asleep) chital, sambhar, nilgai, langur and wild boar would come out of the jungle at the far side and drink, kept company by the ever-present peacocks, with their quivering throats and hideous screams.

'They all seem to be so terribly frightened when they come down to drink,' Shikha whispered to Aslambhai.

'Hahn, baby – yes baby, that is because they know the tiger can get them here, while they drink. They have to be very careful. But at least there are no crocodiles here.'

And Shikha and Sunny learnt to keep absolutely still while the animals went about their business. Ever so often the red-wattled lapwings would get hysterical, flapping about and creating a great ruckus, as a sambhar or chital startled them.

'Those birds will be nesting soon. They'll be making a lot of noise,' Aslambhai said.

One afternoon at Hari Pani, about ten days after they had started going into the jungle, Shikha had pulled out her notebook and decided to try and sketch the scene in front of her. She was on the pavilion steps, at the end of the promontory, leading down into the pool, while Sunny and Ali were enjoying their usual siesta on the mat they had spread out, in the chhatri behind her. Aslambhai too had apparently dozed off, his gun beside him, but Shikha knew how lightly he slept. If she so much as stood up, he would be wide awake in a second. Now she surveyed the scene. Across on the opposite bank, a small herd of chital had stepped nervously out of the forest, looking in every direction and sniffing the air cautiously for danger. The layout of the whole area was such that usually the wind funnelled down through the ravines and gullies, from the jungle side towards the pavilion, which was a great help to anyone watching the animals. They (if their noses were sharp enough) smelt the animals and not the other way around. A couple of red wattled lapwings patrolled the far side too, keeping a smart eye out on the deer. A pair of lovely plum-headed parakeets flew down to drink. Shikha knew them well, they had a nest in a hollow in one of the date palms at the side of the lake. She looked at them through her binoculars. They were always so beautiful, the male, with his rich plum-coloured head, his wife with a dark grey head, and both with papaya-coloured nutcracker bills and maroon epaulettes on green wings. Casually she raised the binoculars higher, focusing on the forest beyond – and froze.

A face was staring out of the jungle, framed by grasses and bushes. A lean striped face, with burning amber eyes and spiky white moustache! A face she recognized in a jiffy because she must have studied it a hundred times before in Dipti's photographs.

Sheba!

But, thankfully, her burning eyes were not fixed on Shikha, who now was hardly daring to breathe. They were locked on the small herd of deer that, unconcerned, were drinking in the shallows of the lake.

'Run! Run! Run!' Shikha prayed silently and fervently, though some tiny part of her was also praying equally hard, 'slowly, Sheba, take it easy, you're almost there girl!' She saw the grass quiver ever so slightly, and watched spellbound as the tigress, crouching low, her belly brushing the ground, stepped out of the jungle. She knew she was too far away to spring just yet, those last few crucial metres would have to be done out in the relative open, with just short grass for cover.

The damn lapwings stood suddenly to attention, all alert and poised to flee.

Sheba wriggled forward, a couple of metres closer now.

The chital watched the lapwings, their ears pricked, standing stock-still.

The tigress slithered forward, her movement barely discernible.

Shikha's heartbeat had become a disco drumbeat!

The lapwings flexed their legs, ready to spring into the air.

'Run! Run! Run!' Shikha prayed for the chital. And then, 'Go Sheba, go!'

Sheba heard her prayer.

In a blur of growling flame, the tigress leapt. In two bounds she was in the middle of the herd, which scattered wildly in every direction. The tigress had chosen her victim well, a doe that had been wandering closest to her. The panic-stricken animal had turned to flee, but had bumped into another, and staggered. It was enough for Sheba.

'Oh!' Shikha gasped, a hand in front of her mouth, her face white as chalk. The weight of the tiger had crushed the doe; there was a resounding crack as her knees buckled and broke as she went down, and then the terrible growling of the tigress as she bit deeply into the chital's neck, virtually smothering her with her body, her claws digging deep into the golden flanks. A despairing bleat from the chital, a hind leg kicking out feebly from under that great weight, and then just the cacophony of the surrounding jungle as peacocks and langurs and lapwings sounded the alarm, too late at least for one unfortunate chital. Her eyes round with horror Shikha saw the blood pouring out, darkening the dry earth and soaking the golden pelt. And then at last, the tigress relaxed her vice-like grip, and looked around panting, her mouth and face smeared brightly with blood, as the chital's head lolled helplessly away.

'Oh!' Shikha moaned, 'she looks as though she's gone berserk with lipstick!' Then her world whirled and she swayed.

'Theek hai! It's okay,' said Aslambhai, who had risen in a flash, his gun in one hand. He put it down and caught her just as she keeled over. His voice sounded very far away and faint, she thought vaguely.

Behind her, Sunny and Ali slept on blissfully.

'Here, drink this!' Shikha opened her eyes and blinked. Aslambhai was looking down at her, raising her head with one hand, the water bottle in the other. He grinned.

'Memsahib aap ne to Sheba ko kill karte dekha! Wah! – memsahib, you saw Sheba make a kill! Congratulations!'

'My God!' Shikha moaned. 'Is she still there?'

'Andar laye gayee – she's taken the kill inside the jungle!'

Shikha sat up and rubbed her eyes.

Hari Pani looked as peaceful and beautiful as ever. The lapwings were patrolling their end of the bank, quite relaxed.

'Oh shoot!' Shikha groaned, slapping her forehead with her hand. 'I didn't take a single photograph!' She had clean forgotten about the camera, which lay accusingly beside her. 'What an ass I am! Dipti will never forgive me!'

'Koyee baat nahin – it doesn't matter,' Aslambhai said consolingly. 'This time you have seen it. Next time you will photograph it. It always happens that way.'

He prodded Ali awake.

'Look at this fellow!' he snorted. 'He slept right through it!'

'But she was so … so awesome!' Shikha said. 'Do you think she'd be eating it now?' she asked.

'Yes,' Aslambhai said. 'It is best we do not disturb her. We can wait here for some more time – maybe she will come down here for a drink.'

'That poor deer! She didn't have a chance!'

'Her time had come. But Sheba will have a full stomach for a few days, now.'

'She was so graceful when she leapt out. And she just seemed to know that she was not going to miss it.'

'Did-ye-do-it? Did-ye-do-it?' the lapwings screamed suddenly and took off.

Sheba stepped out of the jungle confidently, her face a bloody mask. She came to the water's edge, bent down and began to drink.

'Okay, okay, calm down Shikha girl, calm down, just cool your jets girl!' Shikha picked up the camera quietly and focused it on the tigress on the other side of the water. Next to her, Sunny sat up, his eyes glued to his own binoculars, his mouth a huge surprised 'O'. The tigress drank for about three minutes then turned away and walked gracefully back into the forest behind her.

'Wow! Oh, wow! My very first tiger pictures!' Shikha was elated. 'I just hope they come out well. My hands were shaking so much!'

A small flock of tree pies had begun gathering around the thicket into which Sheba had disappeared. They knew there was a kill at hand.

'Do you think we could watch her eating?' Shikha asked, her eyes gleaming. Imagine if she could photograph that. It would partly make up for her having missed taking pictures of the hunt. But Aslambhai shook his head.

'No,' he said. 'Sheba is too dangerous! She will charge! Actually I think we better start going back. It is getting late.'

He was right, because the sun had dipped behind the ridges, plunging Hari Pani into shadow. A chill had spread over the green waters, and Shikha suddenly shivered. Still groggy with his siesta in the sun, and having watched Sheba drink, Sunny took her hand. Then he held out his other hand to Ali and they walked back to the Gypsy, with Aslambhai close behind them, watchful as ever. They looked as though they were returning from a walk in the park.

'Shikha memsahib to Sheba ko dekh kar behosh ho gaya – Shikha memsahib saw Sheba and fainted!' Ali teased, with a snort of laughter. Shikha turned, her eyes flashing.

'Hahn, maybe but at least I saw her make a kill. You were fast asleep! If Sheba pounced on you, you'd still be snoring inside her stomach! Big jungle tracker you think you are!' Then she turned to Aslambhai.

'Aslambhai, do you think we could drop by at Rana sahib's office on the way back?' she asked, as she rummaged about in her knapsack, trying to settle things. It always ended up being an unholy mess by the end of each day. 'I'm running out of film and want to give Rana sahib the exposed ones for developing.'

'Hahn, memsahib, zaroor! Yes, memsahib, definitely.' Aslambhai spoke into the radio and beamed.

'I've told them you saw Sheba make a kill. They're waiting to welcome you with ladoos and garlands!' he grinned.

Shikha blushed. 'I only wish I had managed to take photographs of it. But I was so stunned!'

Well, it wasn't garlands, but it was another of Joginder aunty's massive hugs followed by an equally massive tea. And Shikha, Sunny and Ali simply fell upon the huge mountain of hot pakoras as though they hadn't seen any food for six months.

'Well done!' Rana uncle said. 'It seems that the tigers of Shergarh like you. First you see Shahenshah from close quarters, (of course he didn't know exactly how close, Shikha thought with a chuckle) then Sheba lets you watch her make a kill!'

'I was lucky! I wish I could have photographed it though. I was just so shocked I simply forgot all about it. And it all happened so suddenly!'

'Well, you were lucky perhaps, but deservedly so. You have spent every day out there from morning to evening after all, so you deserve to see something happen. Frankly my dear, I'm surprised you've carried on so long. It's been, what, ten or twelve days, non-stop?'

'I like it, uncle,' Shikha said simply. 'Even when you don't see anything, it's just so nice. It's peaceful and beautiful. I feel calm inside, not upset and worried. And everything seems to know what it has to do. I mean all the creatures go on with what they have to do without really getting into each other's way. Sometimes they do, but then they just butt one another politely and get on with things. Not like us, always interfering with one another unnecessarily and getting all upset.'

'Well, by and large they do mind their own business, except when one creature decides to eat another,' Mr Rana said, his eyes twinkling.

'Uncle, any news from Dipti? I'll be posting her my first set of notes at the end of this week; she said once a week or fortnight.'

'She's fine! She rang the other day. She can't wait to get back here!' Joginder aunty said. 'Now, bachche have another pakora! Is that uncle of yours looking after you properly?'

'Binoy chacha is fine! Mostly painting, or out somewhere on his motorbike!'

'Hmm! Good thing you have Sharifa to look after you.' Mrs Rana looked decidedly flinty – rather like Dipti had.

'Here you go, a dozen more rolls of film. These should see

you through for a bit.' Mr Rana handed Shikha the rolls, which she packed away safely into the knapsack.

'I just hope the pictures come out well,' she said. 'I've never done any photography before, and sometimes that camera sort of plays the fool with me! All these lights come on and off!'

'Don't worry, Shikha dear.' Suddenly Mr Rana spotted Ali, sitting low in his chair, and busy gobbling his pakoras.

'Has this rascal been bothering you?' Mr Rana roared, as Ali sat bolt upright with shock.

Shikha grinned. 'No uncle!' she said sweetly. 'He only likes people like Mr Goldie Singh!'

It was dark by the time they got into the Gypsy. It would take them forty-five minutes to drive back to Shergarh House – except that half an hour out on the road, the Gypsy began to wobble.

'Puncture!' sang Ali happily, jumping off, as Aslambhai stopped the vehicle with a muttered oath. He looked up and down the road, but they were quite alone, and it was pitch dark and pretty cold already.

'Take the jack and lever out,' he told Ali, and began unbolting the spare tyre at the back. Shikha took out her torch and flashed it. To her surprise, she saw that Aslambhai was panting and sweating as he struggled with the tyre nuts. And frankly it was too cold for anyone to be sweating.

'You shouldn't do that!' she said suddenly. 'Sharifa mentioned you'd had a heart attack! Hey, Ali, come on, help me get the tyre down!'

She virtually snatched the spanner out of Aslambhai's hands. Together, they loosened the nuts. The tyre bounced down and nearly ran away into the darkness with Ali in hot pursuit. Then, as Aslambhai instructed they loosened the nuts of the flat tyre – and this was the toughest part. Ali virtually stood on the tyre lever and jumped on it, to make the nuts come loose.

'Here,' Shikha said, game to try, 'let me do it, I'm heavier than you!' Carefully Aslambhai positioned the jack under the vehicle. Flat on her tummy in the dust Shikha flashed the torch to ensure he put it in the right position. Then he began raising the vehicle, which wasn't too strenuous. Together, the three of them (with Sunny watching solemnly and letting off huge yawns) changed the tyre and set off again.

'Home at last!' Shikha breathed in relief as they drove into the porch of Shergarh House. What she needed was a nice long hot bath. Her hair had been blown all over her face in the open Gypsy (her ponytail had long come adrift), her cheeks and nose were pink with cold and stained with grease and dust, her hands were filthy black thanks to the puncture. Her jacket was covered with the dust she had lain down in while flashing the torch under the Gypsy. Even Sunny looked quite the ragamuffin – well, a sleeping ragamuffin because he was fast asleep by the time they drove in. Somehow, he had got tyre black all over his face and his jacket was also filthy because he too had lain down flat when she had. Shikha was a little surprised that Sharifa was not on the porch to greet them as they drove in – as was her usual practice. Maybe she was readying their baths, which was something she was looking forward to like nothing else. A long, hot soak in that gigantic tub, and hopefully Sunny would be fast asleep, so she wouldn't have to call out to him every thirty seconds but simply lie back and daydream.

'Thanks so much Aslambhai,' she said, smiling tiredly. 'We had a great day today!'

'Kal milenge! We'll meet tomorrow, Khuda hafiz – God willing!' Aslambhai said grinning. And then prodded Ali. 'Take memsahib's bag inside!'

Shikha hitched a cranky (because he was now coming awake) Sunny on to her hip and staggered indoors. To her surprise, the lights were on everywhere, in the lobby and the drawing room. She sniffed. There was definitely the whiff of an unfamiliar perfume. A sweet, sickly smell that made her crinkle up her nose.

'Sharifa!' she called. 'We're home! We got late because we had a puncture! And guess what! I saw Sheba make a kill!'

She jutted out her hip a little more, so Sunny wouldn't slip down (he was really getting a bit too heavy for this now) and stumbled into the drawing room.

'Sharifa!' she sang. 'Is Binoy chacha in his studio or gallivanting about the countryside on his motorbike? And why are all the lights on? Oh!'

She stopped, as startled as she had been when she had seen Sheba peering out of the jungle foliage at the deer. And nearly turned to flee as the poor chital had done. Also too late!

Binoy chacha, in a clean dark grey kurta, was sitting on the sofa, his legs crossed elegantly, his beard combed, beedi between his fingers. Beside him sat a strange large, fleshy lady with a bloated face and a bindi that looked like a mango, and a mouth which looked like Sheba's after her kill. She had small black eyes, heavily lined with kohl, and though she had begun to smile dazzlingly, there was no real smile in those watermelon seed eyes, just pity. She got up from the sofa, as Shikha's eyes flickered up and down taking her in; she was wearing an off-white sari with an orange border, and orange blouse. She was a little taller than her, and looked a bit like one of those advertising balloons – blimps they were called – Shikha noted, a little pleased with her observation. She had a single thick gleaming black plait that swung to her waist and a severe centre parting. But where on earth had she got that hideous blood-red lipstick from? A dying chital doe? Shikha shook the hair out of her eyes and forced a smile.

'Hello, my dear!' the strange lady said in the sort of tone that people she didn't know had used when they came to say how sorry they were that mama and papa had died, holding open pale plump arms on which bangles jingled. 'I'm Veena aunty. A very good friend of your uncle's! He's told me so much about you. You brave children! But tell me my dear, do you always carry your little brother on your hip like that all the time?'

Wildly, Shikha looked at Binoy chacha, but he seemed busy searching for another wretched beedi.

'Er ... Hello!' she stammered, suddenly aware of what a sight and fright she must look. She, who normally was so particular about being neat and tidy ('presentable' as mama used to say) when meeting guests, looked and probably smelt like a scarecrow that had been butted by a wild boar! And there was Binoy chacha, who normally went around like a hairy caveman sitting smugly, spick and span, *with even his beard neatly combed!* She ran one hand through her wild hair and then hurriedly hitched up Sunny, who had begun to slide again (pulling her jeans down with him), back on to her hip. 'I'm Shikha,' she said, smiling brightly, but hugely embarrassed, 'and this is Sunny. He's just very tired. We've just returned from the tiger reserve. We had a puncture and had to help with changing the tyre. That's why we're late.'

The lady nodded understandingly, that pitying smile still on her face.

'Here, Sunny bunny, say hello to Veena aunty,' Shikha murmured, involuntarily pecking her brother on his cheek.

'Tiger reserve! Puncture! Changing the tyre! Late! How lovely! Did you hear that Binoy, dear?' Veena turned to Binoy chacha who was staring at the ceiling.

'Really, Binoy!' she said shaking her head as if greatly distressed. 'They're children, for God's sake!' She turned to Shikha again, her eyebrows arched: 'And my dear, what was that you were saying when you came in? About someone called Sheba making a kill?' Her voice was smooth as velvet.

'Hey Sunny bunny get down a second,' Shikha whispered. 'This big dame is giving me the creeps!'

Sunny slid down and beamed and chortled, rubbing his eyes. Frog, he thought. Big froggy!

'Er ... Sheba's a tigress ma'am. We saw her make a kill! It was awesome!'

'Ah, Shikha, Veena er... aunty will be having dinner with us. She's a very well-known social worker in the village. I thought it would be good if you got to know each other,' Binoy chacha said, nodding casually as if noticing her for the first time.

'Ah, here's something I have for you both!' Veena Aunty said brightly, plunging into her handbag and taking out two extra-tiny sized bars of Five Star chocolate. She pinched Sunny on the cheek (he turned away and buried his face in Shikha's lap) and offered him one.

'Here, beta,' she offered. 'Chocolate?'

Sunny turned around and took the chocolate, clutching it in his palm.

'And, beta, what do you say?' Veena aunty asked, looking hurt, and opening her eyes as wide as she could. Sunny just stared at her.

'Er ... Sunny can't speak any more,' Shikha said. 'Not since the accident.' She looked despairingly at Binoy chacha for help. Surely he had told this awful creature about the accident and everything?

Veena aunty nodded knowingly. 'I know, beti,' she said in a low sad sort of tone. 'I know! I just thought that by asking him a question, he might just answer involuntarily and start talking again. You never know with these cases.' She shook her head tragically.

And to her dismay, Shikha suddenly found hot tears flooding into her eyes again. How many hundred times had she tried getting Sunny to talk again – she couldn't remember! And in how many different and often cunning ways! None had worked. And now here was this fat faced woman with a voice like oil sliding about in a cold saucepan who thought she could get him to talk by making him thank her for the measly chocolate bar she had just given him! If only it had been so simple! Shikha gulped and closed her eyes, hoping the tears wouldn't squeeze their way out and give her away. Quick, think of something crazy, nutty, idiotic – that's what papa used to tell her to do whenever she got upset. Just to derail what was bothering you. Then she smiled like a cat that had just eaten an especially plump and juicy canary. She imagined the scene at Hari Pani that morning. Sheba crouched low in the foliage, her eyes burning, her tail twitching. And then leaping out right at the soft fleshy creature in front of her! Squish! Squash! Squoosh! Like landing on a gigantic maggot! What a meal she would have! A little rich perhaps, tiger junk food definitely, but delicious! 'Snail snot!' she thought suddenly, wackily. 'Your voice reminds me of snail snot!'

Thankfully then Sharifa bustled in briskly and scooped up Sunny.

'Come on, Sunny sahib, bath time!' she said, kissing him and wrinkling up her nose. 'You smell like a tiger! Chalo Shikha baby! It's very late! Look how dirty you've made your clothes!' She gave 'Veena aunty' a glare, grabbed Shikha's hand and took the children to their room.

'So who is she?' Shikha asked, as she took off her shoes and socks and flexed her cramped toes ecstatically. 'Is she Binoy chacha's girlfriend?' she giggled. 'My God, she's so smooth and oily! She could grease a … a ferris wheel with that voice! And that lipstick!' She rolled her eyes wildly and lay back on her bed. 'Like Sheba's mouth after a kill! But Sheba would enjoy her wouldn't she! All soft and juicy and mushy! Hardly any chewing required! She'd just slide down like snail snot! Yum yum! Well, ugh!'

'Shikha baby, samaan theek karo – sort out your things.' Sharifa said briskly. 'I'll give Sunny a bath in the meantime. Keep calling to him or he'll jump out of the tub and come running out nangu pangu and full of soap!'

'But who is she?' Shikha insisted. 'Have you seen her before?'

Tiredly Sharifa nodded. 'Hahn – yes,' she said. 'She came to Shergarh about a year ago and stays in a room in the village school. She says she does some work with village women and children or something like that. She has come here to meet your uncle several times to complain about the tiger reserve and poison his ears about the Ranas. Fortunately your uncle doesn't listen to anyone very seriously.' Sharifa sniffed vaguely. 'I really don't know what she does with the children, but she has no children of her own and most of the village children – including Ali – run away when they see her coming! Now come on, take a bath! I have to go and finish making the dinner now.'

Half an hour later, scrubbed, shining and radiant, Shikha and Sunny stepped into the drawing room once again. Shikha knew it would seem rude if they had stayed in their room till dinner, and anyway, she was curious to learn more about 'Veena aunty'. Imagine Binoy chacha having a girlfriend, though trust him to pick one like that smooth bloated blimp!

'Come on, Sunny,' she said. 'This is the first guest we've had since we got here! Let's go and see what she's like!' She snorted and tossed her head. 'Like snail snot I bet! They can walk on razor blades after snotting all over them, did you know that toodledumps?' She grinned and dimpled wickedly.

The low earnest conversation in the drawing room stopped the moment the children stepped into it, and Shikha knew at once that Binoy chacha and Veena aunty a.k.a. Snail Snot had been talking about them.

'Ah, hello again!' Veena aunty said, smiling brightly. 'My, what a pretty young lady you are! I can hardly recognize you!'

Sharifa bustled in looking for Sunny.

'Come on, you have your dinner now. You're almost asleep,' she said. Sunny made sure that Shikha was following him into the dining room, and went out with Sharifa.

'Why don't you stay with us and chat?' Veena aunty suggested.

'Er ... Sunny doesn't like being separated from me,' Shikha said, wondering what the hell Binoy chacha had told this woman. Or was she simply pretending that she didn't know anything? 'Excuse me!' she said and went into the dining room. Poor Sunny fell asleep halfway through his food, and had to be carried to bed by Shikha. Then she joined the adults in the drawing room again. She was half asleep herself, but very curious about Snail Snot. Something was in the air, something fishy was cooking, something she didn't like the smell of one bit, and she was sure that it involved her and Sunny. She simply had to find out what it was. Stifling a yawn and drawing her mother's pink dressing gown around her (which still smelt of her) she walked into the brightly lit room.

10

'COME SHIKHA DARLING, SIT NEXT TO ME!' VEENA AUNTY invited, shifting up on the sofa so that there was plenty of room, and patting the seat, a bright smile on her face.

'What a big smile you have, Snail Snot!' thought Shikha, quite aware that she was being extremely rude (at least in her thoughts)! Gingerly she sat down next to the woman, aware of the sweet sickly smell that wafted over from her. Binoy chacha was as usual studying the ceiling fan.

'Your little brother is asleep?' Snail Snot inquired tenderly.

Shikha nodded. 'Yes,' she said, 'he was very tired. Otherwise he'd be right here, with me!'

'Binoy chacha says that he has never left your side ever since … since it happened?' Were those tears in those tragic looking eyes? They glistened, and Snail Snot dabbed them with a handkerchief.

'Yes. He's very afraid of being left alone,' Shikha said in a matter-of-fact manner, and sticking out her jaw firmly. She would be damned if she let Snail Snot upset her, or feel sorry for her. 'He's just a little boy, I guess!'

'And he's never said a word? Not one word?'

Shikha shook her head. 'No,' she said. 'Not since the accident! He cries and laughs and throws tantrums, but hasn't said anything. Not even in his sleep. I've listened!' Oh hell, she was getting moist eyed again and that lump in her throat was bobbing up and down like a ping-pong ball. Damn Snail Snot! Why did adults always bring up these subjects time and time again? Why couldn't they be like Dipti and Rana uncle, who spoke only of tigers and interesting things like that and accepted Sunny and her as they were?

'And you don't mind it? Having your little brother tag along with you everywhere? What a wonderful girl you are!'

'Mind it? Why should I mind it? Of course it can get a bit tiresome sometimes, but the doctors say he is not well! What's so wonderful about me being with him?' She looked around. 'I mean there's no one else. So what's so wonderful?' She felt her temper rise; she wanted to scream at this silly bloated toad of a woman and smack her face!

'Cool it, Shikha baby! Just cool your jets girl!' she told herself fiercely. 'This woman is just a curious interfering busybody!' But she would be damned if she let her say anything against Sunny. He, poor fellow, couldn't even defend himself.

'Snail Snot!' she blurted loudly before she could stop herself and looked around embarrassed, as if she had belched in public. 'Oops, beg your pardon!' she added, blushing. There was a brief puzzled silence. Snail Snot leaned forward, pretending to look interested.

'What my dear?' she asked. 'Did you say "snail snot"?'

Shikha nodded. 'Did you know that snails lay down a trail of snot, and then are able to walk on razor blades without hurting themselves?' she said. 'Mr Rana told me that! Imagine!'

Binoy chacha's eyebrows reached the ceiling, but as usual

he said nothing. Really, he was becoming more and more like Sunny, Shikha thought.

Snail Snot smiled. 'Oh,' she said. 'How fascinating!' She looked at Binoy chacha and then at Shikha.

'So my dear, what happens when your school opens?' she asked.

'School?'

'Yes, surely you'll be going back to school after summer? Binoy chacha said that you missed half of last year, and will have to repeat the year, but you will be going back in the new academic year, won't you?'

'Um … ma'am well it depends on how Sunny is,' Shikha said. 'If he's okay and has started talking again, well then I guess so! But if he's like this, well then there's no way he's going to let me!'

'What? My dear, you can't be serious! Have you tried leaving him on his own for a bit? What would happen if you went out while he was not looking …'

'He gets hysterical and then it takes the whole day to calm him! They had to give him calmpose injections in the hospital when I had to go for tests!' (And didn't add that it had taken them the whole day – and calmpose injections – to calm her down too, she'd be damned if she admitted it to this creature!)

'Oh, you poor child!'

'Actually it's fun,' Shikha said shrugging her shoulders nonchalantly. 'I don't mind in the least. And Sunny is no trouble at all. We spend the whole day inside the reserve, following tigers. And now Sunny is getting along very well with Ali. I'm sure that soon he'll be willing to go along with him and without me.'

'Oh!' That was Binoy chacha, wonder of wonders, hallelujah! 'It is good to hear that!'

Shikha beamed. 'Yes, Binoy chacha, I definitely think he's better. He no longer looks so frightened all the time! Like a bunny caught in headlights,' she added, remembering the rabbit that had stared, stupefied at the Gypsy's headlights on their way home. 'Or a chital that has just smelt a tigress!'

'Following tigers! In the jungle! Such a young girl like you! I've never heard of such a thing! How old are you, my dear?' Snail Snot had her scandalized look on her face again.

'Fourteen!' said Shikha, making it sound as if she were twenty four.

'Don't you get scared? And isn't it dangerous?' Now she had begun sounding helpless and lost. 'I would be terrified!'

'Well, it can be scary!' Shikha turned and looked at her uncle, not wanting to share with Snail Snot what she had been dying to tell him all evening. 'Binoy chacha, today we saw Sheba kill a chital – and I fainted! Of course Aslambhai was right there with us, with his gun and all! But I felt so stupid! And I didn't even take any pictures! But you should have seen her face – all smeared with blood – it almost looked like she'd gone crazy with lipstick! And imagine, Sunny and Ali slept through the entire drama!'

Snail Snot looked as if she were about to be attacked by Sheba herself. Binoy chacha glanced at Shikha in his usual laconic way.

'Just make sure you are always with Aslambhai,' he said. 'Don't ever wander away from him. And make sure he is awake!'

'But Binoy!' Snail Snot protested in an earnest, concerned tone. 'This is asking for trouble! I've never heard anything so ridiculous! To allow a child to roam about a tiger-infested jungle! And with her little brother by her side! I mean the poor little fellow will not even be able to call for help if anything happens! She should be in school! The little boy should be in school!'

'And Aslambhai,' added Binoy chacha, in his dry way. 'They have Aslambhai with them too! That fellow has eyes at the back of his head and can take out the eye of a bird at five-hundred yards. He's the best!'

'It shouldn't be allowed! It can't be allowed! I don't know how you have allowed it, Binoy, and I don't know how that foolish field director has given permission!' Snail Snot was almost weeping with horror and outrage! Or, at least, trying to sound as if she was. Pretending to, like.

'And when Sheba growled, it made me feel all horribly wobbly inside. As if I just had to go to the bathroom. Sn ... Veena aunty, have you ever seen a tiger in the reserve?'

'Er ... no! And I don't want to,' Veena aunty replied with a shudder.

Sharifa popped her head around the door.

'Khana tayaar hai! Dinner is ready!' she announced.

'I'm famished,' Shikha said, yawning hugely, big tea at the Ranas long forgotten. 'And sleepy, too,' she added.

Sharifa, not being told by Binoy sahib that Veena (who was a fussy eater) was coming to dinner, had made chicken curry and rice. At the last minute, she had had to run around and conjure up 'a simple khichri, like what the villagers eat' as the woman prissily put it, for the guest. Shikha dug in hungrily. After the whole day out, she had returned home as ravenous as any tigress in Shergarh Tiger Reserve.

She said goodnight and went to her room almost immediately after dinner. She had had a long, tiring day, and was virtually asleep on her feet now. Binoy chacha and Snail Snot returned to the drawing room, Snail Snot lecturing on righteously about how important it was for kids to have proper schooling and upbringing and how they needed discipline and order in their lives or would turn out wild and bad and take to drugs and smoking and drinking and using foul language and disrespecting their elders.

'God!' Shikha said to herself as she brushed her hair in front of the wobbly mirror. 'She's like a moral science lesson. So sancti ... sancti ... what was that word? Sanctified? No!' Impulsively she went to the door and was about to pop into the drawing room to ask her uncle (it was a rare occasion when he was around and she could ask him anything!) what it was, when she paused at the doorway, behind the curtain. Snail Snot was holding the floor again, talking away in that earnest wheedling manner, as if to show that there was very deep meaning and caring behind her words and that the good of everyone depended on them. Shikha hesitated, her face going red because she knew she was eavesdropping, and that was one thing both mama and papa would not tolerate. But now she just could not help it, even though she felt ashamed.

'Binoy, you have just got to do something about those poor children!' the awful woman was saying. 'They can't go on like this – roaming around like wild things in the jungle the whole day. And I don't care if they have that forest guard with them! He can't be much of a good influence on them!'

'They appear to be quite happy, given the circumstances,' Binoy chacha said, and behind the curtain, Shikha silently cheered, 'yes, yess! Way to go Binoy chacha, way to go! Sock it to her!'

'Of course they appear to be happy! Running wild all day, doing God knows what they want in that jungle. A tiger-infested jungle at that! Do you know, Binoy, they kicked out all the poor villagers who were staying in the reserve just so the tigers could live there and rich foreigners could come and take photographs and videos! Imagine! I think all these places should be closed down and the people allowed back in. They will be able to look after the environment much better than any tigers! They're humans, not animals!'

'Humans haven't done very well, have they?' Binoy chacha countered mildly.

'Well, certainly Binoy you haven't done very well with those poor orphaned children! Such irresponsibility! And I really think it is time that the little boy was made to separate from his sister. It's not good for either of them! Going to school will be a good thing. And different schools too. They must learn to face the world alone, not cling to each other all the time.'

'They've had a hard time, Veena. And it hasn't been very long either. I admit I may not be the best person to bring them up, but that's the way it is. I'm following what the doctors have advised … Maybe they need a little more time.'

'Binoy dear, but I can help! I want to help! When I saw that young thing enter the room this evening, her little brother on her hip, looking as if she had been living wild in the jungle for a week, it broke my heart! I thought, I have to do something for these poor things!'

'Eh? What? How can you help?' But there was a hopeful note in Binoy chacha's voice, and Shikha's heart sank. She was also dimly aware of a rage building up inside her against this interfering busybody who had just barged in like this. Control freak!

'You know Binoy, I work with villagers and village children. I've seen this sort of thing before! I know! Don't do anything now, and these kids will get spoilt forever! You wouldn't want that would you! And that girl is so pretty!'

'So what do you suggest, Veena?'

'School is number one. Of course we are now at the end of the academic year and the summer holidays will start. But after the holidays, Shikha must go to school. No question about that!

Also, I think the little boy needs specialized treatment. First, he has to be separated from his sister. Then we can begin teaching him sign language so that he can communicate again!'

Sign language! For Sunny bunny! As if he would never talk again! Shikha felt her cheeks hot up as they turned scarlet with rage. Besides, Sunny and she communicated perfectly well – they had, in fact, unconsciously developed a sign language of their own. Well Sunny had, because Shikha always spoke to him and he replied with hand gestures, or making faces or rolling his eyes, or smiling or frowning or whatever. At any rate, they understood each other perfectly. She was about to burst into the room and indignantly claim that Sunny didn't need any specialized classes thank you, and that she would never leave him if he didn't want it, when she paused, trembling with rage. 'Back off Shikha, girl, easy!' she muttered fiercely. It would be better if she just stayed quiet and didn't let the enemy (what else was that smug-faced control freak?) know that she had overheard her.

'How do you think we can separate Sunny from his sister without upsetting him?' Binoy chacha asked, joining the enemy as it were. 'You saw how he clings to her.'

'I think he will have to just wake up one morning and find that she is not there,' Snail Snot said with diabolical calmness, as Shikha went pale behind the curtain and began to tremble. 'He will then just have to get used to the idea that she is not there any more for him to cling to.'

'Don't you think the little boy has had enough of a shock with his parents' deaths?' Binoy chacha asked. 'If Shikha disappeared too he'd … I really don't know what would happen to him!'

'Yes,' said Snail Snot, with astonishing calm. 'The shock might just also make him start talking again! Think about that.

At any rate he'll get used to her absence very quickly. Children always do!'

'And exactly what do you mean by Shikha disappearing suddenly?' Binoy chacha asked, frowning, not quite liking the sound of it.

'Simple!' said the diabolical woman. 'We will get her admitted to a boarding school – I know the directors and principal of Paradise Valley Boarding School, which has just opened. It is about eight hours by train from Shergarh. Admission should not be a problem. She leaves very quietly early one morning, bag and baggage, while Sunny is asleep and that is that!'

'Hmmm … I'll have to think it over,' said Binoy chacha doubtfully. 'And maybe talk to Jogi Rana too – she runs a school here for the kids of the wildlife staff.'

'Binoy, between you and me, I think it would be better to keep Shikha away from those Ranas, as much as possible. I don't think they're a good influence on her. Look at that girl … what's her name … Dipti? You said she was the one who encouraged Shikha to go into the jungle alone.'

'Oh, the Ranas are all right! And Rana sahib is the best field director this park has ever had,' said Binoy chacha. 'And Shikha likes Dipti!' He ran his hand through his beard, and Shikha wondered what the dry rasping sound was. Then he spoke again. 'But what if Shikha refuses to cooperate? I don't think she'll just leave Sunny like that – she's been caring for him so devotedly ever since the crash. You saw it for yourself.'

'Binoy dear, you worry too much!' came the horrible, smooth voice. Like snail snot on a razor blade!

As if you do, Shikha thought, sticking out her jaw fiercely, as if you care, Binoy chacha, you're listening to all this horrible, wicked stuff this … this evil … sanctimonious (that was the word she was looking for!) bloated blimp is spouting and … and *conspiring* with her, I hate you, I hate you, I hate you! The tears were running freely down her cheeks now.

'We are in no hurry. The entire summer is ahead to prepare Shikha for school. By the time the school opens in July, she will be itching to join – I will make sure of that. She will go willingly, happily, with a smile on her face!'

'I hope so,' Binoy chacha said in his old dry disinterested way.

'And now Binoy dear, enough about the children! What about yourself? What's this I hear about you starting on a new series of paintings? Come on, tell me!'

It was Sharifa who, five minutes later, found Shikha clutching the curtain and sobbing uncontrollably, and rushed up to her. She heard the voices in the living room too, and cannily put two and two together.

'Come, Shikha baby! Come now, you musn't cry like this. That stupid woman has upset you? You know, she upsets everyone. Some people are like that! It is in her fate to try and make people unhappy while thinking she is making the world a better place! God makes some people like that, though why I don't understand!'

'Sharifa!' sobbed Shikha burying her face in the old woman's shoulder, and weeping freely now. 'She wants to separate Sunny and me! She wants me to sneak off to the boarding school while he sleeps! And Binoy chacha is listening to her!'

'Then she is evil!' hissed Sharifa, anger boiling up inside her, and holding the sobbing girl close. 'May a cobra bite her big bosom!'

Shikha looked up with a teeny weeny smile. 'I will not leave Sunny bunny until he's well again!' she sniffed, stifling a hiccup and wiping her eyes. 'I will kill that woman if she tries to make me do it!'

'Hush, Shikha baby, you musn't talk like that. That stupid woman doesn't know what she is saying. I think she is simply trying to flatter your uncle. She's been trying to do that for a long time!' She rolled her eyes. 'Why anyone would want to, I don't know!' she added witheringly.

'Sharifa, do you think she would kidnap me?' Shikha asked suddenly, the panic rising again.

'Of course not you silly girl! Now go to bed. I'll just bring you a glass of warm milk. You are too tired today. And that stupid woman has upset you too much.'

'Maybe that's what she's going to do!' Shikha went on. 'Sneak up like a slug in the middle of the night, chloroform me and carry me away to a boarding school, while Sunny sleeps! I've seen it happen in films! Or maybe ... maybe she'll give me laughing gas, so I go giggling and laughing and Binoy chacha will think I am happy to be going!'

'Don't be silly, Shikha baby. Who will dare kidnap you? You are being protected by the tigers of Shergarh after all!'

'What?' Her eyes red rimmed and face tear stained, Shikha looked up dolefully from the bed. She frowned. Was that a twinkle deep in Sharifa's eye?

'Hahn! Yes!' the little old woman replied, smiling toothily. 'After all you have already met the rajkumar of Shergarh and his tiger Badshah! He will protect you!'

'Sharifa!' But then Shikha thought about the other tigers of Shergarh – the real ones, Shahenshah, Sheba and even Shaitan – whom she had still not met, and felt better immediately. Tomorrow, she and Sunny would be out there in the jungle again, with Aslambhai and Ali, looking for them. Far away and safe from people like Snail Snot and her diabolical plots! She looked at her peacefully sleeping little brother on the bed beside her and impulsively leaned forward and kissed him. Then she stared at her parents' smiling photograph on the table beside her.

'Don't worry, mama!' she whispered. 'I won't ditch Sunny! But I do hope he doesn't cling to me like superglue forever! That Snail Snot can do what she wants! I'll show her!'

By the time Sharifa had returned with the glass of warm milk, Shikha was fast asleep, her hair spread out on her pillow, her pink cheeks still smudged with tears. Next to her, Sunny slept as usual, in his pangolin position.

11

'HEY TOODLEDUMPS WE'VE OVERSLEPT!' SHIKHA NUDGED HER little brother looking in dismay at the time. In ten minutes, Aslambhai and Ali would be at the porch with the Gypsy. Then she remembered the events of last night. Oh, hell, she had been so upset that she hadn't even written up her notes, let alone sorted out her things. That damn Snail Snot had properly upset her routine.

Sharifa padded into the room, with a glass of hot milk on a plate. She put it down and gave Shikha, now wriggling into her mother's dressing gown, a hug.

'How did you sleep?' she asked, smiling. 'Did you dream of your rajkumar?'

'Fine Sharifa, no I didn't!' Shikha blushed and dimpled. 'But we'll be late! Aslambhai will be here soon!'

'Aslambhai der se ayega – Aslambhai will be coming late,' Sharifa said calmly, picking up the clothes that Shikha had scattered over the planter's chair. 'He's gone to get the Gypsy's puncture repaired. 'Aaram karo! Ek ghanta lag jayega – relax! It will take an hour!'

'That woman is gone?' Shikha asked, traipsing towards the bathroom.

'Hahn! Yes! She went soon afterwards. Sahib dropped her in the Gypsy.'

'Where does she stay?'

'Gaav me! In the village – she has a room in the school in Shergarh village!'

Shergarh village was about a ten-minute drive away from the house, just where the road forked towards the ridge.

'Oh, damn! So close by!'

'Phikar nahin karo baby – don't worry baby! I'll take care of her!' Sharifa snorted.

The extra hour gave Shikha time to complete yesterday's notes and fill in her journal. The journal, a beautiful leather-bound big notebook with gold-rimmed pages, lined on one side and blank on the other (separated by an onionskin sheet), had been a parting gift from Dipti.

'Write all your notes in fair, in this,' she had told Shikha. 'You can make sketches and stick in photographs! Keep it as a personal diary of your study.'

And Shikha had diligently done so. She was a meticulous worker, and loved to see her projects or assignments neatly presented. She consulted her grubby notebooks and went to work, occasionally calling out to Sunny, whom Sharifa was getting dressed.

She entered yesterday's date, and began writing:

I saw Sheba make a kill today – and fainted! She had been hiding in the bushes at the far end of Hari Pani, watching the chital that had come down to drink. She must have been there all along, yet I never saw her until I spotted her purely by chance. She had sort of become a part of the scenery, if you know what I mean. If you took your eyes off her, you might not be able to see her again, except when she landed on the back of your neck, with a growl, which makes your stomach feel someone had used a mixie in it!

She charged out, so beautiful and so deadly! The poor chital just collapsed under her weight! God, what it must have felt like to have those huge curving canines plunge into your neck, your blood spurting in a great ruby-coloured fountain! Poor thing. But I guess Sheba has to eat too and at least she hunts her own food. Imagine if she simply had to go to the supermarket to pick up plastic packed protein-enriched tiger food advertised by Sher Khan! And Aslambhai says that tigers always choose the weakest of the deer, the ones that are easiest to catch. So only the really tough and healthy ones survive and breed. Well, like an idiot I fainted when she made the kill – it was such a shock – so no pictures! But later, I got some shots of Sheba coming down to drink, her mouth all bloody, and licking her lips.

Like that horrible woman who Binoy chacha had invited to dinner! Actually I shouldn't write about her here, because this is supposed to be about tigers and not ghastly people like Snail Snot!

Carefully she tore out the page from her grubby notebook in which she had made a sketch of Hari Pani, and slipped it into the journal. Well, the blank pages would fill up when the photographs came – provided they came out all right! She shut her journal and went into the drawing room. The house was silent – there was no sign of Binoy chacha anywhere, as usual. Things appeared to be quite normal again, at Shergarh House.

'Where do we go today, Aslambhai?' she asked, settling down in the Gypsy, her binoculars and camera ready, as they drove into the park a little later.

'Hari Pani, memsahib!' he replied. 'Sheba will still be near her kill.'

This time they approached with extreme caution, Aslambhai guiding the Gypsy almost soundlessly over the rough terrain. Carefully, and testing the wind every now and then, he led them to the ancient stone pavilion abutting the glinting lake, his eyes flickering around, on the ground, and everywhere. It would not do to surprise Sheba, if she were guarding her kill nearby. Every now and then he would freeze, and indicate with his hands that they remain motionless. Her heart doing its boombox act again, goose pimples rising everywhere, and the fine golden hair on the nape of her neck standing up, Shikha kept her head down, one hand firmly holding on to Sunny. He was looking absolutely thrilled – he seemed to be slowly coming out of his 'big funk' as she put it. Now if only he would start talking again – though that might be a mixed blessing! He looked around, just the way Aslambhai was doing, he put one foot down in front of the other in Charlie Chaplin imitation (but without falling over his laces, thank God!), he put his fingers to his lips, his eyes dancing with excitement.

And it struck Shikha, that in a strange, crooked sort of way, that well, it was perhaps all for the best that Sunny could not speak at this moment – under normal circumstances it would have been impossible to keep him quiet at such a time. She bit her lip, there again was that strange mixed-up feeling inside her that made her all confused. She would have loved for Sunny to talk again, just to be normal again, but now at this moment she couldn't help but be glad that he couldn't yell out 'Hiya there, babydolldimplechick!' She grinned at him sardonically, and put her fingers on her lips with exaggerated caution. Ali, of course, was expert at keeping a low profile and just slipped along with them eel-like.

The glinting emerald waters lapped the pavilion steps with a soft plash-plash sound, and the jungle was quiet. Crouching behind the parapet (at the end of the promontory), where Aslambhai indicated that they should sit, Shikha peeped over it and surveyed the scene through her binoculars. The lapwings were gone, but the dabchicks were still around, puttering about like little bathtub ducks. But what was that, at the far bank? At first she couldn't make head or tail of what she saw (literally!), and then, when she had sorted it out, she gave a little gasp of delight.

A tigress was lying sprawled on her back, her great paws pointing skywards in complete abandon. Sheba! She looked ridiculously like some giant puppy or kitten wanting to have her tummy tickled. She twisted her head this way and that a bit, then struck another ludicrous upside down pose. What a big silly billy she is, Shikha thought, as she indicated in sign language to Sunny where he should look. Aslambhai, of course, had spotted her already and so had Ali – on whose face there was a strange yearning expression. At that moment there was nothing he would like better than to toss a pebble on to the tigress's tummy and watch her reaction – from a very safe place of course! Sunny spotted the tigress, and his jaw dropped. Then he simply beamed from ear to ear, and he glued his eyes to his binoculars.

'She has a full stomach, and is happy!' Aslambhai whispered. 'See, she's brought the kill out of the bushes again.'

Sure enough a cloud of buzzing bluebottles hummed around the remains of the chital, and Shikha was surprised to see how much of it Sheba had eaten. She could see the bones of the rib cage glisten, red and white, and one haunch had been pulled clean from the rest of the body. But there seemed to be something else, much larger than the bluebottles on the kill. Shikha focused her binoculars.

'Hells bells Sunny bunny just look at those frogs! They're humungous!'

Indeed, the chital's carcass was teeming with them. Huge olive green fellows with burly faces and muscular thighs hopping clumsily in and out of the glistening rib cage. As if they were a gathering of fat pompous landlords stuffing their faces at a five star hotel – while the great tigress dozed not five metres from them. They reminded her of some of Sunny's he-men toys.

'What are they, Aslambhai?' Shikha asked. 'And what are they doing there?'

'Bullphrog!' Aslambhai replied. 'They've come out of the lake to feast on the chital and the flies!'

'Look, Sunny, those frogs are having a pig-out! Like we had at the Ranas, yesterday!'

Sunny nodded. He'd seen them. Froggies again! Like the big froggy they had met last night, who had given him that small chocolate. What a big froggy, what a small chocolate!

'She's so sweet!' Shikha whispered turning her attention to Sheba again, and immediately being captivated. Surely this was not the vicious and merciless tigress that had hunted with such deadly intent just yesterday? This was a great big striped and very undignified looking pussycat!

'Hey Sunny! She's like a big silly puddy-tat!' she whispered in his ear. He looked at her seriously for a second and then smiled gleefully.

With great daring a tree pie landed near the upside down tigress and hopped nonchalantly towards the kill.

'Oh, oh,' Shikha whispered. 'Trouble!' She waited, her camera at the ready.

Sheba, still upside down, cocked her ears and twisted her neck for a better look. A low rumble rolled over the glinting green waters, but she seemed to be too lazy to do anything else.

The tree pie took another couple of hops towards the kill. Lazily, Sheba, still upside down, batted her great forepaws at it.

'She's telling it to go away and stop bothering her, but is too sleepy to really do anything about it!' Shikha thought, thoroughly delighted and exactly knowing the feeling. It was just the sort of thing Sunny had done to her while she slept, a hundred times or more ... before the accident, of course. Tickled her feet and scampered off, or waved a feather under her nose while she lolled about in a deliciously dreamy slumber to awake to a paroxysm of sneezes while he scuttled off shouting with laughter. He could be so utterly exasperating!

Another tree pie landed near the tigress. This one was even bolder, and seemed to be interested in a piece of meat lying just next to the tigress. The first bird decided that its partner had discovered a juicier piece, and hopped in close as well. Sheba froze in her silly position, her amber eyes fixed frostily on the foolish bird. Both the silly birds had now grabbed hold of the gobbet of meat and were having a tug of war with it, and hopping about in a circle like a pair of folk dancers, virtually under the tigress's nose.

'What should I focus on?' Shikha thought frantically. 'The birds or Sheba?' She shot off a dozen or so photographs quickly, sometimes focusing on the birds (difficult because they were moving) and sometimes on Sheba's eyes.

Another deep rumble emanated from the sleepy tigress's throat like a roll of distant thunder. She was beginning to get seriously annoyed. She batted out with her great forepaws again, as if driving mosquitoes away from her face, with much the same effect. The birds dodged her easily, and then went back to their squabbling.

'They know she's not serious!' Shikha whispered to Aslambhai. He nodded.

'They know that her stomach is full and she is too sleepy to chase them off, but has to make a show of it. And maybe she doesn't mind sharing a little bit with them, now that her own stomach is full.'

'If she's not careful, they'll be pulling her whiskers soon,' Shikha said, stifling a giggle. 'What a silly thing she is!' Really there was nothing better she would like to do than walk up to the tigress and tickle her tummy for her! Soon the tree pies tired of their game and flew off, each with a small piece of meat in its beak. Sheba closed her eyes, her paws drooping languidly, still ridiculously belly up.

Shikha looked at Sheba through the binoculars again, and gave a little gasp. 'Aslambhai, there is a whole flock of butterflies settling on the ground all around her face. Lovely little yellow ones, and big black and yellow patterned ones and mint green ones and orange and black striped ones! They're so beautiful!'

'Hahn baby – they also like meat and blood!' he whispered back, grinning. 'They pretend to like only nectar and honey and flutter around pretty flowers, but will happily drink your blood and sweat and tears! Like some people do!'

Shikha nodded, her eye glued to the viewfinder. 'Tell me about it, Aslambhai! Like that woman who came to dinner last night!' she snorted, clicking off half a dozen more photographs.

'Hey, Sheba's gone off to sleep!'

The tigress's eyes were closed and she seemed oblivious of the butterflies dancing in front of her face. As Shikha watched, a pair of lovely orange butterflies, with black stripes on their wings, and white polka dots on their faces, hovered lightly in front of the sleeping tigress's whiskers. Lightly one touched down, on a whisker tip, just as the other did, on the other side of the tigress's face, but facing its partner.

Click shuttuk! Click shuttuk! Click shuttuk! Click shuttuk!

This time Shikha was not missing anything!

The tigress twitched her whiskers involuntarily, and the butterflies skipped up for an instant, in unison.

Click shuttuk! Click shuttuk!

They touched down lightly again, and this time Sheba opened her great sleepy eyes to see what it was that was bothering her like this. She had a pained expression on her face, as if saying to the butterflies, 'Go away and play elsewhere! Stop bothering me!'

Click shuttuk! Click shuttuk! Click shuttuk!

'Aaaoom! Aaaoom! Aaaargh!'

The call of the tiger seemed to come from horribly close by and echoed off the towering cliffs behind Hari Pani!

In an instant, Sheba had flipped over, ears flat, tail lashing, and crouched low over her kill, snarling in that horrible malevolent way that made you feel you had to run to the bathroom! The butterflies exploded in a cloud of colour all around her, and the fat bullfrogs made for the water with desperate hops, their thick rear legs kicking out wildly. Many had grossly overeaten!

Aslambhai gripped his gun, his eyes flicking all over the scene.

Shikha squeaked, 'Oh my God!' then in a knowing voice, said, 'Aha – you can't trick me twice Ali!' She glanced at him, and her eyes widened. Ali was looking absolutely baffled himself – as if some nasty practical joke had backfired on him – and rather pale indeed. Only Sunny seemed unconcerned. They were in a jungle, there were tigers in the jungle, so what was so great about having heard one call? Just the other day he had met one, though at the time it had frightened him badly, Shikha had been there with him, and nothing could happen to him when she was with him. But no he didn't like that snarling sound very much, so maybe it would be better if he just buried his face in Shikha's lap or something.

Aslambhai gripped Shikha's arm, and silently pointed towards the great cliffs. About one-third the way up, walking calmly on a ledge and finding its way down towards the emerald pool, was a magnificent tiger. A tiger she would know anywhere.

Shahenshah!

'Buddhoo ko abhi pata chala! The fool has only got to know now!' Aslambhai whispered laconically, his beard wagging agitatedly.

'What? What do you mean?'

'If he had known about this kill earlier, he may have got a free meal,' said the forest guard. 'Now he will have to be satisfied with bones!'

'What? You mean he would have robbed Sheba of her kill?'

'Hahnji, zaroor! Yes, definitely! He would have tried to, though no one gets the better of Sheba easily. And he is a big fool. Now watch! And be ready with your camera!'

As Sheba snarled and spat, her ears back, her tail lashing, Shahenshah came down, and growling deep and warningly in his shaggy throat, began approaching the remnants of the kill. Spitting defiance, Sheba crouched low, standing her ground, her eyes blazing. Suddenly the big male rushed at her, and the tigers reared up, batting each other with their forepaws, growling and roaring.

'Oh no, he'll kill her!' Shikha whispered in distress, for Shahenshah seemed to be at least one and a half times her size. 'Hells bells Sunny bunny!'

The sudden explosive anger of the warring animals had further startled Sunny. Petrified, he buried his face in Shikha's back, holding her tight around the waist, and making her shake at least four photographs. Even Ali was now very pale and with trembling lips, had slid close to Aslambhai. Suddenly Sheba backed down and moved away from the kill, the angry light dying out of her eyes like a cigarette being extinguished in water.

With a roar of triumph, Shahenshah straddled the remnants of the kill, and began pulling at the bones.

'Wow!' breathed Shikha. 'What a macho fellow you are!'

'Bewakoof! Fool!' spat Aslambhai in disgust.

Shikha, now intently watching, saw Sheba, as she crouched low in the grass, put her hand in front of her face.

'Aslambhai,' she whispered, frowning. 'She's got this funny cunning expression on her face! She looks as if she is *allowing* him to share her kill! As though she's pretending that he has won!'

'Aur kya! What else!' Aslambhai seemed properly disgusted by Shahenshah. 'Now see what happens! She'll make a proper fool of him! Bada hero banta hai! He thinks he's a big hero!'

Shahenshah tugged ferociously at a stringy length of chital, growling aggressively.

A low moan came out of the grass, where Sheba crouched.

'Aaoom! Arooom!' she called, softly.

'Look at her!' Shikha breathed. 'She's gone all soft and gooey eyed!'

Shahenshah, top tiger and ruler of all Shergarh, paid her not the slightest notice.

The tigress's eyes turned frosty. With a lithe movement she rose, and slithered her way to him, her tail arched high behind her. Before he knew what was happening, she had rubbed her face under his great chin, a rumbling purr coming out of her throat, like a big car's engine being revved. Shahenshah growled, but did nothing more.

'Like a cat rubbing against your legs,' Shikha thought. He's saying okay, okay I accept your surrender, but don't overdo it chick!' She turned to her little brother. 'Hey Sunny, take a look at this! She's like Kittycat was back in Delhi!'

Sheba turned around slinkily and rubbed her head against Shahenshah's chin once again. This time the big tiger cocked his ears interrogatively, a look of interest coming over his face. He sniffed her as she passed him by, his eyes going groggy.

'Now he's got this goofy look on his face!' Shikha giggled, hardly believing what she was seeing. 'I just can't believe it! And she's flirting with him!'

Sheba lay down in the tawny grass and glanced over her shoulder at him. Kill forgotten, he strode over. She snarled suddenly, swiped at his goofy face with her paw and slipped away. He looked puzzled, paused and then followed a little uncertainly.

'Just look at her! Now she's playing hard to get!'

'Bilkul budhoo bana rahi hai – she's making an absolute fool out of him!' Aslambhai shook his head in despair. 'Uski to izzat ka falooda ho gaya! His self-respect is down the drain!'

Sheba had sprung lightly on the great rocks at the right side of the pool (if you were on the promontory, that is) and looked back.

Aslambhai gripped Shikha's arm lightly.

'Chalo!' he whispered. 'We better move away. They might come here! This is their place after all!'

Shikha was both disappointed and relieved. She would have loved to stay on and watch, but knew that Sunny was terrified, even though he was now pretending not to be. She handed Ali her knapsack, and picked up her brother, fixing him on her hip with a sigh of resignation.

'Come on, Sunny bunny! Let's go to the Gypsy and see what Sharifa has packed for us today!' Herded along by Aslambhai they made their way back through the boulders. Just before they reached the car, Aslambhai turned around for a backward glance. Down below, in the little courtyard between the two chhatris Sheba and Shahenshah lay, or rather reposed like royalty.

'Look,' he said, as Shikha, panting heavily, put down Sunny. 'They are at the exact place as we were. They must have smelt us! And yet they have not run away. Normally tigers don't like to stay close to human beings. It looks like Shahenshah and Sheba have accepted you, Shikha memsahib!'

'Do you really think so?' She was thrilled. To be accepted by wild tigers! Wow! Wait till she wrote to Dipti!

'Hahnji. Yes. But this doesn't mean you can take liberties with them! They are wild animals. Today they may be in a good mood and accept your presence, but tomorrow, who knows? Every time it is different!'

'Are they going to mate, Aslambhai?' Shikha asked eyes glued to the viewfinder.

'Abhi to masla shuru hi hua hai – the romance has only begun now!' Aslambhai replied grinning, his beard wagging.

'So then, Sheba might have cubs?' Shikha asked, a hopeful note in her voice.

'Hahnji! Yes! But then you will have to stay very far away from her for many months. She is the fiercest tigress I have ever seen, when she is with cubs!'

'Oh. You mean to say we won't be able to see her cubs or anything like that?'

'After they are four or six months, if you are very lucky! Also she might not be here!'

They watched the tigers in the pavilion till way past lunchtime. Aslambhai manoeuvred the Gypsy right up to the place they were watching them from, and Sunny and Ali quickly went to work on Sharifa's lunch box. Then Sunny did something surprising. He took one of Shikha's notepads (along with a pencil from her pocket), laid it down on the Gypsy's bonnet and began drawing, frowning with concentration.

'Hey, Sunny that's great!' Shikha was suddenly thrilled. 'Hah – Binoy chacha thinks he's the only artist in the family. Well, show him Sunny bunny! Show him! Come on, give me five toodledumps!'

His eyes bright, Sunny exchanged high fives with his sister, as Ali watched baffled. Down in the courtyard, both the tigers had apparently gone off to sleep again.

'They sure sleep a lot!' Shikha remarked softly well after they had finished their lunch, and the tigers down below showed no sign of rising or doing anything interesting.

'Yes,' Aslambhai said. 'They rest most of the day. They use up a lot of energy while hunting.' He jerked his chin towards Ali and Sunny, both fast asleep in the rear of the Gypsy.

'Like those two tigers! Shergarh ke chhote sher! The small tigers of Shergarh!'

But sleeping or not, Shikha could never tire of watching the great beasts. By turn she studied them through her binoculars, wondering about the sort of lives they had led. When and where had they been born? How had their mothers raised them? How had they been taught to hunt?

Aslambhai tapped her arm softly. Silently he pointed. A sounder of wild boar had stepped out of the forest, quite near the kill.

'Ab mazaa dekho! Now watch the fun!'

The leading boar stopped short, sniffing greedily. It saw the humming remnants of the chital and its nose twitched wildly. The others jostled behind it, like people wanting to get on to a bus all at the same time. Apparently satisfied that the coast was clear, the lead boar approached the kill. Within minutes, the sounder – consisting of five adults and twelve piglets (which Shikha immediately wanted to pick up and cuddle – they were so gloriously cute and ugly), were snuffling and swarming all over the kill. The piglets spent more time chasing each other, their tails stuck up behind them hilariously like antennae, than eating.

Sheba awoke.

She was still quite full, and didn't really need to hunt.

'Sooer ka bachcha sher ko bahut achcha lagta hai! Tigers love piglets,' Aslambhai whispered.

Shahenshah pricked up his ears as if he had heard the word 'piglets'.

'That fellow has only had bones so far,' Shikha whispered. 'He must be hungry!'

As Sheba watched, Shahenshah figured out his attack.

'Chalo, come on,' Aslambhai said. 'Get into the Gypsy! Kuchch bhi ho sakta hai – anything can happen!'

'What? But they are quite far away!' Still, Shikha got into the Gypsy. She could still see the scene below, even if not as well as from outside it.

Shahenshah had begun a belly crawl towards the rocks on the right side of the pool.

'He's going to climb up, and then attack from there,' Aslambhai said.

Sure enough, the big tiger clambered up the great rocks with fluid grace, keeping very low. At the pavilion, Sheba watched lazily, but was sensible enough not to twitch her tail and give the game away. Just yet.

Shahenshah jockeyed himself into position, behind a huge boulder. He was now looking down on the frolicking piglets, and the greedy boars, selecting his victim.

'*Aaaom*! *Arrooom*!' drawled Sheba dozily, rising to her feet.

Squealing with panic the boars scattered as if a bomb had gone off in their midst, piglets scampering every which way. With a roar, Shahenshah launched himself after them, jinking this way and that as piglets swerved past him. He crashed into the forest and disappeared, just as Sheba jumped up on to the rocks, and padded down to the remnants of her kill.

From somewhere near the base of the cliffs, there came a final despairing squeal and a triumphant snarl.

'Pakda! Caught it!' Aslambhai grunted.

'Poor little piglet!' said Shikha. 'But Aslambhai, why did Sheba try and ruin his chances?'

The forest guard shrugged. 'Kya pata? Who knows?' he said.

Now Sheba, too, took a final bite from her kill and disappeared into the forest towards the base of the cliffs.

They waited for another hour or so, but the tigers did not reappear.

'God!' said Shikha looking at her watch, suddenly tired. 'We've been here the whole day, Aslambhai!'

'Yes,' he nodded. 'And Shikha baby, what you have seen in two days here, people do not see in their entire lifetime! Dipti memsahib will be very envious!'

'Well, I have plenty to report to her!' Shikha said thrilled. 'What a time I'm having!'

As usual, it was dark by the time they reached Shergarh House. If you drove non-stop from Hari Pani to Shergarh House, it took an hour and a half, but who can drive non-stop through a tiger reserve? There was so much to see on the way. It took them the usual two-and-a-half hours!

Once again, the lights in the house were ablaze when they reached.

This time, like Sheba (she thought) Shikha paused, and

sniffed cautiously. And didn't call out something rude about Binoy chacha to Sharifa.

No sickly perfume today.

Once again, Shikha hitched a flaked out Sunny on to her hip, though today, Sharifa came scuttling out and quickly took him from her. She saw the expression on Shikha's face and grinned.

'Theek hai, baby!' she said. 'It's all right!'

Joginder aunty surged out of the drawing room, her chins wobbling, her usual beaming smile on her face.

'Bachche!' she shrilled. 'You must be so tired and hungry! Come on inside and eat! How was your day?'

Thank God! Shikha prayed. Oh, Joginder aunty, thank God it's you and not that ghastly Snail Snot! I could hug you!

She didn't have to. Dipti's mother had surged up to them and enveloped them both in yet another of her gigantic hugs.

'My! My!' she said softly, stroking Shikha's head and raising her face towards her. 'There are tears in your eyes, child, and they're rolling into your dimples! Come now baby, everything is going to be all right! No one is going to take Sunny away from you!'

'Hahn baby – yes, baby!' Sharifa said with some asperity. 'Jogi memsahib usko theek kar dega! Jogi memsahib will settle that woman's hash!' Evidently, Sharifa had lost no time in telling Joginder aunty about what had happened the previous night.

It was so nice to be able to gabble and gabble and gabble with someone who listened so … so truthfully, Shikha thought, as she told Joginder aunty all about the great day they had had. Jogi aunty's chins had wobbled more and more, her eyes grew round with alarm at all the dramatic parts, and she kept murmuring, 'But please be careful, bachche, please be careful!'

'Where's Binoy chacha?' Shikha asked Sharifa, suddenly realizing that he hadn't made an appearance.

'He's out on his motorcycle! Must have gone to the village!' Sharifa said, snorting. Of course, Joginder aunty had brought a whole lot of goodies for tea, so the three of them tucked in heartily, as she watched them fondly.

'You must come and see my school, some time,' she told Shikha, shooting a glance at Ali who was sinking low in his chair, gobbling furiously. 'Even if that fellow never attends!' she added darkly wobbling her chins at him. 'Even my nursery kids know ABC better than he does!'

'I will, Joginder aunty, I promise. It's just that I like to spend the whole day inside the reserve, there is so much happening!' Shikha said.

'There's no hurry!' Joginder aunty smiled, patting her arm. 'In a couple of months, summer will be here and it will be too hot to be in the jungle the whole day. You could start visiting the school then. And maybe help me out. And bring that scoundrel with you, if you have to drag him by the ear!'

She gave the children a parting hug and left.

After dinner, Shikha got down to writing up her notes and journal, and sorting out her films. Sunny as usual was fast asleep. At about ten thirty, she heard the door creak and looked up from her desk.

'You are still awake?' Binoy chacha asked, stepping in.

'I'm just finishing writing up my notes, Binoy chacha.'

'Oh, good! You are taking this quite seriously! Achcha, I shall be going to Delhi tomorrow for about two weeks, maybe more. I have to settle things regarding your papa's house and other matters. And I'll be bringing back some more of your things.'

'Oh! Thanks!'

'Yes, how's Sunny doing? Are you sure he is not overtiring himself? Spending the whole day out like that?'

'Chacha, Sunny is sensible. If he feels tired, he just grumbles a bit, gets a bit cranky maybe and goes off to sleep! He's doing fine. He's …' She was about to tell him about Sunny's drawing, when she bit her lip. Fat lot he'd care! He'd probably pass some sarcastic remark, or simply ignore the matter completely. 'He's fine,' she repeated lamely.

'Good. Now, I'll need the Gypsy tomorrow to take me to the station. So maybe you can spend the day at home or go into the reserve in the afternoon. A break will do you good.'

He paused and Shikha looked up quickly.

Okay, she could live with not going into the reserve for a day, no problem, she could work on her notes and read the damn camera manual again and check out the bookshelves in the drawing room. But there was something else, coming …

'Yes,' her uncle said. 'Veena aunty has very kindly agreed to visit you every evening while I am away. She'll come here at about five o'clock and stay till after dinner. Aslambhai will drop her back. Just to make sure you are doing all right and she will be company for you too.'

'Oh!' Oh! Oh shit, oh bloody hell, oh no! She looked up despairingly. 'But Binoy chacha, sometimes we get late. And sometimes we go to Rana uncle's office in the evening.'

'Well try and reach home by five o'clock. It wouldn't look nice if you are not here when she comes. If you are going to be late, you can radio a message, so she will not worry! Okay? Goodnight Shikha!'

'Goodnight, chacha!'

Fat chance of it being a good night after that! Shikha thought glumly as she shut her journal with a sigh and put it away in her cupboard.

Imagine! She would have to be polite to Snail Snot every evening, for two whole weeks!

'Sheba!' she said silently. 'Where are you when I need you? Visit us tomorrow and I can guarantee a meal you will not forget!'

12

ALMOST BY HABIT, SHIKHA AWOKE EARLY THE NEXT MORNING, and padded around the house wondering what to do with herself all day. It seemed so strange that they didn't have to drive off into the jungle today, she thought, running her fingers lightly over the bonnet of the silent Gypsy. She wandered off into the lawn (Sunny was still fast asleep), one ear cocked for any distressed bleat from Sunny. How he had screamed when they had tried taking him away from her, at the hospital. It had brought the whole place to a halt, with white-faced nurses running this way and that or simply standing frozen with horror. It had terrified her even more than the crash itself. And afterwards he had clung to her limpet-like for the whole day, whimpering like one of those tiny baby langurs she had seen on the wall of Shergarh Kila. It had been difficult even putting him down on the bed when he had dropped off, exhausted. Whatever had happened to that tough little brat who loudly called her dimplechick (sheesh!) in public places like cinema halls and shopping malls and drove her nuts? He had given her the fright of her life and they had to give her calmpose injections to make her stop trembling and to keep the waves of panic at bay.

The sun came up, and in the distance, she could see the mists around Shergarh Kila, tinged with pink and then gold. A couple of magnificent peacocks took off from the cliff face near the house and planed down into the reserve, honking dismally, as if warning that they were out of control and about to crash! Their trains were like rich royal tapestry, Shikha thought, and it was amazing how they didn't get caught in all the spiky foliage of the jungle. Then Binoy chacha came up the steps from his studio, a bag in his hand.

'Hello, Shikha, good morning!'

'Hi chacha!' she said.

It was the first time they had said 'good morning' to each other since she had arrived with Sunny at Shergarh House. He disappeared into his bedroom, a door creaking and banging behind him. Half an hour later, she stood on the porch, with Sunny by her side, as he got into the Gypsy.

'Bye!' he said, waving. 'I'll be back in a fortnight or so. Aslambhai will be back in the afternoon – the Gypsy has to be serviced at Shergarh town. Sharifa and Veena aunty will take good care of you. If you want anything, ask them. Be good and don't give Veena aunty any trouble! She's being very kind!'

'Yes, chacha,' Shikha said, looking at the Gypsy thoughtfully. 'Don't worry about us. We'll be fine!' She waved.

She watched the Gypsy drive off, and smiled mischievously.

'Sunny bunny,' she said grinning. 'We have two whole weeks to check out Binoy chacha's studio! What do you think of that!'

But an hour later, having bathed and changed, she stood with Sunny at her side and frowned at the rough wooden studio door. The bolt had been drawn across, with a huge brass padlock in place, to guard against any snooping children.

'Damn!' said Shikha rattling the padlock. 'What's he got inside that's so precious, eh Sunny? The Mona Lisa I suppose!' She made a face. The studio literally clung to the cliff face, and tentatively Shikha leaned over the rail to see if she could peer in through the big glass windows that overlooked the tiger reserve.

'Damn!' she said again, 'he's gone and drawn the curtains!' Then she went across to the other side, but the wall of the studio was virtually flush with the cliff face, and it did not look like a very inviting gap to squeeze through.

'Foiled!' she muttered, accepting defeat. 'Come on Sunny let's go back up. Whoops, careful! This damn railing wobbles horribly!'

She settled Sunny with some paper and colour pencils in the drawing room, and drifted about, eyes scanning the bookshelves. There were a lot of fat, heavy art books, and other heavy looking stuff, and there, glory be, right at the top, a shelf full of books on tigers (by Jim Corbett, Kenneth Anderson and other writers) and wildlife and birds! Also, a folded document-like thing stuck out invitingly. Shikha pulled it out, and her eyes widened.

'Look at this, Sunny! It's a map of the reserve! Come on, let's see what it's like.' She laid it out on the dining table, frowned over it, trying to find her bearings. It was on funny blue paper, drawn in blue lines, but had quite a lot of details marked on it.

'Okay, here! This is where we are!' she said, jabbing her finger at a spot on the map. 'That's the kila, and we face east, so this FRH thing is where we are! FRH – what's that? The key, where's the key? Ah, yes, it stands for forest rest house. So! This is an old time forest rest house, eh, what do you think of that Sunny?'

She spent an absorbing hour tracing out all the routes they had taken on their drives inside, and was utterly delighted when she found Hari Pani marked on the map too.

'You know what, Sunny?' she said, her face flushing with excitement. 'I can trace parts of this map for my journal! To show where we saw the tigers and things like that! Trust Binoy chacha not to have shown this map to me or told me about these books!' She pulled out a couple of tiger books and carefully folded up the map and put it in her cupboard, alongside her journal. Now she would have something to read at least.

Some minutes later, Ali knocked on the big windows of their room and beckoned to her, as she lay back in the planter's chair, leafing through one of the Kenneth Anderson books.

'Hi, Ali, come on in,' she said, as Sunny gave his friend a big smile and charged out to meet him. (At long last he seemed to be getting back to his charged-up old self, Shikha thought.)

Secretively, Ali put his fingers on his lips, and looked around furtively.

'Aao! Come,' he said softly. 'I'll show you something!'

'Okay! Just a moment!' She slipped on her sandals and called out to Sharifa, clattering utensils in the kitchen. 'Sharifa, Sunny and I are just going out with Ali for a walk!'

'Theek hai! But be back early. I have made special lunch for you!' It was, after all the first hot lunch the children would be eating, ever since they came to stay!

Ali took them down the road that led to Shergarh village, then off it along a path that sloped steeply downwards, the scrub jungle giving way to greenery as they went deeper. Eventually they came to a tiny spring that trickled its way towards the cliff face; but petered out before reaching it. Clumps of bamboo reared high above them, and it was cool in their shade.

'Where does this path go to, Ali?' Shikha asked. The path crossed the stream and then disappeared into the jungle.

'Shergarh gaav – to Shergarh village,' he said. 'Chhota raasta hai – it's a short cut!'

'Oh!'

'Idhar tehero – wait here!' Ali said, and scampered off, as Shikha looked on puzzled.

He disappeared behind a bush and emerged dragging what appeared to be a scarecrow behind him. But a scarecrow wearing a plait made of rope and a petticoat?

'What are you doing?' Shikha asked, puzzled.

'Dekho! Watch!' he said.

Holding the scarecrow in front of him, his eyes glued to the path, the little boy began walking forward slowly. At every step he made sure that the 'feet' of the scarecrow firmly touched the ground ahead of him.

'A scarecrow with two feet?' Shikha said suddenly. 'Hells bells Sunny, I've never seen a scarecrow with two feet before. Just what is he up to?'

She watched. Step by step Ali walked down the path. He was about to enter the inky blue shade of one of the clumps of bamboo, when there was a sudden twanging sound and something flew up in the air in front of him, making him jump back.

Shikha caught a brief glimpse of the scarecrow somersaulting through the air in an arc, at the end of a bamboo pennant that had suddenly straightened up like a bow being released. And suddenly the poor thing was dangling upside down, the stuffing from its legs already coming lose, the petticoat over its head.

'Dekha! Did you see that!' Ali cried, jumping up and down with excitement.

'But … but that's a trap!' Shikha said, horrified.

Ali nodded, his eyes shining.

'Hahn! Khud banaya! Yes, I made it myself!' he said proudly.

'But you can't trap animals here!' Shikha said, scandalized. This fellow was the very devil!

Ali shook his head scornfully. 'Nahin,' he said. 'No, it's not for animals! It's for teacher memsahib. She'll be walking down this path to come to your house every day. The village is only five minutes away from here!'

'What? Teacher memsahib? Oh my God, you mean Snail Snot!'

She saw it all. Veena aunty, rather Snail Snot, walking righteously along this path, like a martyr on her way to 'Do Good Work with Orphans' and adjusting her halo modestly. Then, whang, whiz, zing and scream! Flying through the air, and ending upside down – oh God what would her sari do in such a position! – her head inches off the ground, plait in the dust. (And that's why the scarecrow had a petticoat and a plait too!) But would the bamboo be strong enough to take her weight? Shikha collapsed on the ground in an uncontrollable fit of giggles. It was too much! It was just too much! And she could … she could hide in the bushes and take photographs of Snail Snot flying through mid-air and in the upside down position! Rather different to Sheba's pose but still! Imagine what they would look like in her journal, stuck side by side! She went into hysterics, and Sunny was chortling richly too even if he didn't know what the hell was making Shikha laugh like this.

'Achcha laga? You liked it?' Ali's eyes were shining. He had been in the kitchen with Sharifa the night Shikha had been upset, and had watched his grandmother console her. Instinctively he knew that the horrible 'teacher memsahib' was the cause of the trouble – she made all the village children run away after all – and had sworn to get even.

Now, briskly he began re-setting the trap.

'Hey, Ali, hold it!' Still racked by giggles Shikha held out her hand. 'Much as I would love to see Snail Snot go into orbit, you can't do it. You'll get into horrible trouble. She'll call the police!'

'Oh!' The disappointment was plain to see on his face.

But he brightened up again as Shikha went up to him and hugged him impulsively.

'Thank you,' she said. 'You've already made my day!' And dissolved into another fit of giggles.

So Ali spent the rest of the morning teaching her to make birdcalls. At the end of the exercise, Shikha thought she could sound quite like a golden oriole, which was one of her favourite birds.

Aslambhai returned with a sparkling clean Gypsy at three o'clock, along with a whole lot of shopping he had done in Shergarh.

'Memsahib, andar jayega? Memsahib will we be going in?' he asked, his usual grin on his face.

'Um … Aslambhai,' Shikha said frowning and looking at her watch. 'We'll have to be back by five, so that doesn't give us much time. Well, at least today we must be back at five – it'll be her first day here, stupid woman!'

Then she gave him the most charming smile imaginable.

'Aslambhai,' she said sweetly. 'Would you teach me how to drive the Gypsy, please? We could start right away, you know. We have two hours!'

Aslambhai looked as if someone had knocked him on the head with a tyre lever.

'Kya memsahib? What, memsahib?' he asked, not sure of what she had said.

'I want to learn to drive the Gypsy,' Shikha said. 'Will you teach me?'

'But … but, sahib se poocha? Have you asked sahib?' he stuttered bewildered.

'Er … we can always ask him later. It'll be easier then. After I've learnt!'

'Par licence? But what about the licence?' Aslambhai asked faintly, remembering that his own driving licence had expired three years ago.

'I don't want a licence,' Shikha said impatiently. 'Not just yet! I just want to know how to drive the Gypsy. Especially in the forest! Safety ke liye – for safety!' she added cleverly.

'Safety?' he repeated blankly.

'Yes,' she said beguilingly. 'Imagine if we are inside, and you twist your ankle or are bitten by a snake and can't drive. And imagine if the radio doesn't work. We'll be stranded. But if I can drive too, then we need not worry about that, you know!'

A shrewd look came over the old tracker's face. Shikha baby was clever, very clever. At the same time he could not deny the truth in what she had said. Suppose he did indeed, for example, have a heart attack while inside the jungle. It would certainly be useful to have a second driver. He nodded slowly.

'Theek hain, memsahib. All right memsahib, I will teach you,' he said.

'Great! Now don't worry Aslambhai, at home in Delhi I used to drive mama's Maruti in the driveway.' Up and down, back and forth, round and round, but never allowed out on to the colony roads as her friends had been.

Aslambhai took her (and Sunny, of course) to a flat, hard-baked uncultivated field not too far away, and handed her the wheel. Sunny he held firmly in his lap. Ali sat gleefully in the back.

'Dekho,' he said and pointed out the pedals. 'Right vala accelerator – the one on the right is the accelerator, next to it is the brake and the one on the left, the clutch.'

And thanks to mama's little silver Maruti, she was soon trundling around the field in wide and delighted circles, oblivious to the dust she was blowing all over themselves as she went round and round.

'Memsahib ne pehle gaadi chalaya hai – memsahib has driven before,' Aslambhai observed, not a little relieved.

'Yes,' Shikha admitted. 'It'll take me a bit of time to get used to the Gypsy though. And you'll have to teach me how to use the second set of gears too. And how to drive on the tracks inside the forest.'

She gave him another of her sweetest smiles and pressed the accelerator smartly. The Gypsy leapt forward.

They returned promptly at five, covered with dust. Shikha's hat had blown off so many times that she had simply taken it off and now her hair had blown all over her face. Her cheeks were flushed pink, with the thrill of having driven the Gypsy, and she couldn't wait to drive it inside the reserve. But now … now they had to be nice to Snail Snot.

More by habit than necessity, she hitched Sunny on to her hip and entered Shergarh House. Oh damn – she could smell that sickly perfume again. The woman was already here. Shikha thought of the trap Ali had set in the morning, and giggled. She glanced at the mirror in the lobby and giggled again.

'Hells bells Sunny, why do I always look like a tramp when I get home?' She straightened her skirt and poked her head into the drawing room. No one there! Just where … A soft jingling of bangles and bracelets behind her and then:

'Hello, Shikha dear!'

She whirled around.

Snail Snot had emerged from the dining room, where the table had been set for tea. She smiled at Sunny.

'Again in badi didi's godi? Again in your big sister's arms?' she said, pinching his cheek. 'You're a big boy now!'

'Er … actually I put him there,' Shikha said. 'I like to carry him!' Deliberately she stuck out her hip a little more, her skirt going askew again, her midriff peeping out.

'I know, Shikha darling. I understand.'

She delved into her purse and produced two miniscule toffees.

'Here,' she said, holding one out to Sunny. 'Toffee for Sunny baba!'

Again he took it, his big eyes fixed on her face. She jingled her bangles and smiled.

'And what do you say, Sunny baba?' she asked, looking pleasantly at Shikha.

Shikha fixed her eyes on the toffee. God, where did she get these from? Lilliput?

'Are they made in Lilliput?' she blurted.

'What? You mean these?' Snail Snot squinted closely at the toffee. 'No, my dear! I think they are made in Ludhiana!'

'Oh!'

Snail Snot opened out her arms to Sunny. 'Come to Veena aunty!' she gushed. 'Let your Veena aunty give you a hug and kiss!'

Sunny gave her one look and buried his face in Shikha's shoulder.

'Oh he's so shy!' the woman gushed, as Sharifa came out of the kitchen, the light of battle in her eyes.

'Chai tayaar hai – tea is ready!' she announced, and effortlessly took Sunny from Shikha and put him down. 'Chalo, Sunny sahib! Shikha baby haath muh dho lo – Come on Sunny sahib. Shikha baby wash your hands and face!'

'This is so nice!' Snail Snot said, ten minutes later as they sat down in the dining room. Shikha, now more presentable, looked across the table at Sunny, who was staring at her, and then back at Shikha. He wished she would go away.

'Um … yes,' Shikha said. 'And thank you for coming over. Actually there really is no need …'

'Hush Shikha darling, not another word! But of course I will come here every day until your uncle gets back! I promised him that! You can't be left here alone, in the back of beyond!'

'But we're not alone! There's Sharifa and Aslambhai to look after us.'

Snail Snot shook her head dismissively.

'Don't think about it again. I shall be here every day to make sure you are all right. Isn't that so, Sunny baba?'

They went into the garden after tea.

'Such a beautiful view from here!' Snail Snot commented, making it sound as if it were sinful to have a beautiful view. 'Your uncle lives in a very beautiful place.'

'Yes,' said Shikha. 'And at night you can hear the tigers roaring sometimes! But it is the jackals that give me the willies! Sometimes they howl in the garden!'

'Oh, really! Now come Shikha darling sit here, beside me! And tell me all about yourself!'

'What? About myself? What about myself?' Shikha was puzzled. Just what was this woman driving at?

'Everything my dear! Your birthday, the school you were in, the friends you had. The teachers you had! If you think it will upset you then I understand perfectly!' She reached over and patted Shikha's cheek. 'What pretty dimples you have!' she added.

'Well, my birthday …,' Shikha paused and gulped. Her birthday was not too far away now. It would be her first since mama and papa died … She glanced at the complacent-faced woman beside her who never smiled with her eyes, and who always had this ghastly saintly expression on her face.

'Okay, um … let me tell you about my friends …,' she said softly, a tear escaping down her cheek. 'My best friend is Sheba,' she added, glancing at Snail Snot to see if she remembered who Sheba was. She made no sign that she did so. Shikha went on. 'She's great! She doesn't take any shit from anyone!' she added fiercely.

'My dear! Don't use such language. Your little brother is listening!'

'Yes,' Shikha said with sudden bitterness. 'But it doesn't matter, does it? He can't speak so can't repeat it to anyone!'

'I know my dear,' she said in her tragic voice. 'But he will be able to think it!'

Wordlessly Shikha nodded. She collected herself and went on. 'Well, there's Sheba as I said. Really cool! And very clever too – she knows how to get what she wants.'

'Oh,' said Snail Snot, doubtfully, not liking the sound of Sheba very much. Obviously she did not remember who Sheba was, in spite of having heard of her just the other evening when she had first met Shikha and Sunny.

'And then there's Shahenshah!' Shikha went on, glancing at Snail Snot through the corner of her eye. 'He's terrific! He's this big handsome guy, very macho but also bit of a goof! Quite easy to make a fool of, but very sweet!'

'Shahenshah?' repeated Snail Snot doubtfully. 'What a strange name for a boy! That's his pet name I presume?' She glanced at Shikha and tinkled hideously. 'Is he your boyfriend, my dear? Have you written to him?'

'Well, um ... no,' said Shikha, her good humour restored because her big leg pull was working way beyond her expectations. 'Well actually, Sheba and Shahenshah are ... well going out together!'

'You must miss them terribly here!' Snail Snot said. 'But if you start going to school again, you'll make new friends in no time, don't you think?'

'I suppose so. But Sunny won't still leave me, you know!'

'My dear! You may not know! Sunny may be over his shock now. He may be quite willing to separate from you – and not cling to you. Maybe you are clinging to him, darling!'

'Veena aunty I know!' Shikha said fiercely. 'I know by the way he clutches my hand first thing in the morning. By the way he hugs me when I come out after my bath as if he hasn't seen me for days! By… by … every way!' she ended lamely.

The stupid woman had a blank, pasty smug look on her face. Like she wasn't hearing what she didn't want to hear. She wouldn't even have heard Sunny's screams in the hospital, Shikha thought. She stood up, and deliberately put Sunny on her hip again.

'Now aunty, I have to go in and finish writing my notes for Dipti,' she said sweetly and walked into the house.

She sat at her table chewing her pen, still upset. Then she thought about the tigers of Shergarh and a slow smile lit up her face. Beside her, Sunny scribbled vigorously with his crayons.

'Dear Dipti,' she wrote. *'You won't believe what we saw yesterday! And that Shahenshah! He's so big and fierce and macho, but he's such a doofus!'* She bent her head over her work, her pencil flying over the paper as she wrote.

The days that followed quickly fell into a pattern again. Every morning, Shikha and Sunny would venture forth into the reserve, with Aslambhai and Ali. Usually Aslambhai had received news of tiger sightings, or would find out via the radio and they would head hopefully in that direction. On several occasions they spotted the animals, and sometimes were able to follow them slowly in the Gypsy, as the tigers too, it seemed, liked to use the forest tracks made for the vehicles. Sometimes, while well into the interior, and after having checked the whereabouts of Rana sahib (whom they had met a few times) and other department vehicles, Aslambhai would hand over the Gypsy to Shikha. She had become quite skilful at driving it, and only had trouble on the bad patches, where it was important to drive at the right speed: too fast and you were jolted all over the place, and too slow and the vehicle would stall. It thrilled her no end. Often she wondered what her parents would have thought if they had seen her now, inching behind a gloriously pacing Shahenshah, who would give them a condescending backward glance and stride on, tail swinging from side to side. Sometimes they spent hours just watching the animals sleep, and every evening, Shikha would meticulously plot on her map the places where she had seen them, the points till which they were able to follow them, and of course write up her notes from her grubby field notebooks. It was a busy time for her.

'Look,' she told Aslambhai one evening, tracing a path out with her fingernail on the map spread out on the Gypsy's bonnet. 'Shahenshah usually walks along this huge area, from Hari Pani down here, along the ridge, then cuts across and goes around Hira Talao, up to the fort and then back again, along the road we take.'

'That's his territory probably,' the old tracker said. 'He would turn out any other male tigers from it.'

'But we saw Shaitan at the kila too,' Shikha pointed out, remembering the brief glance she had got of the wickedest tiger in the park.

'Yes, he was probably sneaking in!'

But best of all, Sunny appeared to be recovering quickly too. He had started swaggering around in his old energetic manner and would even duck out of her sight for a short while. If only he would start talking again, Shikha thought for the thousandth time; then things would be as normal as they could possibly be.

And if only that stupid woman would go back to Shergarh village and not ruin her evenings! The five o'clock curfew had been impossible to keep; it meant that they had to start returning from where they were in the reserve by three thirty at the latest, which was ridiculous. After staggering home at seven thirty for three straight evenings (of course, Aslambhai had flashed messages ahead that they would be late), matters came to a head.

Shikha entered the drawing room as usual, apologetic and irritated because she always felt a little guilty, because the stupid woman must have been sitting in the drawing room for two hours now, looking at her watch.

'Sorry!' she said, aware of how meaningless it sounded. 'We had a truly beautiful sunset, and then there were all these vultures swooping down to land on Shergarh Kila! Sunny couldn't take his eyes off them and had to watch all of them land!'

As always, Snail Snot was looking pointedly at her watch, a pained, suffering expression on her face.

'Shikha dear,' she said in that awful martyred voice. 'It is now nearly eight o'clock. You don't know how worried I get waiting for you like this! I was thinking of calling the field director!'

'But we sent a message!'

'That's neither here nor there. While I am here, you and Sunny are my responsibility. I can't have you wandering about in the jungle after dark! And in that open jeep too! It is asking for trouble. It is bad enough that you spend the whole day loafing around inside ...'

'Veena aunty, we don't loaf!'

'Well, Shikha dear, I don't know what you do then! Following tigers, what for? If you want to see tigers, you can go to a zoo!'

'Zoo?'

'Yes! What is the need to go inside all the time? One drive now and then – that should be enough. But every day, for the whole day! And you've been doing this for more than a month now!' (Had it been so long? Shikha wondered. Time had simply flown past!) Again, Snail Snot shook her head tragically, as if Shikha had been one truly wild child or something.

'I can't imagine what your parents would have thought,' she said shaking her head from side to side.

'My p … parents?' Shikha whispered, really not knowing how to react.

Snail Snot nodded. 'Yes,' she said. 'To have their only daughter roaming about from day to night in a jungle, and taking her little brother along with her! I think they would be very upset and concerned, don't you? What if something were to happen to little Sunny? What if a snake were to bite him?'

'Snake? But we haven't seen a single snake since we got here. Well, one or two pythons perhaps …'

'Beti, this is for your own good. Just imagine what your mummy and papa would have thought. Is this the sort of life they would have liked you and Sunny to live? They would have wanted both of you to go back to school and lead the lives of normal children. Not vagabonds and wastrels. Every evening you come home covered with mud and dust, and with scratches and bites all over! You do not study or prepare for school! It can't go on like this! What would your mama and papa think if they had been alive?'

She could feel it rising up again, that old anguish and pain. And anger.

'You never met mama and papa, so how do you know?' she flared up suddenly, more angry that the tears again were rising fast. 'Mama would have understood. She … she was my best buddy!' she blurted but the tears were coming too fast now! With a sudden gulp, Shikha grabbed Sunny's hand and fled to her room. With a despairing sob, she realized that Sharifa had gone off with Aslambhai in the Gypsy on some errand to the village. She was alone with this awful woman in Shergarh House. And her tears came freely and fast, the sobs wracking her body, completely out of control. Beside her, Sunny whimpered, wondering what had gone wrong, and began to wail.

Shikha felt a light touch on her arm and jerked it away with a squeal. Ali stood next to her bed, looking frightened.

'Mat ro – don't cry!' he pleaded, almost in tears himself. He leaned forward, his eyes gleaming. 'Suno – listen!' he said. He spoke softly for five minutes. Still sniffing, Shikha listened, and a slow smile spread across her face.

'You're a wicked little genius, Ali,' she said, hiccuping. 'Isn't he a genius, Sunny bunny!' she said. She got up and washed her face.

'Come on, Sunny bunny,' she said, 'let's go and keep Snail Snot company!'

Out of sheer cussedness, she picked Sunny up again and put him on her hip. She knew this irritated Snail Snot, especially when she deliberately jutted out her hip to one side, more than was really necessary, and let her midriff peek out.

Snail Snot was sitting primly in the drawing room going through one of Binoy chacha's fat art books.

'All she needs is a halo!' whispered Shikha, 'then she'll be Saint Snail Snot! Now try and say that fast! Come on Sunny bunny give it a shot!'

But of course Sunny bunny still couldn't.

'Er … hi,' Shikha said.

Snail Snot looked up and smiled tightly.

'I'm sorry if I was rude!' Shikha said demurely. 'And that we were so late.' She put on her sweetest expression. 'We will be home early tomorrow, I promise!'

Snail Snot nodded and shut the book.

'Good,' she said. She patted the sofa. 'Now come and sit next to me,' she said. 'See what I've brought for you! It's a brochure of the Paradise Valley Boarding School!'

They leafed through the glossy colour brochure with its pictures of sparkling swimming pools and happy smiling children riding ponies, and trekking and dancing and doing all sorts of things she used to, and that made school so much fun. And Shikha couldn't help feel a pang of longing for her old life – the life that had disappeared so suddenly when the car had gone upside down. Everything had turned upside down with it. Snail Snot eyed her shrewdly, and patted her hand.

'Keep it,' she said. 'You can read it whenever you want!'

Later that night, when Sharifa brought her the bedtime glass of milk, she noticed Shikha's red-rimmed eyes at once.

'She has upset you again?' she demanded, nostrils flaring, the battlelight entering her eyes. Tiredly Shikha nodded.

'She was upset because we were late. And she's started that old school thing again. I would like to go back to school, Sharifa,' she said in a rush, her eyes filling up again, much to her disgust. 'But I can't leave Sunny until he's all right.'

'You don't worry about anything!' Sharifa said fiercely. 'You are doing just fine! These things always take time. Everything will be all right. Now go and sleep!'

Shikha grinned. 'Yes,' she said, nodding. 'By tomorrow, everything should be all right! Back to normal!'

13

'ASLAMBHAI,' SHIKHA SAID AS THEY SET OFF THE NEXT morning. 'We'll have to be back by four o'clock today!' She made a face. 'That Veena memsahib will be coming. She got angry that we were so late yesterday and before that!'

Aslambhai nodded. 'Theek hai, baby, okay,' he said.

They were lucky again that day. A message came through that Shaitan had been seen on the northern side of the kila's wall, at the very edge of Shahenshah's territory. They set off at once, Shikha as usual marvelling at all the early morning jungle sights and sounds: the langurs leaping demonically from tree to tree, peacocks screaming, flights of parakeets streaking across the sky, and the occasional neurotic scream of an eagle as it flexed its wings against the early chill. In the golden grass, the chital and sambhar moved gracefully, while sounders of wild boars bashed through everything regardless of how thorny it was. Aslambhai took the Gypsy up the northern side of the kila's ridge, till they were driving (at a precarious angle) just below the wall. Shikha scanned the scrub jungle spread out below with her binoculars, till suddenly Aslambhai grunted and stopped the Gypsy. He pointed to the ground.

'Pugmark!' he said. 'He passed this way not fifteen minutes ago!'

'Does the path go all along the side of the wall?' Shikha whispered, the taut tense feeling back in her stomach.

'Yes,' Aslambhai said. 'But there are some paths that lead from it to the valley below. He might have taken one of those.'

'That will definitely be in Shahenshah's territory!'

Suddenly Ali grabbed her arm and pointed. Down below, on a jungle path, Shaitan walked with his relaxed, indolent gait, stopping now and then at a tree stump to first smell and then spray it. He made a face after sniffing, as though he didn't like what he had smelt on it.

'Badmash Shahenshah ka jaga maar raha hai – the rascal is claiming Shahenshah's territory!' Aslambhai whispered. 'There is going to be trouble between those two before long!'

They watched the rogue tiger move along in what was clearly Shahenshah's turf for a good fifteen minutes before he vanished.

'Shahenshah is probably far away!' Shikha said, jotting down her notes. 'I just hope we're not anywhere near them when they meet!'

They were back home at four o'clock sharp, Shikha with the funny feeling that the day had somehow been incomplete, but she had plans for the rest of the afternoon. Ali slipped off the Gypsy, caught her eye and nodded.

Ten minutes later, Shikha went into the kitchen.

'Sharifa,' she said. 'Sunny and I and Ali are just going for a stroll. Ali said he has seen some strange birds nearby.'

'That Ali is a lafanga!' Sharifa said. 'Okay, go, but be back by five!'

In fifteen minutes they were back at the spot where Ali had sprung his demonstration trap.

'Shall we do it here?' Shikha asked. Ali shook his head.

'Aage! Ahead!' he said.

They reached a spot where the path squeezed through a ravine, with rock faces rearing up on either side. Ali indicated a rock halfway up the cliff face.

'Go there,' he said. 'Hide behind that! You'll get a good view from there.'

'Okay! Come on, Sunny bunny, say isn't this exciting!' She went up the cliff face like a deer, lifting her little brother effortlessly in the places he found difficult to get up to. Ali was right. From here you got a clear uninterrupted view of the path for nearly fifty metres. She looked around for Ali, but the boy had vanished. Grinning, she opened her knapsack and took out her camera. If it worked, this was going to be good! She glanced at her watch. Ten, maybe fifteen minutes to go!

At quarter to five a familiar figure walked down the path, from the far end. She had the gait of one who was on her way to Do Good with Orphans Gone Bad. The dreadful sanctimonious expression was clear on her face. She seemed just a wee bit nervous as she walked hurriedly through the narrow confines of the ravine, glancing from side to side and up its walls. What she had to go through for the sake of those undisciplined vagabond children, who really ought to be in school! Shikha smiled and focused. Snail Snot was a little more than halfway through, and Shikha was just beginning to worry, when:

'Aaaoom! Aaarooom! Aaargh!'

The call bounced off the ravine walls, making it impossible to tell from where it had come, except that it was horribly close.

Snail Snot froze, her bosom heaving.

'Arre baap re!' she wailed weakly, looking about, her mouth open, one hand at her throat in dismay.

Wickedly, Shikha shot off a couple of frames.

'Aaaoom! Aaaoom! Aaaroom Aaaargh!'

The dreadful calls seemed nearer than ever.

Snail Snot stared wildly around in every direction, still paralysed and rooted to her spot. She didn't know whether the tiger was behind her or in front of her, or waiting to pounce on her from the cliffs.

'Aaaargh!' roared the tiger.

'Aaaaeeee! Bachao! Bachao! Help! Aaaeee!' screamed Snail Snot and turning tail, hitched up her sari and wobbled off as fast as she could the way she had come.

Click shuttuk! Click shuttuk! Click shuttuk! Click shuttuk!

Gleefully, Shikha kept her finger pressed firmly on the shutter button.

Two minutes later she, Ali and Sunny were exchanging high fives and whooping with laughter. Then Shikha put the camera on a convenient rock, set the self-timer and took a picture of all three of them, giving a triumphant thumbs up!

That evening Veena aunty failed to show up.

'Imagine, Sharifa!' Shikha complained indignantly, trying hard to keep a straight face. 'I came home early so that she wouldn't be angry. And she doesn't come at all!' She clicked her tongue reprovingly, while Sharifa shot her a suspicious look.

Just then the phone rang.

'Hello?' Shikha wondered who the hell it could be.

'Hello – Shikha dear? You are at home? Is Sunny with you?' (What a silly question! And Shikha nearly said, no aunty I left him at Shergarh Kila to play with Shaitan, but there was a hysterical note in the woman's voice which warned her not to.) 'Don't leave the house for any reason okay? Lock all the doors and windows!' Veena aunty almost screeched. 'There is a tiger somewhere nearby. It nearly attacked me when I was walking towards your house!'

'What? A tiger? Wow!'

'Yes! In the ravine! Thank God it didn't attack!'

'It probably knew you were on your way to Do Good Work!' Shikha said, before she could stop herself, and then stifled a giggle.

'What was that? But listen dear. Don't go out. This place is too dangerous. I am going to complain to that useless field director, Mr Rana. One of his precious tigers is roaming about outside his sanctuary. It will kill someone, soon!'

'So you won't be coming anymore?' Shikha asked hopefully, her brown eyes shining. 'It would be so dangerous to drive back at night, imagine!'

'My dear, I won't be able to come today. But I'll think of something. Now let me ring up that field director!'

Shikha put down the phone.

'Hells bells Sunny!' she said, looking at him, a frown on her face. 'That didn't sound very promising!'

It wasn't. Next morning Snail Snot turned up at Shergarh House in a tonga with bag and baggage.

'I'll be staying here till sahib comes back!' she informed a horrified Sharifa. 'It's too dangerous to come and go every day. I have informed sahib on the phone.'

Ali's genius plan had backfired horribly!

Returning home that evening, at six, well six thirty, well closer to seven o'clock again, happily expecting an empty house with a message that Snail Snot would not be coming anymore, Shikha found the woman firmly ensconced in the drawing room as usual, bosom heaving as she looked at her tiny watch every two minutes, an expression of acute prissiness on her face.

'Oh!' Shikha said, pausing in the doorway, her hand shooting up to her mouth in dismay. And then, 'Snai … er … Veena aunty, you shouldn't have come! It's too dangerous!'

'Shikha beti! Again so late! My dear, I have some very good news for you. I shall be staying here with you both until your uncle returns. In the little bedroom upstairs, though it is a little difficult to get up the spiral staircase. But, I don't mind! Now what do you think of that!' She gave Sunny one of her smiles that the little boy found scarier than Sheba's grimaces.

'St … staying here?' Shikha stammered faintly taking a step backwards.

'Yes, dear! Every morning of course, Aslambhai can drop me back at the village, where I will do my work, and pick me up again in the afternoon or at lunchtime! I'll be able to spend so much more time with you this way!'

'Tt … time with us? B … b … but we go into the tiger reserve in the mornings!'

'Well my dear, yesterday after the tiger had nearly killed me I got back home and did some thinking. Actually I first went to the temple to thank the Gods for my escape. Really it is only they who saved me! But then I thought that if I could be in so much danger outside the reserve, in the middle of the afternoon, imagine what it must be like inside! So, at least until your uncle returns and can take full responsibility (said in a rather disapproving manner), I think you both can stay at home and maybe help me in my work.'

'Ss … stay at home and Do G … G … Good Work?'

Snail Snot nodded, and there were tears in her eyes.

'Yes,' she said, wiping her watermelon seeds with a sniff. 'I think you children have been left on your own rather too much! You need more supervision.'

'B … but aunty there is Sharifa and Aslambhai and Ali and all those tigers!' Shikha wailed in despair.

'You need proper responsible company, my dear! And supervision! Now look at you! Such a pretty girl like you shouldn't look like a wild jungle cavegirl!'

'Jungle cavegirl?' Shikha scratched her hair wildly as Sunny looked up anxiously. It was going out of control girl, out of control! And there was nothing she could do about it!

'Come my dear, go and take your bath. Tomorrow we shall all three of us go to the village where I will show you what I have been doing. Helping those poor villagers and their children! Trying to get back the rights snatched from them!'

'B … b … b … but aunty, we have to go into the reserve tomorrow!' Shikha wailed. 'I promised Dipti I would! I can't break my promise!'

'Shikha beti, don't make such a fuss. Surely you can miss going into the reserve for a few days for my sake? I couldn't sleep a wink all of last night thinking about that tiger! Imagine if you and Sunny had been playing there!'

'Cc … can't we at least go into the reserve early in the morning for a couple of hours and then come back and go to the village and things?'

'Shikha, beti, I don't want you to be overdoing things! Think of your little brother! You don't want him to fall sick do you?'

'But … but Sunny is fine! Aren't you Sunny bunny! Tell her!'

Sunny fixed his big black eyes on Shikha, and then nodded solemnly. He was fine. Was this froggy woman going to run away again like she had yesterday? He hoped she would.

'Good, dear! Now go and take your bath! Oh, yes I forgot! I spoke to your uncle this morning. He says he'll be delayed by a week or ten days. But some of your things will be arriving in five or six days' time!'

'Oh!' Shikha said. She took Sunny's hand and wandered into her room. Listlessly she took her night clothes and went into the bathroom, waving and smiling automatically to Sunny. Thank God he no longer sat with his head jammed against the door, listening out for his sister. He was quite happy playing in the room provided he could hear her inside. And Shikha had hit on the perfect solution to keep both herself and Sunny happy. She sang in her bath.

'Any special requests, Sunny?' she'd ask before shutting the door.

Of course there were none.

So Shikha sang all the songs she and mama used to sing together at home on the piano when the power cuts happened. She had a clear strong voice that went easily through the thick bathroom door – even though a bit muffled by it. This evening though, she didn't feel like singing. The damn woman had spoilt everything. But she had to, or Sunny would get upset. Tremblingly, she began, singing those old beautiful numbers that mama had taught her. Songs by Roberta Flack, Diana Ross, Lisa Minelli, Carole King, Barbara Streisand and so many others. (The deal had been that in return she had taught mama all the latest hip-hop rap stuff that everyone was listening to, though now she found herself singing mama's old favourites most of the time.) And outside, squatting crosslegged on the bed, Sunny was happy to listen – and to fiddle about with Shikha's camera – something he was not supposed to do, of course. (And which was why, on several occasions, Shikha had thought the camera had been playing strange tricks on her!) Now Sunny heard the room's door handle rattle and instinctively slipped down behind the bed. Probably it was just Sharifa checking up on them. He peeked. And ducked back quickly.

It was froggy aunty.

She looked around the room briefly and frowned. From inside the bathroom Shikha was launching into – or rather trying to – 'People', that old Barbara Streisand hit, which had been one of her mother's favourites. She was making a complete hash of the high notes, she knew but carried on regardless. Outside, Snail Snot looked around, a look of horror coming over her face.

No! It couldn't be! She would have to stop it instantly! That terrible girl! And inform Binoy! The girl needed to be put in an institution for children gone wrong! She surged to the bathroom door and burst in. (It was always that little bit too difficult to lock securely from inside. Bathroom doors of old houses always are.)

'Shikha!' she said, her horribly oily voice, full of tragic disapproval. 'Where's Sunny? He's in here with you, isn't he? He's not in the room! Hai, you should be ashamed beti!' She looked around the vast echoing bathroom, whose acoustics were so good for singing.

'Eeeeeeek! Eeeeeeeek! What are you doing here! Get out, get out, get out! Get out you fat tick!' Reclining in the tub singing away, poor Shikha got the shock of her life! She grabbed the first thing that came to hand and flung it. It was a sponge, heavy with soapy water and it smacked straight into Snail Snot's face with a soggy thump and then glooped slowly downwards. Shikha made a frantic grab for her towel, as Snail Snot slowly wiped her face with her sari pallu (the sponge had slid to the floor), as if wiping tears away, and looked around for Sunny. She even peered inside the enormous clothes bin, and then approached the gigantic tub, as though Shikha had hidden Sunny in its cool if soapy depths or he had scuttled down the plughole! Still in the tub, Shikha wrapped a towel around herself frantically, and backed off, still screaming hysterically:

'What do you want? Get out, get out, get out! Go away Fatface!'

Sharifa came charging up on the double.

'Kya hooa, baby? What happened baby?' she said, as Snail Snot turned to her.

'She's got Sunny hidden somewhere here. While she bathes! No shame!' Snail Snot shook her head tragically, as if it were the end of the world.

'Memsahib, Sunny baba palang par khel raha hai! Memsahib, Sunny is playing on the bed.' Sharifa said calmly, but with great anger. Actually he was now standing uncertainly at the bathroom door, wondering why Shikha was screaming, and getting quite upset himself. 'See there he is!' Sharifa said.

Snail Snot turned around. 'Oh,' she said calmly. 'He must have run out when my back was turned.' Sunny quickly scampered back on to the bed and got busy stuffing Shikha's camera back into her knapsack. She'd be mad if she found out he had been fiddling with it.

Snail Snot a.k.a. Fat Tick a.k.a. Fatface walked over and stood by the bed.

'Sunny beta,' she said primly. 'You must not go into the bathroom when Shikha didi bathes. Good little boys don't do that!' She smiled to show him that she was not scolding him (for something he had not done), even if she was.

Sunny looked puzzled. Even during his most frightened days, that was one thing he had not done. He had jammed his face against the door, waiting for Shikha's next call out to him, but he had never gone in.

'*Cool your jets girl, cool your jets!* Easy Shikha! Don't let that fat tick upset you!' Shikha muttered fiercely, balling her fists, as Sharifa began drying out her hair with the towel. Her face had gone bright scarlet with rage and embarrassment. Breathing deeply she forced herself to calm down. This time she would not collapse in tears. She would be a real cool hep kick-ass chick hard as nails and deadly as … what was that … razor wire. Yeah man, razor wire! She came out of the bathroom and looked at Sunny, squatting innocently on the bed as if butter wouldn't melt in his mouth.

'Hi toodledumps!' said the hard-as-nails hep chick, deadly as razor wire, dimpling disgracefully as she smiled. 'Sorry for the interruption in tonight's performance due to unforeseen circumstances!'

But dinner that night was a very frosty affair indeed. At first Snail Snot pretended that absolutely nothing out of the ordinary had happened and tried a lot of inane chitter chatter. Shikha concentrated on her food and answered in single syllables. Sunny looked from one to the other as he played with his peas. Then Snail Snot laid down her spoon and gave Shikha a look as if she was trying once again to rescue her from going to the very devil.

'Shikha beti,' she said shaking her head. 'Just imagine what your parents would think! How hurt and disappointed they would be! Didn't they teach you to respect your elders?' She sniffed and wiped a tear that really wasn't there. Shikha bent down and stuffed another spoonful into her mouth.

'So wouldn't you like to apologize to me?' Snail Snot went on. 'I can understand how difficult that is. But it has to be done.'

Shikha looked up with calm eyes. She chewed and swallowed and took a gulp of water.

'My parents,' she said slowly, 'mama and papa also taught me not to tell lies!'

It took a while for the meaning of what she had said to sink in. Snail Snot's face took on its blank pasty expression.

'Very well,' she said calmly. 'I have asked Aslambhai to

report at eight o'clock tomorrow. We will go to the village and you can attend the school where I work.'

'Err ... Veena aunty, I won't be able to come. I have a lot of work to catch up with. I have my field notes to sort out and the journal to bring up to date. You know, it's sort of like school homework. Dipti will be mad if I don't do it!'

Good for you, Shikha girl, way to go, way to go, that's telling her baby! Shikha looked up calmly though she could feel her cheeks go red.

'Very well,' said Snail Snot pursing her lips and trying to look hurt. 'As you wish.'

Shikha got up.

'Goodnight, Veena aunty,' she said politely. 'Come on Sunny, time for bed!'

'Goodnight, children!' Snail Snot said, shaking her head tragically. To think that Binoy's niece had turned out like this! Such a lovely but utterly rotten apple! And she was clearly such a bad influence on the little boy.

But matters only got worse after that. In the days that followed, Shikha was not able to go into the tiger reserve at all. Snail Snot would say she needed the Gypsy and Aslambhai and drive off. Shikha had steadfastly refused to go along with her, stubbornly saying she had to finish the 'project' Dipti had given her. And Aslambhai (grumbling and furious) had told her that usually, all that 'madam' did was to drive to the village, and make him wait there the whole day, doing nothing, or sending him on silly errands. For a while, Shikha had eyed her uncle's motorbike, and wondered ... But it would be too risky to take Sunny on that. So mostly, she mooched about Shergarh House, kicking pebbles in the driveway and getting bored and irritated and feeling all bottled up. If only Sunny would start talking again, this dreadful fear of him being sent away to learn sign language would disappear. The idiot didn't even know what he was heading for. Well she would give it another shot, dammit he had to talk! It had been long enough. Could it be that he was not really trying enough? Or could it be – as she had heard Snail Snot say that first evening – that he needed another shock to make him regain his power of speech? Her face set and determined she turned to him one afternoon:

'Sunny,' said folding her arms across her chest and hooding her eyes. 'You'd better say something or I am not going to speak to you again! Ever!'

Sunny, who had been playing on the bed, looked up at her, his eyes wide, a look of surprise on his face.

'Say something Sunny! Just say something, will you!' Shikha leaned forward and took him by the shoulders. 'Do you know what it's been like to have just a dumb bunny of a brother to talk to all the time? Do you?' She was shaking him now, and he was clearly bewildered. What on earth had come over her? Why was she so angry with him? He hadn't fiddled with her camera for several days now.

'You just sit there and laugh and cry and nod and shake your head!' Shikha raged on exasperatedly. 'Do you know how I feel? Do you care? Come on, now say something you little dumb bunny! Or I'll leave you here and go away forever!'

Sunny's lips trembled and he opened his mouth.

'Oh, no you're not going to cry!' Shikha shouted, completely losing her cool. 'No crying! Say something!' She smacked him smartly across the cheek, and poor Sunny just gulped like a goldfish out of water. He put his hands in front of his face to ward off any more smacks, but bit his lip fiercely. He would not cry! He wanted to say so much but the words would not come out somehow. His lips moved soundlessly.

'Come on you little shrimp, talk!' commanded Shikha,

raising her hand. He cringed and suddenly Shikha found that she was the one who was weeping, angry, frustrated, and suddenly ashamed. Not Sunny.

'Oh, Sunny bunny I'm sorry!' she whispered, dropping her arm. 'I don't know what came over me! I'm so sorry! But please try and talk! Then we can be normal again!'

Sunny just clung to her and buried his face in her hair. She was not going anywhere. She would be with him, at least until mama and papa returned from wherever they had gone.

Shikha missed her days in the jungle sorely. Sitting at the edge of the garden and looking at the reserve through binoculars was poor compensation for the excitement of the morning drives and afternoons spent at Hari Pani. Poor Ali had kept away from her, afraid that she might be angry because his plan had backfired so horribly. But Shikha had realized, that by hook or by crook, Snail Snot would have seen to it that their forays into the jungle would be brought to a grinding halt.

One thing she remained firm about. She would not apologize to the woman.

'Never, Sunny!' she said fiercely. 'She's the one who comes bursting into the bathroom, making wild accusations, and she wants me to apologize! She's the one who wants to take you away from me! Oh, how I wish Sheba would eat her!'

What was worse was that Binoy chacha had been further delayed due to legal problems concerning her father's affairs and there was no sign of the truck bringing their things either.

'Binoy chacha, Veena aunty has stopped us from going into the reserve!' Shikha had complained when he had rung up, hoping that he would speak to her about it.

'Oh,' came the answer. 'Why?'

'Because she hates me!'

'Now, Shikha you know that is not true. And as long as she

is in Shergarh House, I think you should respect her wishes. There is probably a very good reason why she doesn't want you to go into the park. She had said something to me about a tiger roaming about near the house. She only has your safety in mind! Now be good and listen to her!'

The only good thing about their enforced curfew at Shergarh House was that Shikha had turned her journal into a work of art. Her precious field notes, accompanied by her sketches and watercolour portraits (done separately and then stuck in, of course), and even a few of Sunny's drawings, on which she proudly made him scrawl his name, had been presented beautifully, along with the maps she had made. The entry for each day started on a new page and included everything interesting she had seen or heard on that day. She had an excellent memory and had quickly got the hang of jotting down brief field notes that further helped her remember details she might have otherwise forgotten. Like the baby langur that had been riding on its mother's back backwards, and looking puzzled because it couldn't see its mother's face! Like the way the sun spangled on the emerald waters of Hari Pani and the way the spotbill ducks bathed in it, spraying a shower of diamonds all over themselves. All she now needed were the photographs. Those, she decided, she would arrange album fashion, on the blank pages, with appropriate captions. They would be separate from and yet linked to the text. It had to be like that because she didn't have the photographs while she wrote the text, so they would have to tell their own story later on, as it were. She wondered if she ought to ring up Mr Rana to ask if they were ready, but knew he was a very busy man and so, at least twice, had backed away from the phone. She spent hours pouring over her work, planning how each page should look like, drawing a rough outline, then going ahead with the fair copy. It was the only way she could be with her tigers.

Until one evening, about a week after the bathroom battle, the phone rang.

'Hello, Shikha dear!' the field director boomed. 'What have you been doing with yourself, my dear! I've been out of station and the range officer I deputed to call you told me that you've stopped going into the reserve. Is everything all right? Jogi aunty would have come down to see you, but she hasn't been very well.'

'We're fine uncle,' she said in a voice smaller than she had wanted.

At the other end, Mr Rana frowned.

'Are you sure?' he demanded. 'You are both well? There is this nasty virus going around, beti! Jogi aunty was laid up with it!'

'We're fine, really.'

'Well, then I have something for you. Your photographs have come. Would you like to come and collect them?'

'Oh! Yes, sure! But uncle, Snail Sno … I mean Veena aunty has taken the Gypsy and Aslambhai. How do we come?'

'Who? Snail who?' he boomed.

'Um … Veena aunty! You know, who is staying with us.'

'Oh!' He took a moment to digest the information. 'You mean that lady who looks hali-bhali, bholi-bhali all the time, but who could eat a shark and pretend it was rose petals?' he asked, forcing a giggle out of Shikha at the other end.

'Um … yes, I suppose so!'

'Don't worry Shikha beti. I'm sending the Gypsy right over. This is official business after all!'

'Oh, thanks uncle! Er … is there any news from Dipti?'

'Yes!' he said. 'She's been very busy with her job, but

said that she did write to you! The mail takes a long time to reach us here, beti! Anyway, I'm sending the car over, right now, okay?'

'Thanks, uncle.'

'No problem, Shikha beti!'

It was such a relief to be driven out of Shergarh House, after having been confined to it for an entire week. Shikha breathed deeply as she settled down in the forest department's jeep. On her lap sat her precious tiger journal; she felt she had to show Rana uncle something that would assure him that he had been right in allowing her to go into the reserve. Besides, she was dying to show it to someone, anyone really, except Snail Snot, of course. She had worn her lovely black skirt again and slipped on big golden hoops in her ears, and was looking quite un-safari like. Sharifa had smiled as she had scrubbed Sunny's brown face and combed down his unruly hair.

'Good,' she said. 'Rana sahib will take good care of you!'

But by the time they had driven through the gates of the 'Field Director's Residence', Shikha knew that something strange was happening inside her. She stared fixedly ahead out of the windscreen, and held Sunny's hand tightly. Something had been building up inside her all week, and was now, like some monster of the deep, threatening to surface in one hell of a rush.

'Helleo bachche!'

She looked out of the window. Tea, as usual, had been laid out in the lawn. Joginder aunty, looking a little pale, but with three chins wobbling in place as always, stood in the middle of the lawn, her warm five-hundred watt smile splitting her face, her arms open in greeting. Shikha helped Sunny down and they walked up to the lawn, hand in hand. They had barely reached it, when Sunny, to Shikha's amazement, let go of her hand and charged towards Joginder aunty in just the way he used to when their mother returned from work. She lifted him effortlessly and kissed him resoundingly on both cheeks, put him on her hip and looked at Shikha. She stood uncertainly there for a second, not trying to resist the tears that had suddenly made everything so blurry, and then, abandoning all her steely self-control, rushed into the huge woman's embrace. Joginder aunty was big and soft and warm and safe and nicely scented and could easily accommodate both the children in a single huge hug. And that's all she did. She just hugged them, and held them, not saying anything, but listening with rising fury, to Shikha's abandoned weeping, and Sunny's whimpering accompaniment. Her husband came out on to the lawn to welcome his young guests and stopped short.

'What? What's happened?' he stammered weakly. His wife shook her head warningly, and still holding the children to her, walked them slowly indoors as he stared after them.

'Sahib,' said the jeep driver. 'Sahib, memsahib ne kitab chod diya! Memsahib has left her book!' He handed Mr Rana Shikha's tiger journal and drove off.

Cautiously Mr Rana peeked inside the dim living room where his wife had taken the children. Cautiously, because he had recognized the look on his wife's face. It was the sort of look that Sheba would have on her face, if she knew that someone was threatening her cubs. It was better to stay away. He went into his office and began leafing through the journal. Fifteen minutes later, he was still completely absorbed in it, when his wife entered.

'They are better now!' she said, her eyes glinting angrily. 'The woman that Binoy has put in charge is busy destroying these children! Day by day! We will have to do something! That sweet girl has wept non-stop for the last fifteen minutes! She won't have any tears left and will ruin her eyes! She will be a nervous wreck very soon.'

'And look at this!' her husband said. 'A classic document if I have ever seen one! Such a labour of love! A work of art!' He frowned. 'But what can we do? We can tell Binoy, of course, and you know Binoy! So unpredictable! So touchy! He might just tell us to mind our own business and keep away from the children. As it is he has hated this whole business from day one. And that woman – isn't she the one who has been telling the villagers to forcibly occupy the tiger reserve and graze their livestock inside?'

'That Binoy!' said his wife in disgust. 'Such a fool he is, sometimes!'

'Did she tell you why she was crying?' Mr Rana asked.

His wife shook her head and her triple chins.

'I didn't ask,' she said. 'She just needed to be hugged. She's better now. We could ask her. It can't just be not being able to go into the reserve! She's probably missing her mother terribly!'

In the drawing room, Shikha was looking acutely embarrassed, but strangely feeling much better.

'Hells bells, Sunny! Fat lot of a hep kick-ass chick I am!' She sniffed dolefully, smiling wanly through her tears. 'I just see Jogi aunty and go blub blub blub! What a drip! But it's all right, I'm fine now!'

'Feeling better now, my dear?' Jogi aunty said, sitting down beside her, and almost capsizing the sofa. 'You, little tiger man, come here!' She plonked Sunny into her vast lap and jogged him there, while he stared fascinated at her wobbling chins. Mr Rana sat down quietly, and put the tiger journal on the table.

'Now, beti, would you like to tell us what is bothering you so much?' Jogi aunty asked gently.

Shikha gulped and nodded.

'I'll try,' she said, 'but I'm all mixed up inside! Ever since that … that … er Veena aunty came to stay she's been trying to stop our trips inside the park. And now she's succeeded! Then she goes on and on about how I should be at school – she even brought this beautiful brochure to show me – and how I should leave Sunny alone.' The tears were filling up slowly again, and she wiped them away impatiently. 'Aunty, I do want to go back to school – I miss Rini and Ritu and Sunaina and all my other friends terribly! And she sticks this lovely brochure under my nose to make me miss it more and want to go back! I … I got so upset I smacked Sunny the other day, trying to make him talk. And aunty, he still won't leave me, and I can't force him to! I know he's getting better – like … like the way he ran to you today. He would never have done that a month ago. She wants him to learn sign language, but I know he's going to start talking soon! In the tiger reserve, you should just see him! He's so happy – he pretends he's Shahenshah and runs after Ali. And I love it there, too. I can just be myself there and no one says anything.' She looked up and sniffed. 'Not even Shahenshah!'

The Ranas exchanged brief glances. So Dipti had been right, after all. She usually was. If only she could knock some sense into that silly Binoy's head too.

'Beti, of course you will go back to school one day!' Jogi aunty said, stroking her head and holding her close. 'And one day, this little tiger man here will be waving goodbye to you while he goes off to school.'

'The worst part is that she makes me feel so bad about it,' Shikha went on. 'She makes me feel so guilty. She keeps saying "Your mama would be so ashamed if she were around" and horrible things like that. What does she know about mama? Mama … mama was my best buddy and I do miss her so much!'

'Right,' said Mr Rana who seemed to have made up his mind about something. He tapped the journal with his finger. 'I had a look at this, Shikha dear! I think you need to go on with it. It is excellent! From tomorrow you will resume your trips into the park. I shall be sending you a vehicle at six in the morning. Will that be all right?'

'What?' She could hardly believe her ears. 'But uncle, won't you need the jeep for your work?' she asked faintly.

'This is as much my work as it is yours. And there are plenty of jeeps here.'

'But what if Veena aunty objects?'

'I'll send an official note with the ranger. Once you are inside the reserve, you are my responsibility, not hers. And you will be on official work.' His eyes twinkled.

'Oh! Wow! Thanks so much!'

'Hai beti, just look at your pretty eyes! All red and puffed up! Now come on, tea is ready!'

'Er ..., uncle, you mentioned that my pictures were ready? How have they come out?'

He grinned. 'It seems my dear that you were in a terrible state of excitement while taking them. I think Dipti has a tripod somewhere in her room. I'll give you that. It will steady the camera.'

'Oh, then they're not very good?'

'Some are blurry, but some are all right. And some are very good indeed. Come and see for yourself!'

Back home later that evening, Shikha politely informed Snail Snot that she and Sunny would be spending the next day (and following days) in the tiger reserve on invitation of Mr Rana, the field director. He would be sending a jeep for her, so she need not worry on that account. (But yes, she was already feeling terrible about 'ditching' Aslambhai. She'd have to think about some way to rescue him ...)

'He says that the journal I wrote is very good,' Shikha said a little smugly.

'But of course, I can't just send you off in any jeep that turns up here at six o'clock in the morning, Shikha beti,' Snail Snot protested as though that would be like pouring hot oil over a litter of puppies. 'Surely you realize that.'

'Oh, he's sending an official letter,' Shikha said blandly. But never in her wildest dreams had she imagined what was going to happen at six o'clock the next morning.

Of course, she and Sunny were ready and waiting at five thirty! Sharifa yawned and grumbled, but was happy no doubt about that. Aslambhai, poor fellow was only going to report at eight o'clock and would miss everything. So would Ali. But Snail Snot had arisen too. She had to see the children safely off you see, and check the letter properly. The sacrifices she had to make for these ungrateful children, really! She watched disapprovingly as Shikha put her knapsack down and did a last minute check of her list. She was humming happily.

At sharp six, out on the porch and pacing about impatiently, Shikha paused. What was that sound? A motorcycle? God, don't tell me Rana uncle had sent her a motorbike transport, she thought. Snail Snot would freak! But hey, that sounded like more than one motorcycle. Already she could see a cloud of dust as the vehicle or vehicles approached.

Four rather battered, but polished forest department motorcycles rumbled up the drive to Shergarh House at a sedate speed, side by side, flanking a spanking new metallic green forest department Gypsy King, glittering with medallions and stickers, its lights flashing and pennant flying proudly from its bonnet. (In fact Mr Rana had just taken delivery of it two days ago!) Behind it followed a Canter full of forest guards, each one obviously in his best uniform.

The Gypsy and motorcycle escort stopped smartly in the portico of Shergarh House, and a smiling range officer got off it.

The forest guards had jumped off their Canter, and under the supervision of the senior-most officer stood stiffly to attention in two columns in the verandah, their lathis resting over their shoulders as if they were guns. The range officer stepped up to Shikha, and smiling widely, held out a sealed envelope on a silver platter.

'The field director presents his compliments and would like to invite you to Shergarh Tiger Reserve in pursuance of your official work there!' he said formally and saluted. (He had heard stories about this girl and her ability to attract tigers, or so everyone said ...)

Shikha's mouth had fallen open, and beside her, Sunny was looking thrilled to bits. She took the envelope and opened it. A very formal looking letter, full of very official looking rubber stamps and seals and signatures and countersignatures lay inside. (Mr Rana had simply used every rubber stamp and seal in his office regardless of how irrelevant to the issue they were!) She scanned it briefly and then turned around to give it to Snail Snot.

Snail Snot was looking as though she had swallowed a mouthful of pig's puke instead of porridge (though she was the kind of person who might have enjoyed that more!). Her face was pale, her mouth open, clearly she was in shock.

'Veena aunty, this is an official letter from Rana uncle,' Shikha said sweetly. Snail Snot nodded. Shikha turned to get into the Gypsy.

'Ma'am, will you and Sunny sahib please inspect the guard of honour?' the range officer requested, smiling.

Beetroot with embarrassment, but enjoying herself hugely, Shikha (and Sunny) slowly walked down the grinning line of forest guards (she had seen the Queen of England and world leaders do this, on television!) as Snail Snot watched in amazement. Just what was going on here?

How mama and papa would have loved this! Shikha thought. Papa would have gone berserk with his handycam! She saluted the guards as smartly as she could, but that was not good enough for Sunny. Clicking his heels smartly, he snapped them a sharp salute, looking as fierce and stern as he could under his floppy jungle hat, but plainly thrilled to bits.

Shikha went quickly over to Sharifa and whispered in her ear. 'Tell Aslambhai that tomorrow he will not be feeling very well and will have to go to the forest department headquarters to get medicines from Joginder memsahib. So, unfortunately he will not be able to come for duty for Veena madam.'

'But ...,' Sharifa began, then her eyes widened as she understood.

'Shikha baby, tum bahut badmash ho – Shikha baby, you are very naughty!' she said, but gave the girl a pinch and then a peck on the cheek.

Happily Shikha took her seat in the back of the Gypsy, and waved to Snail Snot.

'I'll try and be back early,' she called. 'But I can't promise anything. Don't worry, I'll send a radio message if we get late! Have a nice day aunty!'

Game, set and match to Shikha Saini, she thought gleefully, thumping her hand into her fist.

Well, game and set, maybe. The match had not yet started.

14

IT WAS REALLY GREAT TO BE BACK INTO THE RESERVE AFTER A week's absence, and Shikha couldn't help feeling that she had to catch up on what she might have missed during that period. Everything seemed much the same though, it appeared as though she had missed no momentous event, and she was relieved. She would have hated to know that, for example, Shaitan and Shahenshah had settled their dispute while she had been killing time at Shergarh House. This time around, her trips into the forest were, of course, a little different. They had the forest department's Gypsy and driver, so Shikha couldn't take the wheel from Aslambhai as she had begun doing quite regularly. Aslambhai had grinned and nodded approvingly when Sharifa told him that he was not feeling well and had to get medicine from Mrs Jogi and so would not be able to report to work for Snail Snot. He duly sent word with Sharifa to her that the doctor had advised him rest and so would be absent for two or three days at least. And so, he (and Ali) would wait at the padlocked gate of the tiger reserve near Shergarh House, and hop on with delighted grins, when Shikha and Sunny drove past every morning in the forest department Gypsy.

'Can we give you a lift, Aslambhai? You need to get some more medicines?' Shikha would ask, feigning surprise and grinning wickedly under her safari cap, as Sunny bunny would chuckle beside her and thump his fist into his palm. He found it very funny indeed.

And because she was now on 'official dooty' as the range officer put it, she saw no reason to be back at Shergarh House at 5 p.m. sharp, and returned usually by seven or seven thirty, dog-tired but happy, and with a sleeping Sunny (deliberately) on her hip. Snail Snot of course would sniff disapprovingly, purse her lips and heave her bosom tragically. From time to time she would bring up the subject of the Paradise Valley Boarding School.

'You know, Shikha dear, you must be looking forward to going back to school, no?' she would say sweetly, never raising her voice and leafing through the brochure. 'Look at the lovely pool they have, and all these mountains. Such a lucky girl you are, to be going there.'

'Uh uh,' Shikha would mutter, and pretend to be interested in Binoy chacha's bookshelves. She had recently found a ten-volume encyclopaedia on *Birds of India and Pakistan* by Salim Ali and S. Dillon Ripley and had been fascinated by it as well as by some of the other books.

'Really, we must start thinking about getting your things together. Before you know it, it will be time to catch that train!'

'Uh uh.'

'It was so kind of the principal Mr Bhatinder to give you admission without a test even,' Snail Snot would go on in her implacable manner. 'You will, of course, be in a class lower than what you were in. But that'll make things so much easier for you, don't you think!'

And Shikha would clench her fists and mutter under her breath: 'Cool your jets, easy girl! You are not going to that school, so why get bothered by what this fat blimp says?' At any rate, the problem (if there still was one) was still three and a half months away. But one thing Shikha had made up her mind about:

Even if Sunny did start talking again by that time, and was well, she was not going to Paradise Valley Boarding School. One, because it was a boarding school, which meant she would be away from Sunny for unthinkable periods of time; when he did start talking he would be the only person she would be able to talk to about their parents, which she desperately wanted to do at times. And secondly because Snail Snot had suggested the school and she'd be damned if she would listen to her.

One morning, the Gypsy driver handed her a letter in a very official looking envelope. She saw with delight, that it was from Dipti and ripped it open.

'Dear Shikha,' wrote Dipti in a sturdy no-nonsense kind of handwriting. *'Apologies for taking so long to reply, I have been buried under with work! I have received your field reports on the movements and doings of the tigers, and papa told me about the journal that you have been maintaining. He even sent me copies of some of your photographs. I can't tell you how impressed I am! You've done a wonderful job my dear, in spite of Sn … er, what's her name, Veena aunty, trying to spoil things. (Aha, papa caught on pretty fast my dear!) There's just one thing I'd like you to remember: in your letter you called Shahenshah an old "doofus" and that alarmed me! No, I know he is an old doofus, but Shikha, always remember that he is a wild tiger too and capable of very un-doofus like behaviour. He's not a harmless cuddly pussycat by any yardstick! So please be very careful while watching him – and of*

course the other tigers too! You can't imagine how green with envy I got when I read that you had watched Sheba make a kill. (I would have fainted too!) How's Sunny bunny doing? Don't worry Shikha, he'll start talking soon and once he finds his tongue, he's not going to stop. Well, I have to stop here. Keep it up Shikha girl, we are all very proud of you. Lots of love, Dipti

P.S.: I've met Binoy chacha a few times here – he's going nuts with all the legal hassles and all, not his cup of tea at all! I helped him pack some of the things I (and he) thought you might want from here. They should be on their way soon. Love, D.

'Keep it up … we are all very proud of you!' For two days Shikha kept the letter in her blouse pocket, reading and re-reading those lines, her face aglow! In the field, she re-doubled her efforts, pushing herself to do more and more each day, and staying up later every night to write up her notes. Sundays were the only days when they didn't go inside the reserve (but one was always on stand-by in case an interesting message came through) and she spent her day just lolling and relaxing and playing with Sunny, who was slowly but surely regaining his old hellion ways. Else they would be driven to the Ranas, where she would update them about what she had seen and done that week.

And Snail Snot's waves of disapproval, sniffs and martyred looks she just ignored.

One Sunday morning, a small truck lurched up to Shergarh House. At last, at long last their 'things' had turned up! Mostly it was furniture and suitcases full of clothes and, of course, Sunny's big trunk full of toys, which had got left behind. He fell upon it, his face split in a huge smile of delight and very soon had scattered all its contents on the bedroom floor.

'Put that dressing table in the hall,' Snail Snot instructed, but Shikha would have none of it. Mama's dressing table would go into her room and nowhere else! So would her school bureau. But what made her pause a bit, and swallow hard, was a heavy tall crate that the men, huffing and puffing, put down.

It was her and mama's old piano. The piano on which they thumped out tunes while singing during the power cuts (while Sunny went berserk on his drums!) 'The Cacophonies', papa (who had been a sneaky fan of 'Asterix') had called them, stuffing cotton into his ears while a session was in progress. The piano on which she played her 'scatterbrained birdwing jazz', madcap, dizzy, loopy, sad, happy and often just crazy tunes that spun out of her head, which she could never repeat and never particularly wanted to, no matter how lovely they were. 'The notes just come into my head, mama,' she explained earnestly, 'and then fly away like birds. I don't want to catch them again! And they're always more of them anyway, sort of waiting to be freed!' She couldn't even replay the tunes after papa had (secretly) recorded some of them – and actually, just wasn't interested in doing so. The tunes would come, how they sounded depended entirely on her mood at that moment – which could and often did change as she played – and they would fly out of the piano and be gone forever. That's how she liked it.

They un-crated the piano and it stood, gleaming and polished a rich rosewood brown, looking awkward in its new surroundings.

'I think that will look so nice in the lobby,' Snail Snot said, who seemed to have a lobby fixation. 'Put it there,' she instructed the men.

'No way,' Shikha said, shaking her head. 'It goes into our room. The room is big enough! Idhar lao please! Bring it here please! Near the window!'

And Snail Snot shrugged as if to say, well what can you do

with badly brought up kids these days who insist on having everything their way!

Tentatively Shikha raised the lid and put her fingers on the keys for the first time since the accident. It would be horribly out of tune, she thought, plinking one tentatively. It was in perfect pitch. No doubt about it, someone had had this piano tuned and overhauled before sending it over. Binoy chacha? Well, maybe he did play the piano too.

She dragged a stool over and sat down and began to play. One by one the old favourite tunes poured out, and all too soon she was back in scatterbrained jazz mode and lost to everything else. Sunny had found his dusty drums in the trunk and had begun hammering on them and jerking his head around in proper drummer style, yeah man yeah!

Snail Snot glided into the room with a pained look on her face, her hands on her ears. 'Children,' she admonished in her soft, mossy voice. 'Children, you are making so much noise! It will give me a headache!'

'Good!' Shikha muttered under her breath, thumping the keys harder and tossing her head like a bad bronco filly, making the piano sound like a thunderstorm. And that afternoon Binoy chacha called to say that he would be returning the next day, so could Aslambhai be at the station to pick him up?

'Hells bells Sunny let's go to the station and pick him up,' Shikha said, still thrilled by the arrival of the piano. Also, many of her favourite summer outfits had come too, her shorts, swimsuit and T-shirts, which had been packed away for the winter. She wondered how Binoy chacha, of all people, had managed to send such sensible things over, and then remembered Dipti's letter. It must have been Dipti who had packed! To her horror she discovered Snail Snot pacing about in the verandah early next morning, obviously waiting for Aslambhai.

'Are ... are you coming to the station with us?' she inquired, horrified. God knows what sort of tales this woman would tell Binoy chacha.

'I'm going back to my room in the village school, of course,' Snail Snot sniffed righteously. 'I can't possibly stay here when your uncle is here. You know how people will talk! Aslambhai can drop me home and then go on to the station. Tell Sharifa to bring my bags down, please!'

Oh happy day! Oh joyous moment! She was going! She was going! At last! At last they could have Shergarh House to themselves! No more prissy disapproving looks! No more prying watermelon seed eyes!

Her mood was slightly dampened by Binoy chacha, of course. He had been away for a little more than a month, but greeted them both with just an absent-minded pat on the head. He seemed very anxious to get back to Shergarh House and disappear into his studio.

'Binoy chacha, thank you for sending down the piano,' Shikha said. 'It's been all tuned and polished too!'

'You'll have to thank Dipti for that,' he said shortly. 'She organized the whole thing.'

'Oh! Thank Dipti! Yes, I will.'

'I hope you haven't given Veena aunty any trouble,' Binoy chacha said. 'She didn't sound very happy on the phone. She thinks you need to go to school as soon as possible.'

Hah! Here was an opportunity to get her oar in before that fat tick did.

'Binoy chacha, she's even got me admission into that boarding school! Imagine! I mean, who asked her to?'

'I did,' said Binoy chacha unexpectedly. 'Well, I just told her to do what she thought was best for you both. She has a lot of experience in matters like these and it's been good of her to help.'

'But she stopped us from going into the reserve!' Shikha blurted, not liking the fact that she was telling tales. He raised a sardonic eyebrow.

'Yes, and I believe you complained to Rana uncle, and he sent you the forest department vehicle and a band after that!'

'She just didn't want us to go in. She pretended she needed Aslambhai and the Gypsy every day … dog in the manger!' she muttered under her breath.

'She must have had her reasons for not wanting you to go inside. Maybe she was just afraid that something would happen to you and it would be her responsibility.'

Afraid? All she had wanted was to control their lives from day one. That, and to separate her from Sunny. Control freak! That's what she was.

'Control freak!' Shikha blurted, and quickly covered her mouth. Shit, she had done it again!

'What?'

'Er …, nothing chacha!' Shikha frowned. She might as well get it over with now. The big question had to be asked: 'Er … chacha, can Sunny and I continue going into the reserve with Aslambhai as we used to?' she asked in her sweetest tone. 'Please?'

He turned around in his seat and looked at them, sitting side by side at the back. 'Well Rana was saying something about a journal you were keeping which he said was very good and should go on doing. And Dipti was raving about you in general. So yes, you can. I won't need Aslambhai much this summer – I want to do a lot of painting.'

'Thank you, Binoy chacha, thank you!' She leaned forward and kissed his hairy face.

Yet somewhere far away, she remembered asking Sharifa in the darkened bedroom, 'When do the horrible things start happening? Everything's going all too well!' She thrust the thought away from her. For three whole months, she and Sunny were free to roam the reserve. For the moment that would do.

In his office, Field Director Rana was leafing through the latest batch of photographs that Shikha had taken. He flipped through them steadily and then stopped. Sheba with her face all bloody, drinking at the pool had been impressive. The ones where she had fended off Shahenshah had been a little fuzzy and blurred, probably shaken by the excitement of the moment (and little Sunny clutching Shikha around the waist). But this one, this one needed to be blown up 16 x 20. It was the picture of the two orange and black butterflies settled on Sheba's whiskers, while she looked at them sleepily, upside down.

'Just look at this Jogi!' he told his wife, who had come in at the moment. 'She has talent! Look at this: "The Small Tigers of Shergarh" it should be called! The butterflies are tigers, and so are those children!'

'And dedication,' said his wife. 'I have never met a child with such dedication!' She sniffed. 'If only that foolish Veena would see it and get off her back!'

Her husband gave an exclamation and a sudden honk of laughter that really sounded like the alarm call of a sambhar.

'Speak of the devil!' he roared, putting back his head and laughing. 'That girl is too much! What spirit she has! What cheeky spirit!'

'What are you talking about?'

'Look at these!' he said, wiping his eyes and tapping a set of pictures.

Picture one: A pasty-faced woman walking earnestly down a jungle path, flanked by ravines on either side.

Picture two: The woman, obviously halted in her tracks looking around, very nervous.

Picture three: The woman, her mouth open, in a complete fink!

Picture four: The woman screaming..

Picture five: The woman beginning to turn around.

Picture six: The woman fleeing the scene, her sari hitched high.

Picture seven: Three young faces grinning delightedly into the camera giving it the thumbs up!

Mrs Rana put her pallu in front of her face, but her chins were wobbling frantically and her shoulders were shaking.

'We will,' Mr Rana said seriously, between snorts of laughter. 'We will, of course, pretend we haven't seen them at all and say nothing! Actually, I had no business looking at Shikha's pictures in the first place. She should have been the first to see them. We'll put them back and keep quiet.'

'That Ali,' Mrs Rana said. 'What a little devil he is!'

'One day,' said Mr Rana, almost hopefully. 'One day a real tiger will answer his call and then he will be in real trouble!'

Little did he know that it could be much worse than just that.

15

'TOOFAN AA RAHA HAI – THERE'S A STORM COMING,' SAID Aslambhai as they drove back to Shergarh House one evening about a week after Binoy chacha's return. Indeed it had been a strange sort of day, very still and by the evening quite prickly and uncomfortable even though it wasn't yet really hot. The sky was the colour of ivory, with a yellowish tinge to it, and even the most delicate of acacia leaflets were motionless. Back into her old routine, Shikha had plunged happily into her work, following and observing her tigers, getting hopelessly distracted by everything from a praying mantis eating a bee ('She's like Snail Snot again Sunny!' she giggled, 'all innocent and beseeching and then wham, she has you in her barbed wire arms' – little realizing how close to the truth she had come), to a nilgai giving birth to twins, and absorbing huge amounts of information that Aslambhai so casually ladled out, jotting as much as she could down frantically in her notebook – in much the same way she had done in school, which seemed to have happened to another person on another planet at another time. Strangely, even Sunny seemed to be pleased by Binoy chacha's return, he would now go off happily with Ali for as long as ten or even fifteen minutes at a time, and then come swaggering back beaming to Shikha, as though he had climbed Mount Everest blindfolded and with hands and legs tied, all by himself! Nor did he need her to accompany him to the bathroom anymore – provided she remained in the room outside and called out from time to time.

'Why don't you sing for me when you're inside?' she had suggested cunningly. 'I get frightened too, all by myself, waiting for you, tiger bunny!'

It didn't work, he still couldn't talk, let alone sing, but he made up for it by hammering a mad drummer's tattoo on whatever he could lay his hands on in the bathroom, especially the big stainless steel pail and mug.

Binoy chacha had vanished into his studio like a bear into its den, emerging in his usual erratic fashion, distracted, paint-smeared and looking wilder than ever. He'd mutter darkly about cancelling the 'damn exhibition' and light another beedi.

The storm took its time to arrive that evening, and Shikha was prickling horribly all over by the time it did. It was a grand, blustery affair (like the arrival of a barat, she thought, but so much more tuneful!), and the thunder sent all the peacocks in the reserve into paroxysms of joy. There were many alarming bangs and crashes as windows slammed, and branches snapped, but at last the rain came, still too cold really to go out and dance in, as Shikha and Sunny invariably had done back in Delhi. And Shikha thanked her stars that Sunny had never been afraid of thunderstorms – and remained that way after the crash – clapping and grinning all over his face at the loudest peals, which made even her heart miss a beat.

The next morning was the most beautiful she had ever seen. The sky had been washed powder blue, every tree looked as if it had decked itself up for a party, and Shikha couldn't wait to go into the reserve to see how the creatures there had taken the storm.

Ali came up to her shyly with a box in his hand as she put her knapsack into the Gypsy the next morning. He had been dying to 'make it up' to her ever since his tiger call trick in the ravine on Snail Snot had backfired, convinced that she had been angry with him about it, even though she hadn't mentioned it at all. He had taught her several more bird and animal calls, though she never could quite master his superb tiger imitations.

'Kal raat, paed se gira – they fell out of the tree last night,' he said, thrusting the box into her arms.

'What's in it?' Shikha asked, lifting the lid and peering inside.

'Sambhal ke – be careful – they'll bite!' Ali said urgently, suddenly realizing that it wouldn't do if his peace offering bit her!

'Oh, my God, they're so sweet! Look Sunny they're a pair of baby owls! Where did you get them from Ali?'

'Toofan me paed gira – a tree fell during the storm. They were inside a hole. Their parents flew away and never came back!'

'Hey, Sunny be careful!'

But Sunny had put his hand inside the box. One of the owlets glared at him and hissed, and then waddled up on to his arm, quickly followed by its twin. They flapped their wings to balance, as Sunny, with admirable self-control slowly, took his hand out of the box and held up his arm, squinting and wincing because of the birds' sharp claws, but making no sudden movements.

'Hey Sunny they like you! Oh, just look at them, they're adorable!' Shikha gushed and Sunny nodded. Gently he put out his other hand to stroke one of the birds on its head, but it hissed and snapped at him with its beak, its eyes blazing. Grinning nervously, Sunny took back his arm. He knew exactly what the little bird was feeling. He had felt the same way when mama and papa had flown away and not come back.

'What do they eat?' Shikha asked Ali, still all gooey eyed over the little birds.

'Cockroaches, mice, chipkali – lizards, things like that!' Ali answered vaguely.

'Ugh! And who's going to feed them?' Shikha asked, suddenly realizing the practical problems that could arise.

'Nani hai na – there's nani,' the incorrigible boy replied nonchalantly, with a wave of his hand.

'Shareeefa!' Shikha sang in her sweetest voice. 'Could you please look after these adorable little owlets until we get back in the evening?'

'Ab ye ulloo ka pattha lay ke aaya – now's he's gone and brought baby owls!' Sharifa snorted, peering at the little birds in the box. 'Ek din sher ka bachcha layega – one day he'll bring a tiger cub!' But she took the box inside, and Shikha could hear her telling the 'ulloo ke patthe' that the kitchen was full of flies and cockroaches so they better get to work.

Spring-turning-into-summer was certainly the most beautiful time to be in the tiger reserve, as one by one the great forest trees burst into bloom. The silk cotton trees, with their big goblet-like blooms that attracted a mad collection of birds, insects and animals, and then the flame of the forest, which made entire slopes look as though they were flickering.

On Dipti's advice (and like the tigers themselves), Shikha had marked out a route, which she 'patrolled' every day. It took her through Shergarh Kila, the Chhota Mahal, around Hira Talao and ended up, of course, at Hari Pani, which they would usually reach in time for lunch. Here they would settle in the pavilion, and she would write up her jottings, relax and just watch the animals come down to drink. There had been no signs of Sheba or Shahenshah here after that first dramatic encounter, but there had been other exciting moments.

Driving along the kila wall one morning, Aslambhai suddenly stopped and peered intently ahead at some thorny scrub about a hundred metres away.

'What is it?' Shikha whispered, her tummy tightening as it always did, her heart going boombox again.

'Shaitan jhadi me baitha hai – Shaitan is sitting in the bush,' he replied. 'Waiting for us to pass. Then he'll charge! He likes chasing cars!'

'What?' She peered through her binoculars, her heart thumping, and then she saw him. He was staring straight at them, crouched low in the bush, the tip of his tail twitching.

'He's puzzled because we have stopped!' Aslambhai said, unobtrusively engaging reverse and glancing in his rear-view mirror.

In the back, Sunny and Ali were playing some complicated game that they had invented, oblivious to Shaitan's presence.

Slowly Aslambhai began reversing the Gypsy.

But Shaitan would not be deprived of his morning's entertainment. He sprang out of the bushes with a deep growl ('Oh God, there goes the mixie in my tummy again,' thought Shikha snatching up the camera), and charged at them. Aslambhai put on speed, and gave a sharp toot of the Gyspy's horn. Shaitan swerved off the path and with fluid grace vanished into the bushes. He had had his fun!

'Badmash! Rascal!' roared Aslambhai, shaking a fist at him in mock fury.

'Whew!' said Shikha, suddenly realizing she had been trembling. (More shaky pictures, she knew!) 'Does he always do that?'

'He likes scaring people,' Aslambhai said. 'One day he is going to get into trouble!'

'Yes, and he's still crossing the line of control as far as Shahenshah is concerned,' Shikha said. She flipped through her grubby notebook, and frowned.

'Aslambhai – you know that other tigress – Begum, the one whom we saw on one of our first trips inside. When she was at her kill …'

'Yes,'

'Well, we haven't met her since! And none of the forest guards we've spoken to have mentioned her.'

He nodded. 'Maybe she's gone into hiding to have cubs,' he said.

'That would be marvellous!' Shikha said, eyes shining. 'Um … I think we'll put out an alert for her!'

'Theek hai, memsahib! Okay, memsahib!' he grinned, saluting her.

And apart from surprises in the jungle (which happened every day) there were surprises at Shergarh House, too – pleasant and unpleasant.

One evening they got home to discover Snail Snot installed in the drawing room again – as though she had never left – along with a smooth puffy-cheeked man with a thin moustache and the same watermelon eyes. He was a little taller than Shikha, with an awful paunch and a strange way of looking not quite straight at you. Binoy chacha, as usual, was staring at the ceiling over his spectacles, as if unaware that he had guests. He had become more and more distant and absent-minded recently, and spent nearly the entire day in his studio, often missing meals and sometimes, Shikha suspected, even sleeping on the studio floor (judging by the state of his clothes!).

'Why hello Shikha beti, and Sunny beta, so tall you've grown!' Snail Snot rose and came forward to hug Shikha. 'So you must be looking forward to school, no?' she said in that slickly pleasant way that always gave Shikha the heebie-jeebies.

'Er … please, we're filthy, you'll spoil your clothes!' Shikha stuttered, stepping back to avoid the praying-mantis embrace.

'Shikha, this is my cousin brother Randhir,' Snail Snot said, 'Randhir uncle, like you, is very interested in tigers.' Randhir got clumsily to his feet, and extended a fleshy hand.

'Er hello,' Shikha said, eyeing the rings on his fingers. Rings? They looked like knuckledusters!

'So you're the famous tiger girl of Shergarh, eh?' Randhir said thickly. 'I am so glad to meet you! Perhaps you can tell me about the Shergarh tigers!'

'Er, yes, I'd love to, but I should really have a bath first,' Shikha said, excusing herself.

It was later that night while Sharifa was brushing her hair, and Sunny was gazing raptly at the owlets, up in the ventilator (they had simply been called Sunny's owlets and spent most of the day up there), that Sharifa dropped the bombshell.

'Shikha baby, aap samaan theek se rakho – Shikha baby, please look after your things!' she said, and Shikha screwed up her nose. 'Veena memsahib and Randhir sahib were looking through your big book this evening. Randhir sahib usme se kuchch likh raha tha – Randhir sahib was writing something down from it!'

'What? My journal?' Shikha leapt up and ran to her desk. Her precious journal was safe, and appeared unharmed. 'How dare she! How dare she look through my journal, and … and show it to that ghastly Randhir!'

Randhir in fact had not endeared himself to her at all, because he had spent the evening boasting about all the tiger hunts he had been on, while just a child, with some local maharaja's son. That, and a lot more, which had made her control her temper with the greatest of difficulty.

'They should have never banned tiger hunting!' he said. 'Look what's happened. Now there are only 3,000 left.'

'There would have been none left if they hadn't banned it,' Shikha retorted hotly.

The slimeball shook his head. 'No my dear! You see all the rich and powerful types, who would have hunted the tigers, would have ensured that the animals survived. They can't hunt what's extinct after all!'

'Rana uncle says that if hunting were not banned and these reserves not set up, there would have been a rush to kill the tigers because everyone would have wanted to! Besides you don't have to be rich and powerful to kill tigers these days. You can do it with DDT. They would have been wiped out in three months!'

'Ah, that Rana! Of course he has to talk that way! He's been posted here too long!'

'But I feel sorry for the poor people,' said Snail Snot, digging into her second kulfi. 'Turned out of their jungles, their cattle starving. How would you like it if you were turned out of Shergarh House?'

I would certainly love it if it were you, Shikha nearly retorted, but concentrated on her food.

And now, and now to think that these horrible people had been leafing through her precious journal without even asking her! She felt as though she needed to have another bath.

But there had been that other evening that had more than made up for it. She had finished writing up her notes and journal for the day and had settled down at her piano. The stream of music that had trickled out softly had been sad to start with, until with an irritated toss of her head she had scattered her tears over the keys, and gone on to something that reminded her of the wild boar piglets she had seen playing in the reserve that morning and that big bull boar scratching his bum on a rock, sheer bliss all over his ugly mug. After that she had been in full flow with her 'scatterbrained' jazz, but keeping it soft because Sunny was sleeping. Up and down her moods went, black, angry, bitter and sad again, then cheeky, happy, loony and joyous. She never knew it, but outside in the garden, Binoy chacha on his way back to his studio stood transfixed in the garden, beedi unlit as the music plinked out of the window in a never-ending cascade, the hair (plenty of it!) at the back of his neck and on his arms standing up and prickling. He never noticed Sunny's owlets fly past him through the magic window. They had now grown up enough to fly on their own, and were let out to practise their own hunting skills, every night, which they enjoyed, chittering and squabbling in that querulous way of theirs. Usually they returned quite quickly, demanding their supper, which Sharifa would have kept ready for them wrapped up in newspaper. Now the birds flew in through the open window and landed on Shikha's bare shoulders, surprising her as always by their silent approach and making her wince and miss a few bars. Sunny was still fast asleep as usual.

'Oh!' she said, 'you really should knock before you enter! Look, you've made me lose my place in the music!'

'Hi, Shikha!' said a soft, familiar voice from the door. 'You play the piano like an angel – I had no idea, child! And will you show me some tigers tomorrow, dear?'

Dipti, in a maroon salwar-kameez was leaning on the doorway, a huge smile on her face, her big eyes glistening.

'Dipti! When did you come? You never told me!' Pink with pleasure, Shikha rose. 'Let me just give Sunny's owlets their dinner – or they'll peck my ear till I do!'

'Just look at you!' Dipti said with obvious pleasure, coming into the room and giving her a hug that was so much like Jogi aunty's. 'You've got a tan to kill for!' She glanced at Sunny. 'And him! He's grown and he no longer sleeps all curled up! But where did you learn to play the piano like that? I've got goosebumps all over!'

'He now sleeps like we once saw Sheba sleep after having eaten her fill of chital!' Shikha grinned. 'Flat on his back, arms and legs spread in every direction! The piano – umm … well I don't know. The music just comes out of my head and plinks out on the piano – I call it "scatterbrain birdwing jazz", because I can't play any of the tunes again and don't want to! But when did you come and how long are you staying?'

'Oh, this long weekend came along, so I thought I'd take advantage of it,' Dipti said. 'I should have been here earlier, but the stupid train was late. I've come straight from the station! Now is this the famous journal that papa has been raving about?'

'Yes,' Shikha said, blushing a beetroot red. 'You mean you've come to see us even before going home?'

'Your dimples,' said Dipti chuckling, and looking sideways at her. 'They must be horribly embarrassing!' But there was a faint flush on her cheeks, too, and she glanced at the dark garden outside.

A wonderful weekend followed, as usual far too short and over before you knew it.

'Dipti,' said Shikha on their last evening. 'This Snail … I mean Veena aunty has got me admitted to this Paradise Valley Boarding School. But I don't want to go! Sunny still won't leave me! He's much better, I know, but he still doesn't talk! She wants to send him off to a place where he can learn sign language! But he can't possibly be on his own!'

'Oh,' said Dipti, surprised. 'Binoy chacha never mentioned anything like that to me!'

'He must have forgotten!' Shikha said, making a face. 'It is just the sort of thing he would forget about!'

'Hmmm … I'll speak to him about it. That Veena aunty, she's quite a busybody isn't she!' The old flinty look was back in Dipti's eyes.

'Control freak!' said Shikha fiercely. 'She wants to control everything we do!'

And so, all too soon Dipti returned to her job in Delhi, and summer sizzled into the Shergarh Tiger Reserve. It was impossible now to spend the whole day inside the reserve (unless there was some very exciting tip-off), and they followed a new routine. They were up and inside at the crack of dawn. They did the 'patrol' route and returned to Shergarh House by ten. Breakfast and baths and 'free time' till around three (very hot, but necessary if they were to reach anywhere cool inside in time), when they set off again, wet towels on their heads, now usually straight for Hari Pani, which invariably had become quite popular with the animals, because of the weather. To Shikha's delight, on several occasions they had seen Sheba come down here, and carefully lower herself into the emerald green waters to relax and bathe. While the Hira Talao and other water bodies in the park shrank and shrivelled in the heat, none really dried up completely. But Hari Pani always remained at more or less the same level, fed by a deep cool underground reservoir that never ran out. Summer was an easy time to spot tigers too, because the undergrowth was sparse, and well they all turned up at the talaos and waterholes to slake their thirst – and check out the menu! And as she patrolled 'her jungle' day after day ('like going to school, really, but the most beautiful and exciting school in the world' she wrote to Dipti earnestly), Shikha learnt that what you did not see in the forest could be as important as what you did. For instance there was the apparent disappearance of three tigers (including Begum) whose paths had regularly criss-crossed her patrol route – they seemed to have gone off somewhere else.

'I haven't seen Raja and Queen Victoria for three weeks now,' she told Mr Rana worriedly. 'And Begum, for over a month! Of course that old Shaitan chased us though!'

'Tigers are great wanderers,' Mr Rana said. 'They might just have decided on a change of scene. Don't worry about it. They may show up – sometimes they can be gone for months at a time! But I'll sound the alert. If they are spotted somewhere else, we'll soon know about it.'

But no forest guard reported spotting any of the three tigers. Shergarh was not a vast tiger reserve, it was relatively compact and easy to patrol and unlike many of the others, well staffed. Mr Rana's antennae began twitching. Was there trouble brewing in Shergarh? Had that sweet hardworking girl stumbled on to something, even though she did not know it herself?

The sweet hardworking girl was, at that time, once again being very sweet with Aslambhai. They were at Hari Pani, on a hot afternoon, Shikha gazing longingly at the cool green waters. At the far bank, a covey of grey partridges had come down to slake its thirst, kept company by a resplendent golden oriole.

'Aslambhai,' said Shikha sweetly. 'You are sure there are no crocodiles in Hari Pani?'

'Bilkul! Absolutely!' the old forest guard replied, not realizing he had put one step closer to the trap that was being laid for him. 'There never have been and never will be! It is impossible for them to come over the ridge all the way from Hira Talao!'

'Umm … and you said that in the old days, the ranis and rajkumaris of Shergarh used to bathe here?' Shikha asked, her eyes wide and innocent.

'Yes,' said Aslambhai. 'That is why it is so well hidden!'

'Aslambhai, may I swim here?' Shikha asked, her brown eyes as pleading as that of any spaniel's. (It had always worked with papa, mama, well not quite!)

'What?'

'May I swim here, please?' she asked. 'I was champion swimmer in school so you don't have to worry about that!'

'You want to swim in Hari Pani?' he asked again, beard wagging.

'Yes,' she said. 'If the ranis and rajkumaris did, why can't I?'

'And what if a tiger comes while you are swimming? You've seen Sheba swimming here!'

'Well you are here to guard me!' she said beguilingly, smiling sweetly. 'You can just tell Sheba to come another time! Besides,' she added, 'if Sunny's in the water too, no tiger will come anywhere near the place! They don't like being splashed all over!'

'Sunny sahib?' he said weakly.

Now she wanted to take Sunny sahib into the water, too!

'Yes,' she nodded. 'He's quite good, too. We can use that old spare tube from the Gypsy, if you like, for extra safety. And I'm sure Ali would love to jump in also. We can have a lot of fun! Please Aslambhai?'

'Mana hai! It is not allowed,' said Aslambhai. 'Rana sahib will kill me if I allow you to swim!'

Shikha made a face. 'He needn't know,' she said. 'Besides, it doesn't say anywhere that swimming is not allowed! Neither here nor at Hira Talao for that matter.'

Hira Talao of course, was full of grinning crocs!

'You see, Aslambhai, if I am allowed to walk about in a national park with an armed escort, why should I not be allowed to swim? It's just a different way of getting about. And anyway, here I'll be safe. I can see the banks, you can watch over the whole pool quite easily with your gun, and Sunny will be making enough noise to keep all the tigers at a safe distance! So what do you say? Please?'

'Aur koi guard dekh liya to? And if a forest guard sees you, then what?'

'Aslambhai, we come here every day, and we have never seen a guard. They all go back before the climb up to the ridge begins. And on a summer afternoon? No way!'

He hummed and hawed, knowing fully well that it would be impossible for him to refuse her.

'Theek hai – okay,' he said at last. 'But only for ten minutes!'

'Oh, great! Aslambhai, you are the greatest!' Happily Shikha delved into her knapsack and took out her dark blue swimsuit, which she had hidden right at the bottom, along with Sunny's little red trunks.

'Come on, Sunny, we're going swimming!' she sang. 'Now you wait here a moment, while I go into the princess's changing room, okay?'

The 'princess's changing room' was a dark little room in the pavilion, its floor covered with whispering dried leaves, its roof strung with hundred-year-old cobwebs (some with ferocious looking inmates that looked equally old). Shikha nipped in, changed and came skipping out.

'Come on, Sunny, get changed tiger boy!'

But the tiger boy had no need for all that. He just flung off his clothes and charged into the water nangu pangu beside his sister.

'Sunny!' Shikha exclaimed with mock shock, giggling helplessly. 'Snail Snot would freak out if she saw you running around and waving your pee-pee about like that! Hai hai!'

In a minute, Ali had tossed aside his shirt and charged in too.

At the far bank, the grey partridges scuttled off into the undergrowth, thoroughly alarmed and the oriole, of course, had long gone.

Squatting on the pavilion steps, his gun by his side, Aslambhai watched over the pool, his eyes flicking to all the places where conceivably a tiger or leopard could lie in wait.

'Shergarh ke chhote sher – the small tigers of Shergarh!' he muttered to himself looking at the children frolicking in the water. 'After all they are the small tigers of Shergarh!'

For the small tigers of Shergarh, and especially for Shikha, that first swim in Hari Pani was sheer heaven. The water was blissfully cool, the eternally bubbling springs in its depths ensuring that it never got rank or mouldy. It was clear too and Shikha could see the dark shadows of fish as they swerved, alarmed by these new creatures. She played with Sunny for a while, splashing water in his face, while Ali of course kept diving off the boulders and splashing in, trying not to whoop too loudly with sheer joy.

'Hells bells Sunny bunny, just what would mama and papa think if they saw us now!' Shikha said, as he splashed happily, a huge grin on his face. After a while she took him back to the steps and sat him beside Aslambhai.

'Sit!' she ordered, laughing. 'And stay! I'm going for a swim!' She dived in and streaked off through the pool, while Sunny spent an anxious ten seconds waiting for her to surface. But Ali was now beside him, as well as Aslambhai, so he didn't really mind.

Shikha swam steadily for ten minutes, then floated on her back and looked at the sky. The huge forest trees – peepul, banyan and sheesham – soared high and wide over her, and behind her the great sandstone cliffs rose, pockmarked with their mysterious caves. The great horned owls, which lived there, had taken one shocked look at the goings-on below and retreated into their homes. Deft sickle winged swifts darted about, and outraged dragonflies, magenta, mint green and electric blue zoomed back and forth over the water's surface, trying to chase her away from their territories.

'It's so strange and funny and I really don't know what to feel!' Shikha thought. 'Here I am in one of the most beautiful places I have ever been too, and only because mama and papa are gone and we'll never see them again. Swimming in the same pool as Sheba. Hell, I just hope she doesn't do susu in it!'

She trod water and made for the chhatri in the middle of the pool. This, she decided, would be her own private place, which she would share perhaps only with Sunny and Ali and Dipti. It was small, but it was, she also saw, a good place to set up her camera and wait for the animals to come to drink. You could duck behind the marble lattice work, which was also excellent to point a camera lens through – yes, it was perfect as a photographer's hide! And the far bank was much closer now.

'Hmm, I'll have to pack the camera tightly in a plastic bag and bring it across,' she thought. 'But we could sit here all evening and get some really good pictures! And yess, yess, yess – that would justify her swims as part of her work! In the line of dooty!' She grinned and slipped into the water again and made for the pavilion where Sunny and the others were waiting. In the princess's changing room, a problem became apparent. She had packed their swimsuits, yes but had forgotten towels!

'Well, too bad, the sun will have to dry us off!' she told

Sunny as she changed him. Actually it wasn't bad at all to get into clothes that got damp. Only her thick lovely hair remained soaked and heavy and she wondered how on earth she would explain that to Sharifa, whose eyes missed nothing.

'I guess I'll just leave it open and hope this hot wind dries it on the way back, Sunny,' she said, as they prepared to leave.

By and large it did, though by the time they reached Shergarh House, Shikha was looking worse than Binoy chacha in his wildest moments!

'God, I'm the witch of Shergarh House, Sunny!' she said glancing at herself in the mirror. 'Eeaagh, how I wish I could appear like this in the middle of the night in front of Snail Snot!'

And as Sharifa brushed out her massive tangles that night, she glanced at Shikha in the wobbly mirror and nodded.

'Aslambhai ko budhoo bana sakta hai, par mujhe nahin! You can make a fool of Aslambhai, but not me!' she said, 'Shikha baby aur Sunny sahib swimming ke leye gaya! Shikha baby and Sunny sahib went swimming!' She chuckled. 'But you forgot to take your towels!'

And mama's pink enamel hairbrush was full of duckweed. And one dead tadpole.

16

'MY GOD, SUNNY, IT'S SO HOT THE AIR WOULD CATCH FIRE IF you set a match to it,' Shikha panted as they trudged back to the Gypsy one morning after having spent two hours enviously watching the big crocodiles glide in and out of Hira Talao, and the sambhar, chital and wild boar wallow in the mud. The highlight of the day's outing had occurred when a tiger had appeared at the far bank, to drink and chill out in the water. It was Shahenshah, obviously with a very full belly, because after the initial honks and alarms by the sambhar, chital and langurs, they appeared to settle down. It had lolled about in the shallows, covering itself with mud if not glory, before a big daddy of a crocodile decided that enough was enough and slunk into the water and began swimming towards him. Shahenshah reared up, snarled mightily and smacked the water hard with his paws, his ears flat back, sending lapwings, dabchick, moorhens and spotbills scattering in alarm. Big daddy crocodile nonchalantly changed its mind, and course, and headed out into open water. What was the best thing, as far as Shikha was concerned, was that over the past months, the tigers of Shergarh appeared to have recognized them and accepted their presence, and had begun treating them as part of the scenery. They could park a few metres away, and watch them to their heart's content, resting, posing majestically on the battlements of the fort, and even feeding, provided they were quiet and made no sudden movements. They met up with tigers nearly every day now, and often more than just a single animal and at different times of the day, too. But on every occasion, Shikha still felt the familiar exciting tightening up of her tummy, a few trial runs of the mixie, too (if the animals snarled or growled), but soon forgot about them, as she got busy taking photographs and jotting down notes. And Sunny behaved like the best-trained tiger watcher and tiger sketcher in the world! He would take out his grubby little pad and pencil and, hooding his eyelids in the proper artist fashion, begin drawing the scene in front of him. Aslambhai, gun at his side, ever watchful, seemed to be able to sense the animals' moods and how close they could approach them without alarming or irritating them. And every tiger appeared to have its own personality; Shahenshah, big, macho, but bit of a softie she suspected, Shaitan who lived up to his name every time they met, (his mock charges still terrified her – 'Why does he do it, the bully!' she exclaimed petulantly once to Aslambhai after he had given them a nasty surprise and made her drop her notebook and pencil, 'he's like those awful kids in school who like to hide behind doors and jump at you! Gross, really!'), Sheba whom she liked the best, for her fierce uncompromising ways – she would flatten her ears and twitch her tail and snarl if they stepped an inch closer than what she thought was right, but would tolerate them closer than most of the others, and there was that peculiar soft yet frosty shimmer in her eyes that made Shikha feel all funny inside. (And Aslambhai wondered too, for he had noticed that it was only when Shikha – and Sunny, of course – were with them, did the tigress allow such close access – on his own and while taking tourists around, she had never permitted them to come so close.) Sheba stood no nonsense from anyone – especially any of the other tigers, and how much of you she would tolerate and for how long, depended on her mood at that moment. The most disappointing thing as far as Shikha was concerned was that they hadn't come across any families as such – the only mother with three almost grown cubs they had spotted had quickly taken her adolescent offsprings away every time they had 'met'.

'She's a nervous mother, isn't she!' Shikha remarked to Aslambhai. 'What's her name, Aslambhai?'

He shrugged his shoulders. 'Pata nahin baby – I don't know baby,' he said. 'This is the first time I am seeing her. We will have to ask the forest guards.'

It would have been too marvellous, if for instance, they could see Shahenshah and Sheba bring their cubs down to the talao, or Hari Pani for a dip, she thought (surely it was time Sheba had cubs!), lowering her binoculars as the nervous tigress and her overgrown kids disappeared.

'Well!' she said with a grin, 'as she has no known name yet, I'm going to call her Lily the Fink! Always in a fink she is!' she giggled, 'hey Sunny, I just hope she doesn't take to drink though, eh, what do you say toodledumps?' It was a take-off on an old, old number she and mama used to sing with great gusto on the piano, called 'Lily the Pink'.

Now, pink (herself!) and breathless, her cap low over her brow, she stared at the forest of scratches and scabs on her bare arms and legs, glazed a deep honey brown by the sun: 'Maybe we should try a mud wallow too, someday. It should be fun. And then we'll know exactly how the animals feel too!' she said somewhat wistfully.

Manfully Sunny trudged on alongside, while Ali stripped down to vest and shorts and headband, looked as always like the coolest cat in Shergarh and did not even wipe his brow. Aslambhai, with a wet towel wrapped around his head (looking like a diminutive dacoit), followed them watchfully. It amazed him how Shikha had insisted that they set out morning after morning even in these torrid conditions. They passed a small pond that was drying up fast, with just a little water and a lot of squelchy mud in it. It was pockmarked with the hoofprints of animals that had come to it, and then deserted it as it had become too small for them. Too small for chital and sambhar and nilgai, certainly! But …

'Ooof!' Shikha exclaimed, wiping her brow with an exaggerated gesture. She veered off towards the pond and walked down the slope to its muddy edges, shedding her knapsack and cap en route. 'Aslambhai do you think there are any creatures left in this?' she asked, crouching down at the edge.

'Keeda makauda hoga – there will be insects and creepy crawlies,' the forest guard answered. 'Aur maendak! And frogs!'

'Oh!' Shikha took her binoculars off her neck, and her notebook out of her pocket, handing them to a bemused Ali. Then she slipped her sandals off and tentatively prodded the mud with a toe.

'It's so deliciously squelchy!' she exclaimed. She took a step into the mud wriggling her toes in it, Sunny by her side. 'Hey, deep down the mud is cool! Just checking if there are any turtles stranded here!' she said, and suddenly was shin deep in it.

'Shikha baby, sambhalo! Shikha baby, be careful!'

It was too late. For suddenly Shikha baby had just sat down plonk in the mud with a resounding glooping sploosh, and then had slipped flat on her back into it, pulling Sunny with her.

'Eeeek!' she squealed. 'I slipped! But hey, Sunny this is heaven! It's so cool and soft and squelchy and oozy!'

'Shikha baby!' Poor Aslambhai was too shocked for words. He knew that Shikha had slipped deliberately in the mud, and couldn't help grinning. What a child! Even Ali just grinned from the edge of the pond, but refused to join in. And little Sunny was simply relishing his mud bath, banging his fists into the muddy water, and rapidly turning both himself and his sister into gleaming chocolate brown figures.

'Hey Sunny, we look like we're made of melting chocolate!' Shikha yelled gleefully the whites of her eyes shining bright.

At the edge, Ali grinned slyly as he reached for Shikha's camera from her knapsack.

'Ali!' Shikha screamed. 'Don't you dare! Don't you dare take our pictures!'

Click shuttuk! Click shuttuk! Click shuttuk! Ali grinned happily.

'Voh dekho, Rana sahib aa raha hai! Look there, Rana sahib is coming on patrol!' Aslambhai said suddenly.

'Oh God! Come on Sunny let's get out of this goo!' Splashing, slipping and covered with mud from head to toe, they scrambled out of the pond. 'Where?' Shikha demanded, 'where is he?'

'Oh, mishtake ho gaya memsahib! Oh, I made a mistake!' said Aslambhai contritely. 'I saw the dust flying and thought it was his Gypsy!'

'Aslambhai! You spoil sport!' Shikha wiped her mud-covered hair, watching it fall off in great globs. 'I really will have to wash my hair properly,' she grinned. 'Sharifa is going to throw a fit! But it really has cooled me off!'

Ali screwed up his nose and took one step away from her and Sunny.

'Lagta hai sabh sambhar ne yahan tatti kiya hai – it looks like all the sambhar have crapped in this pond,' he remarked judiciously.

'Ali! No! That can't be! He's pulling our legs!' She looked pleadingly at Aslambhai.

'Ho sakta hai!' he grinned. 'It could be!'

'Come on let's go home! I need a bath!'

The mud had started caking nicely on their bodies by the time they reached, and it was great fun scratching it off.

'We look like a pair of light and dark chocolate bunnies!' Shikha said, as they drove up to Shergarh House. 'What's that word for it? Variegated!'

There was a big black jeep standing in the portico, and sitting in the verandah were Snail Snot, her slimy cousin brother Randhir and Binoy chacha, obviously awaiting their return. (And outside because the power had gone off.)

'Hells bells Sunny we're in for it!' Shikha whispered, appalled, looking at her mud covered clothes and hair that had semi-dried and was standing up in stiff spikes at peculiar angles all over her head. Parts of her face were a nice shade of milk chocolate, with the drying mud cracking up in her dimples. 'Remember, we just slipped and fell into a muddy pond while looking for stranded turtles okay?' Solemnly Sunny nodded.

Nonchalantly, they ran up the stairs leaving a trail of caking mud behind. There was a frozen silence from the adults as they gazed stupefied at the 'variegated' chocolate children.

'Hi there!' Shikha said breathlessly, looking down at herself. 'Sorry about the appearance! We were trying to rescue turtles from a pond that was drying up!'

Snail Snot was shaking her head sadly as if the end of the world was nigh, and Shikha was beyond redemption. The slimeball was looking plainly disgusted. Binoy chacha had his usual sardonic look on his face.

'Feeling the heat and wallowing like the animals now, eh?' he said with remarkable perception, and even under the caking mud, Shikha could feel herself blush and the mud crack like crazy paving on her cheeks.

'We'll just go and have a bath!' Shikha smiled, as a glob of mud dripped off her hair on to the floor with a plop.

'Do that!' her uncle said. 'We have to talk to you!'

'Aiiieee! Shikha baby, Sunny sahib! What is this? You've been wallowing like the sambhar!' Sharifa charged out, looking shocked as Aslambhai quietly drove the Gypsy off to its shed behind the house. He knew he would get hell from his wife later on for allowing them to get so filthy.

Rubbed and scrubbed and shining new, half an hour later, Shikha and Sunny entered the drawing room where Binoy chacha, Snail Snot and the slimeball Randhir had now settled. Sharifa had cut a bowl full of ice-cold watermelon for the children and they were digging into it blissfully, as they walked in, the juice running down the chins, and Sunny as usual shooting the little black seeds into an empty bowl, like bullets. Shikha sometimes thought that this was the best part of 'field work' in summer! But Snail Snot's presence had somewhat spoilt the enjoyment and that old faraway warning voice was already beginning to make her tummy tighten up. Just what did they want with her now, on this incandescent summer morning? She soon found out.

'Well, Shikha dear, there is just a month left for your school to begin,' Snail Snot said, smiling in that hideously angelic manner of hers. 'I think you better start preparing yourself a bit for it.'

'School? What school?' Shikha looked surprised.

'Paradise Valley Boarding School, of course! Mr Bhatinder the principal has, as I told you, kindly given you admission. Now dear, it is time to get your uniforms made. Here, I have even bought the material for it. We can take it to the tailors at Shergarh town this afternoon!'

'I can't leave Sunny!' Shikha said setting her face stubbornly. 'You know that!'

Snail Snot looked pained and exchanged glances with Binoy chacha.

'Shikha dear, we both think that Sunny does not need you at his side all the time any longer,' Binoy chacha said, but not sounding too sure about it.

'And he'll be going to his own special school soon after anyway like a big boy, won't you Sunny?' Snail Snot leaned forward to pinch Sunny's cheek. He jerked away.

Shikha put her arms across her chest, her face mutinous.

'I can't leave Sunny,' she repeated. 'I won't! I won't! Not until I know he's all right. Not until he tells me that I can. And I'm not going to any Bhatinda's boarding school, so there!'

Binoy chacha looked exasperated; Snail Snot like a long-suffering martyr.

'Shikha dear,' she said. 'Please don't make things difficult unnecessarily. It is for your own good!'

'I have my project here and am quite happy doing it, thank you!'

'Shikha dear, you know the park closes down on 1st July. It remains closed for three months. So it is perfect for you to join school then. You can't do anything here in the monsoons.'

'I'll ask Mr Rana to give me something to do!' Shikha replied stubbornly. 'Or Dipti!'

'Dipti works in Delhi. Mr Rana is going on leave in the middle of June for a month or so. There will be no one here and nothing happening my dear! It will be the best time for you to join school!'

'Look, this is how we have planned it,' said Binoy chacha, who really was the last person on earth able to plan anything properly. (It had all been that Snail Snot's scheming, Shikha knew, as she listened to the devious plan they put out to her now.) 'I have to go to Delhi for my exhibition on 15th June. It gets over on the 25th. I'll be back here on the 28th or so, and will personally escort you to school. You have to be there by the 1st of July. Veena aunty will be here with Sunny when I go to drop you. Sunny's special school opens on 7th of July. So I and Veena aunty will both take him there ourselves. Once he settles in, we will return.'

'You just want to get rid of both of us!' Shikha said bitterly, the tears rushing into her eyes angrily.

'Shikha dear!' Snail Snot looked shocked. 'We're only doing what your parents would have wanted us to do! It's for your own good, as I said!'

'You never knew mama and papa! How do you know what they would have wanted!'

'Okay, Shikha we've heard you!' Binoy chacha was trying to lay down some discipline, but feeling rather uncomfortable. Some little voice deep down was telling him that perhaps he was trying to 'get rid' of the children after all. But school would be good for Shikha and perhaps it was time the little boy learnt sign language, too. He had showed no sign of beginning to talk again. Here, they were really running wild. Turning up every day looking like little piglets, covered with mud! He leaned forward. 'Okay. Listen, if you are unhappy at school you let us know. I'll come and fetch you. How does that sound? And if we find that Sunny is not settling down, we'll bring him back too. Okay? Deal? Now dry your eyes! And thank Veena aunty for all she has done for you. It was she who has got you and Sunny admission into schools and is so keen that you live normal lives again.'

'Binoy dear, I am only doing what I am trained to do. I am only doing my job. No need for anyone to thank me for it!' She dabbed her eyes with her pallu.

But Shikha just stormed out, taking Sunny with her, and slammed her bedroom door.

'Once they separate us, they'll make sure we are never together again, Sunny!' she said illogically, sitting her little brother on the bed. 'I can just feel it in my bones!' He had his frightened rabbit expression on his face again, something she had not seen in a long time. All through the conversation his eyes had switched from one person to the next, like someone watching a tennis match. She looked at him and wiped her eyes. 'Whatever happens Sunny bunny we have to stick together.'

He nodded and clutched her hand. She looked fiercely at the door.

'They can't force me on to that train!' she said. 'I'll just sit here and refuse to budge! What will they do then? Like … like Gandhiji!' Suddenly she remembered something Dipti had said. That she would talk to Binoy chacha about this boarding school business. She stormed back out into the drawing room.

'Binoy chacha, did you tell Dipti anything about this?' she asked. 'Or did she speak to you about it?'

He looked uncomfortable and ran his fingers through his beard. 'No. I didn't,' he admitted sounding a little sheepish. 'But she did mention it. She um … wasn't very much in favour …,' he went on uncertainly, but Snail Snot butted in smooth as silk.

'That Dipti! What does she know about children? She sent them into the jungle to look for tigers, honestly! Really Binoy, that girl is … is not quite right in the head, I think! And look at these two! Every day they roam about and return looking like creatures of the wild! Hai hai, what would their parents think!'

'Don't bring my parents into this, I told you!' Shikha shouted and charged back into her room.

'That girl needs to be spanked!' Randhir said suddenly for the first time, shaking his head. Binoy chacha looked more and more uncomfortable.

'She's just very upset. Maybe it would be better if we waited a while about this school business. Maybe they are still not ready!'

'Binoy my dear, there you go again! Always putting things off. Always procrastinating! It is high time those children got a normal life. Here, they are complete junglees! And those Ranas and that Dipti have been a bad influence on them, I tell you!'

'But Shikha looks so happy when she goes into the jungle,' Binoy chacha said. 'Both she and Sunny seem happy! And Shikha likes Dipti very much!'

'Of course they will seem happy. They run wild the whole day, doing whatever they want! Naturally Shikha will like someone who tells her to do that! They're running completely out of control, I tell you Binoy! Listen, just trust me, and leave everything to me, Binoy dear. You'll see – everything will work out beautifully!'

'I hope so,' said Binoy chacha glumly. 'I hope so.'

And he wondered how mad Dipti would get, if she knew about the plan to send the children to school and worse, if things didn't work out. 'Give them time,' she had said in that easy, relaxed way of hers, 'and they will tell you when they are ready!'

Her beady eyes fixed on his face, reading his mind, Snail Snot took Binoy chacha's hand and looked earnestly (as much as was possible for her) into his eyes.

'Listen Binoy! You have the huge responsibility of bringing

up these children after such a great tragedy and look at what's happening! Shikha's education is going down the drain. Sunny needs to learn sign language if he is to communicate. And here, you're sending them out in the forest to look at tigers on the whim of a foolish girl who really ought to know better! Really it would have been so much better for everyone if there had been no tigers here at all!' Snail Snot shook her head tragically. Slimeball Randhir nodded his head silently in agreement.

'Oh well,' said Binoy chacha, suddenly fed up of the whole business. 'I think I better get back to my studio! I have a lot of work to do!'

To her relief, there was no trip to Shergarh town that afternoon to give measurements for her uniform. Snail Snot and slimeball Randhir drove off in their jeep soon afterwards, and Shikha heaved a sigh of relief.

Sharifa came up to her. 'Voh memsahib aap ka salwar kameez sample ke leye le ke gaya – that memsahib has taken your salwar kameez as a sample!' she said making it sound as though Snail Snot had stolen something, which in a way she had.

'What? Now she's been poking about in my cupboard taking my clothes! The slimy witch!' Shikha was outraged. 'Well, she can do what she likes – I'm not going to that school and that's final!'

But five days later, Snail Snot was back with a set of six green (the awful green that they use for hospital curtains) and white salwar-kameezes, and gushed all over about how pretty Shikha would look in them.

'Try them on dear,' she said. 'Just for me!'

'No way!' Shikha said. 'Not a chance!'

The battle lines had been drawn.

And as the days passed, Shikha found it more difficult to

concentrate on her work, knowing that the showdown with Snail Snot had to happen. She had even tried sneakily putting a call through to Dipti on a couple of occasions, to plead with her, but was unable to get through. The Ranas, alas, had left for their vacation a week earlier than scheduled – a conference had come up in Delhi, which Mr Rana had to attend, so poor Shikha could not even appeal to them. She hunkered down angrily, stomping about Shergarh House, followed puppy-like by Sunny. Those nearly forgotten screechings in her head had returned to haunt her at night, and Sunny she noticed had started sleeping in his pangolin position again, clinging tightly to her. And then, on one brooding humid evening, as they were driving past Chhota Mahal, Shikha looked up at the chhatris. Standing there, staring out towards Hira Talao in the strange yellow twilight, was the rajkumar, with an arm around his massive tiger Badshah. Was it another warning that bad things were about to happen in Shergarh, or was he there to defend her, as Sharifa had told her once, so many nights ago? She looked up again, but the chhatri was empty. Or, blast it, was she going nuts?

'Aslambhai,' she asked on another evening. 'What is the most dangerous animal in Shergarh? The tiger? Or the leopard?'

He shook his head. 'Neither,' he said. 'Hum hain – we are!'

'We are? What do you mean? We haven't done any harm really, even if we have been swimming at Hari Pani ...'

'Nahin memsahib, not you and I and Sunny and Ali! But people generally. And especially like that memsahib who is trying to send you to school. She is telling the villagers to get together and invade the park with their gai-bhains! It will be the end of Shergarh if that happens. And many villagers are preparing to do that! And that bhaisahib of hers, I don't know what he is up to, but kuchch theek nahin hain – something is not right! His friends keep coming and going at odd times – pata nahin kyo –

I don't know why. But I don't like it. Raat ko gaadi chalate hai – they drive around at night!'

And Shikha remembered her rajkumar and Badshah on the chhatri that evening.

And then, the very next morning, well before her wake-up hour (4 a.m. these days!) she found Sharifa shaking her gently awake, looking worried.

'Shikha baby,' she whispered urgently. 'Ali has just come running all the way from home. Aslambhai has fallen off a ladder and seems to have broken his leg! What he was doing climbing a ladder in the middle of the night, I don't know! I have to go! I have told sahib – he's getting ready!'

Then Binoy chacha poked his head around the door.

'Chalo, Sharifa!' he said and nodded to Shikha.

'I'll take Aslambhai to the hospital and will return. I'm leaving for Delhi this evening, as you know. I will try and organize that Veena aunty stays with you until Sharifa can get back from the hospital.'

'But we … we'll be fine on our own, chacha,' Shikha protested in spite of still being half asleep. 'Really we will!'

'Don't be silly, Shikha, now go back to sleep!'

Ali sidled in shyly.

'What happened?' Shikha asked.

'We were sleeping on the roof! Badeabba heard some noise downstairs – like a buffalo had kicked over a bucket and thought there might be a snake. He went down in a hurry and the ladder slipped.'

It was strange being alone at Shergarh House for the very first time, with neither Binoy chacha or Sharifa or Aslambhai around. (And of course no Snail Snot yet!) And strangely it felt nice. Like home had felt back in Delhi.

'Hah! I'm the mistress of Shergarh House!' Shikha sang,

poking her head in the fridge to see what she could rustle up for her and Sunny's breakfast. 'What would you like for breakfast, Sunny?'

And indeed, it seemed that things were looking up, because even by midday there was no sign of Snail Snot. Binoy chacha had rung up from the hospital in Shergarh town to say that Aslambhai had had his leg set, but Sharifa would be required to stay at the hospital to look after him. Veena aunty (and presumably the slimeball) had not been at home when he had rung them up (presumably doing their Good Work, Shikha thought), so he would check on them on the way back.

'Don't worry, Binoy chacha! We'll be fine! We really will!' Shikha said. And added, 'There's no need to worry Veena aunty unnecessarily!'

She had been playing her scatterbrain jazz on the piano shortly after lunch, when she had her idea.

'Hey Sunny, how about taking another shot at peeking into Binoy chacha's studio?' she said. 'Imagine, we have been here so many months, and haven't been inside even once! Hopefully he's forgotten to lock it! He was in such a hurry this morning!'

And hallelujah, he had!

'Okay, Sunny, so we must be very careful while we're inside,' Shikha whispered, taking his hand. 'This is where Binoy chacha does his great work!'

She pushed open the door and peered inside.

It was a long room, naturally lit by huge windows that overlooked the tiger reserve, and with big greenhouse-like skylights. To cool things down a bit, Binoy chacha had installed a massive cooler at the door end, which in summer was really quite effective. The long wall on the cliff facing side of the studio was stacked with canvases. Long crooked wooden tables staggering under boxes of tubes, cans, jars full of brushes, rags, blades, scalpels, palette knives, were scattered haphazardly about. At the other end, three empty easels stood looking like curiously misshapen giraffes.

They entered as if it were a magical but forbidden kingdom, which in a way it was. All the paintings that Binoy chacha was showing in his exhibition had been packed and sent off to Delhi, but there were still stacks and stacks of canvases to check out.

'Will you look at this!' Shikha whispered in awe. 'So many paintings! There must be more than a hundred here! He really is a great painter!' She frowned. 'At least, he paints a lot!' she added.

But as she turned over the canvases one by one, and gazed at them, one disturbing thing became quite clear. Binoy chacha lived in one of the most beautiful places she knew, but painted some of the most dark and dire landscapes and people she could imagine. Everything was twisted and distorted – faces, places, things, animals, babies, villages, and even a bunch of flowers was made to look somewhat malevolent and as if struck by some grotesque disease. He seemed to love dark colours, brooding, threatening browns, greys, blacks and blues. They were paintings that Shikha didn't want to look at very much, but somehow found her gaze returning to them again and again as though she had been hypnotized.

'Doom and gloom, Sunny! Doom and gloom!' she said, trying to cheer herself up. 'Honestly, some of these could be used for making monster movies!' Sunny of course, was not so interested in the paintings as he was in the delicious tubes of paints all over the place. For him, this indeed was Alladdin's cave. He wandered off amongst the tables, picking up a tube and squeezing it, just to see what came out, then spreading the lovely gleaming paint on the table with the nearest knife or paintbrush he could find. He had begun enjoying himself.

'Oh my God!' Shikha exclaimed as she started looking at another batch of canvases propped up against the far end of the wall, and suddenly going scarlet, and stifling a giggle. 'Just look all these nangu-pangu people he's painted. And even parts of nangu-pangu people scattered all over the place.' Quickly she turned the canvases over, so that Sunny wouldn't see them, thankful that he was preoccupied with the tubes and stuff. 'Binoy chacha really is the limit! No wonder he didn't want us to come here!'

Sunny, by now, had applied vermilion and scarlet lake on parts of his face, and his hands were a brilliant cobalt blue. He was really getting into the swing of things. But as Shikha moved from one stack of paintings to another, one thing became very apparent.

'Sunny,' she said, more to herself than to Sunny. 'You know, there is not one happy painting in this studio! What pleasure does he get painting all these awful scenes? No wonder he's so grouchy all the time! Why he wants to spend so much time down here with this lot of nightmares I'll never understand!' She shivered. 'They make me feel uncomfortable and upset! Like I was, after the accident!' She casually turned around a small canvas, standing alone facing the wall.

'Why are you facing the corner?' she murmured, and then gasped.

She had found the only happy painting in the studio. It was a beautifully done portrait of Dipti looking right at the viewer and laughing like the sun and glowing in bright happy colours – sunflower yellow, honey gold and kingfisher blue.

'I thought I forbade you children to come down here!'

'Eeek!' Shikha quickly twirled the painting around and whirled, scarlet with embarrassment. Sunny jumped with surprise and fright, spilling a jar of canary yellow off the table, but was scarlet because of other reasons.

Binoy chacha stood in the doorway, his hands on his hips, looking exceedingly annoyed. Snail Snot stood beside him, shaking her head slowly in her end of the world manner.

'You children really are the limit!' Binoy chacha went on, striding in, his eyes glinting angrily. 'Why can't you do what you're told! Veena aunty is right! You're going completely out of control! You need to go to school Shikha, and that's where you'll be going!'

Oh shoot, that had torn it! Caught red-handed – literally!

To apologize or to brazen it out, was the question!

It was Snail Snot's saintly expression of self-righteousness that made Shikha make up her mind. Grabbing Sunny's bright blue paw in hers, she marched out, head high. Apologize in front of this woman – never! She would gloat!

'Then why didn't you let us see them?' she muttered as she walked out. Hah! But she knew, of course! Who on earth would be interested in seeing bits and pieces of naked monsters strewn all over the canvas? Gross it was! Really what on earth was Binoy chacha thinking when he painted those ghastly pictures!

Binoy chacha came to say goodbye to them just before he left for the station shortly after tea. (The slimeball Randhir had kindly agreed to drive him to Shergarh station.) Thankfully, he came alone; Snail Snot was busy stuffing a tasteless late lunch into her brother in the dining room.

'Now, both of you behave yourselves, please,' he said. 'Sharifa will start coming as soon as she is able to leave Aslambhai. In the meanwhile you are to listen to Veena aunty. Shikha, please start packing for school – there is not much time left. You'll be given all the books you require when you reach. I don't want to hear any complaints from Veena aunty, is that clear?'

He's talking like a machine, thought Shikha suddenly. As

though he really does not know what he's saying. Had that witch cast a spell on him or something? Or are naked monster painting artists always like that?

'Er, Binoy chacha, I'm … er sorry about this morning,' she said, looking straight at him. 'We … we didn't mean any harm!' she made a final attempt. 'Can this school thing wait a bit, please?'

He fidgeted with his spectacles. 'Now Shikha,' he said, 'we've been through this a hundred times before. I'll get back on the 28th in time to escort you to school. That is all. Thank you for apologizing!'

'Binoy, my dear, come on!' came the witch's sweet as kheer voice from the dining room. 'You don't want to miss your train, do you?'

'Bye, Shikha, bye Sunny!'

But Shikha was staring at the sloping garden outside her jaw jutting out and Sunny stood by her side, looking up at her uncertainly.

Yes indeed, the battle lines had been well and truly drawn.

17

HOW WOULD IT PLAY OUT IN THE END, SHIKHA WONDERED, for the thousandth time, as she stared at the view before her, not really seeing anything. When they came to drive her to the station, she knew what she would do. She would just sit down on her bed and refuse to budge. What could they do? They could hardly drag her physically to the Gypsy and take her away. Certainly Binoy chacha wouldn't, but Snail Snot and the slimeball, well. And there was Sunny. He was not likely to stay quiet, if she left, and certainly not if she was dragged away. If Sunny screamed like he had done in the hospital, it would terrify all the tigers of Shergarh! But it would send him straight back into that terrifying dark hell from which he had been so surely emerging. Sometimes she wished the time would just come and she could get over it all, this waiting for the days to pass was the worse.

Snail Snot had taken over Shergarh House as though it was her own house. Sharifa had been required at the hospital because Aslambhai's heart had felt the strain of his fall too, and he required care. Ali bused up and down between the hospital and Shergarh House, trying to spread whatever little cheer he could. He knew that Shikha was deeply upset and worried, and he hated Snail Snot and the slimeball for it.

'Three more days, Sunny, three more days! Then it's showdown time!' She had kept a brave face all right, but had lost a lot of sleep. The screechings and bangings of the past were back to haunt her, and she could hardly bear to look at her journal. Her face was pale, and went white with anger when she passed Snail Snot anywhere in the house. She played the piano with fury, hammering and thumping the keys as hard as she could, as Sunny listened unhappily. The phone had broken down, so there were no calls from Binoy chacha either. Snail Snot had told her that his exhibition had opened and was drawing crowds. The Ranas had gone off to Delhi and Mr Rana had ordered the closure of the reserve a week earlier than had been scheduled (because there had been some trouble with villagers) so there was no way she could go in and watch her beloved tigers. It was not a happy time for the children.

'Here, Sunny beta and Shikha dear, have your milk before you sleep!' Snail Snot gushed, after dinner on Friday night, 25th of June, as she had done every night since shifting in, sliding into the room with two tumblers of milk as though they were gifts from heaven that she had personally organized with angelic goodness. Shikha, lying on her bed, with Sunny sketching by her side, looked up.

'I don't feel like it!' she said, shaking her head.

'Okay, then I'll just put it here, and you can have it when you want. But then it will get that cream on the top, which you don't like, so you might as well drink it up now!' Snail Snot lectured with revolting prissiness. She sat down on the bed and held the glass to Sunny's lips. 'There you are Sunny boy, now you'll be as strong as those tigers you draw!'

And Sunny, who liked his milk and was thirsty, because it was a hot, oppressive night, drank up.

'All right children, goodnight, then! Sleep well! Don't forget to drink your milk, Shikha dear!'

She left the room and shut the door softly.

Shikha picked up her glass of milk and walked slowly to the window. With a furious gesture she flung the liquid out, surprised by a yelp from the garden as a sneaky jackal got it straight in its face. It fled, licking its lips, its wife chasing after it trying to lick its face!

'Drink your milk!' Shikha mimicked bitterly, half angry with herself because she too did enjoy her last glass of milk!

Half an hour later, Snail Snot crept into the room again, and picked up the empty glasses. There was a smile on her face, that wasn't quite nice, but Shikha had shut her eyes tightly, not wishing to look at that pasty face anymore.

It was dreadfully oppressive that night, for it had become very humid, and sometimes Shikha suspected she had smelt rain in the air. The eagerly awaited monsoon had been galloping across the country in unseemly haste and was due, glory of glories a week before its usual date. Squelching uncomfortably in her bed, Shikha tossed and turned, unable to sleep. At around one in the morning she rose, glanced at Sunny, all curled up and dead to the world, and tiptoed out of the room. She needed a glass of water, badly. One dim light was still on in the drawing room, as well as a tubelight in the lobby. She could see that up in her bedroom, Snail Snot too was still awake, which surprised her because it was so late, and she tiptoed carefully to the kitchen. She drank her glass of water and tiptoed back.

And stopped and frowned. There was a white envelope propped up prominently on the hatstand. Breathlessly she went up to it, puzzled and then surprised. It was addressed to her. *To Dearest Shikha*, actually.

Carefully she slit it open, and read it as her heart began the boombox act again and her tummy tightened up.

Dearest Shikha beti,

By the time you will be reading this, Sunny darling will be well on his way to his new school with Randhir uncle and myself. We thought it would be better that we took him while both you and he were asleep, so no one would be upset at that time, and there would be no tears and crying. Sunny (and you) won't know a thing, because I put some sleeping medicine in the milk today so that you both wouldn't be disturbed. Don't worry dear – Randhir uncle and myself will be with Sunny throughout, I promise! He will wake up to a completely new and wonderful world, and who knows, this may even make him excited enough to talk! I have sent a message that Sharifa is to return to Shergarh House immediately to be with you. (Ali can look after his grandfather for a change.) Please believe that we are doing all this for your own good. You will be upset of course, but in a day or two, without Sunny's worry on your young shoulders anymore, you will be looking forward to going to school. Do remember that we are doing this for your and Sunny's future welfare and it is what your dear parents would have most probably wanted.

Lots of love,
Veena aunty

She was trembling as she folded the letter and put it back into the envelope and felt a little dizzy as the blood drew out of her face. They … they … Snail Snot and that slimeball Randhir (and maybe Binoy chacha, though that didn't seem very likely) had planned to *kidnap* Sunny! To take him away from her and not the other way around! To spirit him away while they both slept, drugged by the milk they had been given. Thank God she had thrown hers away. But Sunny, Sunny had drunk his. No wonder he hadn't moved.

Think, think, think, Shikha Saini think, this is no time to blub or get hysterical, girl! She balled her fists and breathed deeply. Okay, okay, just cool it! The letter obviously had been put here for her to read tomorrow. Which meant, which meant, that Snail Snot's devious plan was yet to be put into action! Which meant that even at this very moment, that slimeball Randhir might be driving towards Shergarh House to do just that! Which meant that she and Sunny had better get out of Shergarh House pretty damn quickly. But go where? And go to whom, for help? Everyone was out of station at this time …

Of course!

Just beyond the house, lay the whole of Shergarh Tiger Reserve! And her tigers!

She glanced at the letter in her hand. And nodded as ins piration struck. Okay! She darted inside her room, plucked a page from Sunny's pad (which had a gruesome sketch of Snail Snot being eaten by Sheba!), put it into the envelope and returned it to the hatstand. Okay, give nothing away to the enemy, especially knowledge. And gain time – as much as possible.

Like a madwoman she began packing her knapsack, automatically stuffing in all the items that Dipti had made her list out, so many months ago. Torch, penknife, first aid, (that was already in the Gypsy) candles, matches, camera, film, binoculars … That and yes, she'd need some food. Back to the fridge, where she found a carton of milk, which Snail Snot had stocked since Aslambhai's buffalo supply had become erratic. (The stupid buffalo did not like anyone else milking her – especially Ali!) She took some oranges and bananas, and even two melons, and of course, both her and Sunny's water bottles that lived in the fridge when not out in the field. Also, a few packets of biscuits and a loaf of bread. She shoved them all into Sharifa's food hamper and then went back to the hatstand where she carefully picked up the keys of the Gypsy.

She took the hamper and her knapsack and staggered noiselessly out into the hot humid night. The bolt on the door to the Gypsy's shed grated horribly as she slid it back, but soon she was inside, and stowed her knapsack and the bag in the back. Thank God, Aslambhai had put the top up – at least over the front section – before he broke his leg. She rushed back to the house and back to the bedroom, panting and sweating. Anything else? Did she need anything else? She stood blankly in front of her cupboard, and then picked out a pair of denim shorts and a blouse for herself, and two sets of clothes for Sunny. These she packed into his little knapsack. Okay, all done! Well nearly! She took the picture of her parents from the bedside, kissed it and shoved it into the knapsack too. It was time to get out!

She slipped into her jeans and a thin cotton blouse, and bent over her sleeping little brother, brushing her hair away from her face as it fell forward.

'Come on, Sunny, time to get out of here,' she whispered and wrapping her arms around him, lifted him gently on to her shoulders. He just clutched her tightly and slept on. So sweet of you to have drugged my little brother you evil witch, Shikha thought with bitter irony, now I can kidnap him with the same ease as you had planned to! She lowered him carefully into the passenger seat of the Gypsy, tucking him between the picnic rugs and cushions that had become part of the Gypsy's equipment murmuring, 'Hang on Sunny, I'll be back in a jiffy,' and made one last trip to their bedroom. Okay, okay, leave no signs of a hasty exit; of course they would realize they had gone, but no need to do so until the very last moment. She closed their cupboard door, and from the big comfortable tea planter's chair took the huge bolster and placed it on her bed, covering it up with a sheet. If anyone just peeked in, it would look like she was sleeping innocently in her bed. Again, she tiptoed out. She was halfway down the lobby, when the hated voice wafted down the stairs.

'Randhir? Is that you? Come up, but be very quiet.'

Shikha tiptoed out into the verandah, and scampered off to the shed. Inside, Sunny was still fast asleep in the passenger seat of the Gypsy. She was about to get into the driver's seat, when she paused. A vehicle was approaching Shergarh House, she heard it grunt and groan as it changed gears while coming up the last bends. She raced out, and her heart sank. She could see its headlight beams criss-cross the night sky as it breasted the final rise. The slimeball Randhir had arrived. She watched as he switched off the lights before turning into the gates, parked in the porch as if it was his own house and disappeared indoors.

Think, Shikha girl, think! If she started up the Gypsy and roared out now like some silly heroine in a film, they would be after her in a shot. If she could get away undetected, they would take perhaps ten minutes before Snail Snot would be ready – she would have to pack some of Sunny's clothes too, after all, if they were going to kidnap him. It would be better if she pushed the Gypsy out of the gates, and only start it when they were well down the road. Back in the shed, she spotted a pickaxe lying in one corner. She picked it up and sprinted to the slimeball's jeep. The rage inside her, bottled up for so long, just exploded as she swung the pickaxe with all her strength at the jeep's rear tyre.

There was a shrill hiss as the axe sunk in, which startled her. She yanked it out, flung it aside and fled. Okay, that gave her another ten or twenty minutes. She released the Gypsy's handbrake and put her shoulder to the door pillar and pushed, one hand on the steering wheel, one eye on Sunny. She was lucky, because the driveway sloped slightly downhill to the gate and the Gypsy was soon rolling along silently at a decent walking pace. Panicking almost that it would run away from her, she jumped in and steered it smartly out of the gates (lit dimly by one naked bulb on the gatepost) and on the road to Shergarh Tiger Reserve. She was drenched in sweat, her shirt sticky against her back, her hair sticking to her face. Quickly she switched on the Gypsy's headlamps and breathed easier as they lit up the bumpy road ahead. Then she switched the engine on, and drove slowly towards the gate of the reserve. She unlocked it with the key in the Gypsy's key ring, drove through, locked it again and prepared to set out on her long night drive. It was only then that she noticed that the Gypsy's wireless set had been removed – it had been taken away for repairs.

At Shergarh House, the slimeball Randhir walked up the spiral stairs and into Snail Snot's room. She was all packed and ready to go.

'Take these to the jeep,' she said indicating her bags. 'I'll just go and pack the little boy's things!'

'You haven't done that already?'

'I couldn't! The girl would have become suspicious. She was here all the time. Don't worry – I put some sleeping tablets into their milk. She won't wake till 10.00 a.m.'

'Okay, but hurry! Does the uncle know about this plan?'

'What? That we take the little boy away from the girl and not the other way around? No – I thought it would be better if he didn't know. He's a fool and a simpleton. The less he knows, the better. God knows what drama that girl had planned for the time when she was to be taken to the railway station. Now, with the boy out of the way, she'll go quietly!'

'Well come on, then. Bhairon and Sharma are waiting in your room at the school.'

Cautiously Snail Snot opened the door to the children's room and peeped in. All seemed well. The girl and her brother appeared to be fast asleep on the bed. The sleeping medicine had obviously worked. She opened their cupboard, frowning at the mess she saw (due to Shikha's hasty packing). Really, that girl was too much. Not only did she return from the forest looking like a pig, but she lived like one too! Boarding school would set her straight. She had brought an empty carrier bag for Sunny's things, and carefully put away some of his shorts and singlets. All she really needed was clothes for him to travel in – the school would provide its own uniform. She packed his toothbrush and mug and took the bag out to the jeep. The slimeball Randhir, (who had drunk rather a lot earlier that evening) had plonked her bags on the porch and was sitting in a chair, staring at the jeep. Had he drunk more than he had thought, or was the jeep listing to one side?

'Here,' Snail Snot said. 'Put them in. Come on, it's time to take the little boy.'

'You have left the letter for the girl, so that she doesn't die of hysterics when she wakes up?'

'Yes, it's there.'

They entered the children's bedroom again. Snail Snot went over to the bed, and gently drew the sheet back.

And went white!

'Ran … Randhir … come here, quickly! They're not here!'

'Wha … what do you mean!'

'They've gone!'

'What?'

'They've run away!'

'Where to dammit! We're in the middle of the jungle! And why?'

The lights blazed on at Shergarh House as the demented couple searched the rooms.

'So this is what that wicked girl had planned!' Snail Snot hissed. 'She had planned to run away with her brother before her school date arrived!'

'They couldn't have gone far. Or for very long! They're on foot after all! Come on!'

'Yes, and even Shikha would not dare enter a tiger reserve on foot in the middle of the night!' Snail Snot muttered. 'Especially with her baby brother! Come on, she must have been walking down the road and hidden when she saw you driving up!'

Then they discovered the jeep's flat tyre!

'Will you look at this!' whistled Randhir, pointing to the jagged hole in the side of the tyre. 'Looks like a buffalo got its horn in there!' If the fool had turned around, he would have seen the pickaxe lying on the grass where Shikha had discarded it.

'We can take the Gypsy – the keys are in the hatstand drawer!'

Snail Snot waddled off towards the Gypsy's shed shaking her head. Like her hair that was now unravelling in stringy bits all over her face, so were her plans.

She nearly bumped into Randhir as he came running back from the house.

'There are no keys in the hatstand drawer!'

'My dear Randhir, there is no Gypsy in the shed either!'

'That stupid girl has taken the Gypsy inside!'

'Come on, Randhir, change the tyre! We have got to go after them!'

Randhir shook his head. 'No,' he said. 'I'll change the tyre, we drive back to the school, pick the others up in their vehicle and return. And maybe, maybe we can bag a couple of tigers while we're inside!' He laughed. 'After all, we have a legitimate reason for being inside with guns now – we are searching for the children! It is an emergency!'

Snail Snot nodded.

'Okay, now hurry up!' She went inside and picked up the envelope from the hatstand and put it in her purse. There had been a slight change in plan, but things would work out, she was sure of it.

On his charpoy on the terrace of his house, just across the village school (what a place to live!), Ali frowned. Again a vehicle was driving in through the gates. Earlier that night he had heard and then seen the big black jeep belonging to that woman's brother drive off. Another canvas-topped jeep stood outside the school guest room where that horrible woman had been staying when she was not living at Shergarh House. Ali got off his bed and peered over the terrace. Yes, there it was again, that big black jeep, driving up and parking next to the other one. As it passed by a fitful tubelight he saw that there were two people in it. The second person appeared to be the horrible woman – who could mistake that saintly posture? Ali frowned. Just what was going on? His grandfather had always been suspicious of vehicles moving about at night around Shergarh. They never boded well. Besides, wasn't the horrible woman supposed to be at Shergarh House looking after Shikha and Sunny? Ali slithered down the ladder his grandfather had fallen off and ran quickly to the vehicles. Something strange was going on. Before he could decide what to do, the guest room door opened, letting out a flood of light over the vehicles. With a squawk of dismay, Ali jumped nimbly into the back of the canvas-topped jeep and lay low. It was a pick-up type jeep, with just a small window between the cab and the bed at the back. But if someone got in, and looked back through it – he'd be discovered immediately. And then poor Ali, who had played so many nasty pranks on unsuspecting visitors, got the nastiest surprise of his life! There were several lumpy sacks lying on the bed, and quickly he began to burrow beneath them.

Except, that beneath one of them, there was something rolled up like some bori-bistar in one corner.

'Baap re! My God!' Ali reeled back and then leaned forward again, his heart thumping. The rolled up bori-bistar was a tiger skin, still attached to the head. And the head, even in the faint light that filtered in through the small window, belonged to Begum, the tigress that had gone missing some time back! He was just about to leap out and run, when he heard footsteps. Quickly he ducked beneath the gunny bags, hardly daring to breathe. The rear flap was raised, and something hard and metallic clattered down on the bed, and then was covered with a gunny bag. (The man almost touched his toes!) The jeep started up and roared off. Wriggling under the gunny bags, Ali squirmed his way to the back against the cab wall, from where he would be least likely to be spotted by anyone in front. He stared dully at the shiny barrels of the guns that had been put into the jeep. The jeep was roaring up a twisting road at a dangerous speed, and he knew it was the road leading to the reserve, past Shergarh House. It would be foolish to try and jump off it, he knew; besides they might stop at Shergarh House, enabling him to check on his friends. So Ali sat quiet as a mouse, gently stroking the head of what had once been a fine, proud tigress of Shergarh.

In the black jeep up ahead, the slimeball Randhir and Snail Snot were revising plans rapidly, as a fine rain began to fall, and in the distance, thunder rumbled over the ridges of Shergarh like a faraway artillery bombardment.

'Any idea where this girl might go?' the slimeball asked as the vehicle bounced and bucked.

'We could check the fort and Chhota Mahal,' Snail Snot said, hanging on to the grab handles.

It was now two thirty in the morning, and Shikha had a lead of one hour and ten minutes on her pursuers. And was thinking hard again.

'Okay, Sunny,' she said, even though he was still fast asleep. She had stopped for a minute to stuff the picnic rugs and cushions around him again so he wouldn't roll off the seat as the vehicle bounced. And she liked talking to him even if he was asleep. 'Okay, Sunny, now what?' Carefully she manoeuvred the Gypsy down the ridge slope. Thank God, they had returned after dark on so many occasions after their day-long forays into the jungle, she thought. Otherwise she would have been completely bewildered. Even so, driving into the reserve was quite different from driving out of it, she discovered, and on several occasions when the tracks split, she paused, wondering which one to take. Also, without Aslambhai and Ali, she felt quite nervous, but was spurred on by the thought of her pursuers.

Think, Shikha, think! She banged her fist on the steering wheel, staring at the forest track ahead, lit brilliantly by the headlamps. Occasionally, ruby- or emerald-coloured eyes glowed out of the dark as surprised animals stared at the vehicle, blinded by its dazzle. Once, a magnificent leopard, stalking down the track, just walked on ahead, and then veered off with a sneering backward glance as she gained on it. She gave a stifled scream as a nightjar flickered low and shot over the windscreen with barely millimetres to spare.

'Idiot!' she exclaimed. 'Look where you're going!'

She knew now where she was going and what she was going to do. She would head for Hari Pani, where she would leave the Gypsy. She would take Sunny up along the cliff path and find a nice secluded cave where they would camp. If the caves were safe enough for great horned owls and tigers and sloth bears, they would be safe enough for her and Sunny. From the caves you got a lovely view of Hari Pani and its pavilion. No one could approach those without being seen by a watcher on the cliff side. She would hunker down there with Sunny bunny and wait. In a day or so, Binoy chacha would be sure to turn up with the forest department guards and maybe Ali. Well, anyway, by the 28th, when he was due to take her to school!

Then she would have it out with him and that Snail Snot witch!

But as she drove, the fine misty rain that had begun falling got heavier. The Gypsy had one reluctant wiper, and she had to slow down. Sometimes she felt the vehicle slither and slide alarmingly beneath her. Then she remembered to engage the four-wheel drive. That was better! The Gypsy felt more surefooted now. She blipped the accelerator and it leapt forward skittishly like a deer. She knew she'd be leaving fresh tyre tracks behind on the softening mud. So every now and then she yanked the vehicle off cross-country, swooshing through the wet grass, bouncing and bucking, crossing tracks before rejoining the road, and surprising many small animals and birds but thank God, no tigers! It slowed down her progress but it couldn't be helped. Occasionally she peered behind at the pitch-black road. Thankfully there was no sign of any pursuit, though once, she swore she had heard the guttural mutter of a diesel engine in the distance.

18

BUT IF THE RAIN HAD SLOWED DOWN SHIKHA, IT HAD DONE the same to her pursuers. At first they had tried to follow the Gypsy's tyre tracks, but soon realized that they would get nowhere at the pace at which they were going. Sometimes the tracks just disappeared into the high grass, where Shikha, in her wild flight, had taken her vehicle cross-country, cutting across jungle paths with wild abandon, even as she struggled to find her own bearings. They had had to stop here, check around in the drizzle and eventually found themselves driving in circles. Finally they had bucked and jolted their way to the great fort and the Chhota Mahal, whose bulk they could see, looming up against the night sky in the distance. But both places had yielded no traces of the Gypsy. Then Snail Snot thumped her forehead.

'There was that place that Shikha kept mentioning in that journal of hers. Hari Pani or something like that! She must have gone there!'

'Where is it? Do you know the way?' asked Sharma, lighting a cigarette.

'I think it is somewhere in that direction,' said Randhir, pointing vaguely in the direction of Hira Talao. ' Beyond that big crocodile-filled lake. And yes, you're right, she's probably there. She kept writing about the tigers she used to see there.'

'Then what are we waiting for?' said Bhairon with a laugh that made Ali wriggle even deeper into his gunny bags. 'Maybe we'll get a potshot at a tiger as a bonus. Or at least some sambhar and chital! Come on!'

They drove off again into the drizzle, confident that if they kept roughly to the right direction they would eventually reach their destination. It was a foolish assumption, for by the time the sky lightened at around 5 a.m. and the first birds tentatively sang, they knew they were hopelessly lost. There suddenly seemed to be so many ridges and ravines and gullies in the damn place, each one looking exactly like the other.

'Dammit!' Randhir said, angrily. 'Where the hell are we? And where the hell has that girl gone?'

'Do we really need to do this?' enquired Sharma, who was getting fed up. 'Why can't we just take a few potshots, get what we can and leave!'

Snail Snot tried looking horrified.

'How can we leave those poor children here?' she asked, tears in her eyes. 'The place is full of tigers! What will their uncle say if I inform him that they've disappeared? I will have failed my responsibility! My reputation will be mud!'

They drove around in circles till around eight o'clock, and then re-grouped for another acrimonious discussion. In the canvas-topped jeep, one arm around Begum's head, Ali knew he was trapped good and proper. Even if he could slip out unseen, he could not foot it alone through the park to fetch help. He had caught the gist of what these men (and that woman) had been saying and knew that his best bet was to lay low and wait it out.

Alas, it was not to be!

Bhairon suddenly spotted a magnificent sambhar stag standing stock-still behind a thorn bush.

'Look!' he whispered. 'Look at the size of its head!'

He reached into the back of the jeep, yanked back the gunny sack for the gun and stared straight into Ali's terrified face.

'Hoi!' he shouted, as the sambhar honked and bolted in alarm. He thrust in a brawny arm and yanked poor Ali out. 'Look what I've caught! He was sitting there with his arm around the tigress's head!'

'Ali! Ali, what are you doing here?' Snail Snot wrung her hands. 'You know that Shikha baby and Sunny have run away! We are looking for them!'

'Veena,' he's seen the tiger skin!' Randhir said. 'It doesn't matter what he is doing here anymore.'

'Yes,' she replied calmly. 'And he's been to Hari Pani with the children. He'll take us there.'

'Chalo!' said Bhairon, pushing Ali into the front of the jeep. 'Take us to Hari Pani!'

Silently, Ali nodded.

'Bahut door hai, it is very far,' he said at last in a low voice. 'Der lagega! It will take time!'

'So what are we waiting for?' Bhairon growled, starting the engine. 'Come on!'

Petrified though he was, Ali kept his wits about him. He nodded, allowing a few tears to roll down his cheeks.

'Achcha,' he said. 'Okay, I will show you the way!'

And pointed in the direction exactly opposite to Hari Pani.

He led them on a merry wild goose chase that day, making them drive all over the place, hoping a forest department vehicle would come their way. But the rain had started and the roads were beginning to gum up. There were no vehicles in the reserve now, especially since Rana sahib was not in station. Twice he made them drive through muddy streams, getting the vehicles badly stuck.

'Ab to thori hi door hai! It's just a little way ahead!' he would say reassuringly, ready for a clip on the ear. Tired, covered with mud (even Snail Snot, who had got royally sprayed when the jeep's tyres spun in the mud!) Bhairon had had enough. At three o'clock that afternoon he stopped the vehicle and yanked Ali out. He pulled out his gun from the back and held the barrel at the petrified boy's stomach, even as Snail Snot put her hands in front of her face.

'If we are not at Hari Pani in half an hour's time I will put a bullet in your stomach and leave the jackals to do the rest,' he grated, clouting the boy hard with the gun's butt. 'Now get in!'

Dazed by the blow, Ali could only nod, tears (genuine this time) pouring down his face.

'Aadha ghanta nahin lagega – it won't take half an hour,' he whispered rubbing his head and horrified by the blood that came off on his hands. 'It will take two hours!'

In consolation, Sharma took a quick potshot at a chital doe that had foolishly stepped out from behind the bushes in front of them. The poor animal went down, at once.

'Fetch it and put it in the back. It will be good bait for tigers at Hari Pani!' Bharion said, shoving Ali out of the vehicle. 'If you try and run, you'll get a bullet in your back!'

And poor Ali could only do as they said.

At the wheel of the Gypsy, Shikha had no major problem (except the rain) getting to Hari Pani, which she reached like a homing bird, just as a dull grey dawn was breaking over the forest. But she had faced some problems navigating in the earlier stages of the journey; in the dark the reserve had shrunk to just what she could see lit ahead by her headlamps. But soon enough she had found her bearings and had driven the Gypsy as fast as she had dared along the slushy jungle paths. By the time they reached, she was dead tired and sleepy, and envious of Sunny, who was still fast asleep. The Gypsy chugged up the final boulder strewn slope, its wheels skidding on the rain-slicked rocks, just a little bit too fast. At the top, Shikha braked, also just a little too hard, and the wheels locked. The vehicle slid alarmingly forward, and she gave a little scream and yanked the wheel. There was a horrible crunch and a jolt, which made her bang her head against the steering wheel. Sunny thankfully was well bolstered by the cushions, but the jolt woke him up too.

'Ouch!' Shikha exclaimed rubbing her head. 'Are you okay Sunny? We are at Hari Pani – that horrible witch wanted to take you away but I wouldn't let her.'

He nodded solemnly, as if it were the most normal thing in the world.

'Come on,' she said, opening the door. 'Let's find ourselves a cave!'

She went around to the front of the Gypsy and frowned. She had steered it straight into a large boulder, to stop the skid, and the front end had caved in. The radiator had burst and a horrible green fluid was dripping on to the ground.

'Oh, damn!' she said. 'Now we're stuck here!' She shrugged. 'Can't be helped! Come on!'

As usual, the first look of Hari Pani from the ridge top made her heart leap. It lay there, a deep emerald green even in this murky dawn light, refreshing and inviting. Later, perhaps, once they had found their cave and settled in it and the coast was clear, they would swim. At the moment her priority was to find a suitable hiding place.

It was sweaty work scrambling up the boulders and

climbing up the gravelly path, along which she had once watched Shahenshah make his approach. He seemed to have resumed his patrols here she thought, wrinkling up her nose. There was the definite reek of big cat in the heavy air.

'Quiet now, Sunny,' she whispered. 'We don't need any unpleasant surprises.'

The first cave she cautiously poked her head in stank of bats and she retreated quickly.

'Ugh!' she exclaimed. 'What a stink!' Another cave lay near this one, up a sheer incline, but it belonged to the great horned owls and anyway was impossible to get to. But the third one, at the very end of the narrow path along the ridge, seemed fine. Best of all, its mouth was hidden from Hari Pani below by a wild tangle of thorny bushes that clung tenaciously to the steep slopes. No one at Hari Pani could guess there was a cave here, unless they walked up the ridge path to the very end.

'Great!' Shikha said, 'we can see what's going on down there, but no one can see us. So we'll know when someone comes – friend or foe!'

She looked around uncertainly thinking of her next move. She would have to go down to the Gypsy again to fetch food and other stuff (and the rugs and cushions too, she thought, they'd make life a little comfortable and God knows how long it would be before they would be rescued). She put down her knapsack, and peeped into the cave. It seemed to run quite deep, but otherwise appeared perfect. The rocky floor was smooth, and some tentative prodding with a stick and tossing in of a couple of rocks yielded no nasty snakes or lizards – or, thank heavens, anything bigger like an enraged sloth bear or leopard! She went inside and checked it out quickly. All clear. It was vacant (even if reeking a bit) and appeared to have some sort of small opening in the rear, through which light filtered in.

'Okay, Sunny, I'm going back to the Gypsy to fetch the water bottles and food hamper and cushions and stuff. You stay here and look after my knapsack, okay? You will be able to see me go all the way down to the pavilion and then back up to where the Gypsy is. Is that okay with you?' He seemed to be a little dopey still and she didn't want to have to carry him up all the way again, in case he went off to sleep again.

Solemnly he nodded. It was no problem. He could see the Gypsy right from this spot and would be able to keep an eye on her all the way. No problem. He shrugged his shoulders and rolled his eyes. She wouldn't be in any danger with him watching over her, even though he was still feeling quite sleepy.

'No problem, eh?' Shikha grinned and kissed him on the cheek. 'That's the way toodledumps!' she said and waved.

It took her ten minutes to reach the Gypsy and she emptied it out the best she could, of anything that might be useful. Sunny's knapsack was still in the back, and she opened it to see if she could stuff a couple of cushions into it, to make the carrying easier. She slung his small binoculars around her neck, heaved her burden on to her shoulders and set off again, waving in the direction where she knew the cave was. It really was a knockout hideout, because she couldn't see it at all from the car, while you could see the car and the pavilion quite clearly from it. What a piece of luck!

The rain had begun pockmarking the emerald pleats of Hira Pani and the little dabchicks were trilling away shrilly as she made her way back. She was exceptionally careful as she climbed back up towards the cave. It would never do to slip now, and twist an ankle or something. About halfway up, she stopped for a breather, and raised Sunny's binoculars to her eyes to check out the cave. She could see its dark mouth now (especially since she knew it was there) but there was no sign of Sunny sitting at the entrance where she had left him. She frowned. It was not like him to let her out of his sight, especially in such circumstances, when there was no one else around. Maybe he had fallen asleep again.

She put down the binoculars, picked up her burden and hastened up, eyes on the ground. It was only then that she spotted the pugmarks leading away in the opposite direction, down the path, in a small section of it that had been shielded from the rain by a rocky overhang. Her heart pounding, she knelt down and examined them.

They were the pugmarks of a tigress and quite recent. Okay, okay, so probably the tigress had used one of these caves to shelter in, and had walked off. That explained the smell. But if, but if … She dropped her bags and sped up the path as fast as she could. She had kept an eye on the path as much as possible, and hadn't seen any movement. But she also knew that tigers could move virtually invisibly and soundlessly. If anything had happened to Sunny …

Her breath coming in great whooshing gasps, she charged up the last few feet on the narrow ridge path, to the place where she had left Sunny. There was no sign of the little boy.

'Sunny? Sunny bunny?' she called, her voice trembling. Looking around she tiptoed (for no reason really) to the cave entrance and looked inside.

About halfway inside, and trying valiantly to walk towards her, was Sunny, tousle-haired and frowning. In his arms was a struggling little tiger cub, about the size of a pomeranian, and at his feet, another little cub, standing up against him and dragging his shorts halfway down his knees, yarring ferociously.

'Down boy, down!' Sunny said valiantly to the cub trying to climb up his legs. Then looked up and saw Shikha. He laughed delightedly. 'Look what I found, dimplechick! Just look what I found!' he said in that nearly forgotten high-pitched excited voice of his, eyes bright, 'Caves in the tiger cub! Caves in the tiger cub!'

Her mouth dropped and she put her hand up to her face, unable to believe what she had heard.

'Sunny, you just talked!' she whispered.

'Ooof!' Sunny exclaimed, nodding. 'Just take this one off my legs! He thinks I'm a tree! He's pulling down my shorts and scratching me!'

She rushed in and took the little cub into her arms, cradling it against her, as it yarred and spat.

'Where did you find them?' she asked breathlessly, and shut her eyes. Please Sunny, answer, please answer.

'They were back there. They were making a noise. There's a hole in the back of the cave and they nearly fell out of it on the other side. I pulled them back by their tails!'

'What?'

'Dimplechick, can we keep them? Please?' He looked at her imploringly.

'What? K ... keep them?'

'They can live at home and we can bring them here and train them to hunt! I think they are hungry,' Sunny chattered on, firmly holding his cub by the scruff of its neck. 'That's why they're making such a noise! Can we give them something to eat?'

'Just let him keep talking on his own, Shikha girl, just let him keep talking. He's back, he's back with you! Just let him talk on his own.' That switch the doctor mentioned had been turned on again. By these two spitfire tiger cubs, one of which had already torn her blouse and yanked her hair.

'They are little spitfires, aren't they, Sunny?' she said, holding the cub at arm's length. He nodded.

'Can we keep them?' he asked again. 'When they're grown they'll be our bodyguards!' He could see himself striding into a smoke-filled bar, his arms around two full-grown tigers who would obey his every command and leap with growls on those mobsters who had dared upset her.

'Can you hang on to that one, Sunny?' Shikha asked breathlessly, still not daring to believe her ears. 'I'm going to get Sharifa's food hamper, it's just outside. We'll empty it and put them inside it – it should be big enough. Otherwise they'll be running all over the place driving us crazy!'

'Bananas, babydoll,' he drawled rolling his eyes. 'You said it!' He was back, no doubt about that! The horrendous nicknames and accent that used to drive her wild!

She brought the food hamper in, tumbled its contents on to the floor of the cave, turned it over and put the cub (now quiet as she had stroked it gently behind the ears) into it. Sunny shoved (a little more roughly) in his cub and pulled his shorts over his butt with great dignity.

'Okay,' said Shikha breathlessly. Suddenly she picked Sunny up and hugged him tightly, making him squeal in protest.

'Ooof you're squishing me dead!' Sunny complained, wriggling like the tiger cubs, which were now making the food hamper do a rock and roll on the cave floor.

'Sorry toodledumps! Sorry!' She put him down, her face red with happiness.

'Can we feed those tiger cubs now?' he asked. 'Or they're going to run away with the basket!'

'Um … yes, let's see, oh, yes I've got some milk!'

'Whose cubs are they? Where are their mama and papa? Do you think their mama and papa will come back? Let's take them away before they do!'

He had begun shooting questions, just like in the old days.

She opened a carton of milk, emptied her water bottle and filled it up.

'I don't know, Sunny. But I think they may be Sheba's! Here, come on you little wildcat.'

She pulled out one of the cubs, wincing as it spat and snarled, and held the bottle to its mouth. She had plugged the bottle's mouth with a handkerchief, so the cub could suck at the milk. To her surprise, it did and hungrily. Its sibling tried determinedly to get out of its basket, yarring shrilly.

'Hey Sunny, do me a favour,' Shikha said, still beaming. 'My camera is in my knapsack. Will you take it out and I'll tell you how to take a picture!'

'Uff ho babydoll, I know how to,' he drawled, drawing the camera out, and switching it on. Those times he had spent fiddling with it were paying off now.

'Shift that lever to automatic,' she said and he nodded impatiently.

'I know, I know, you don't have to tell me everything! Smile, cheesy weezy!'

Click shuttuk, click shuttuk, click shuttuk, click shuttuk!

'Okay, Sunny now let me take some of yours!'

They spent a happy if somewhat confusing few minutes taking pictures of the cubs and themselves, when Sunny asked, 'Do you think their mama will be mad if she finds us playing with her babies? I mean we are strangers.' He rolled his eyes eloquently. 'Mama used to tell us not to talk to strange people.'

'Hells bells Sunny, you're right! If their mama is Sheba we'll be eaten alive. And we've made such a mess of her den!' There was milk all over the place, and other stuff scattered around. The cubs had discovered one of the old cushions and were busy disembowelling it, crouching, pouncing and sending the stuffing all over the place.

'Like Goldilocks!' remarked Sunny.

'Well not quite, but yes, I think we'd better get the hell out of here quickly! I hope Sheba's not finicky as mama was!'

'Can't we take them with us? Please?'

'No Sunny! Their mama will follow our scent and find us and kill us. Come on, we better get out of here quickly!'

But what was puzzling Shikha was Sheba's absence in the first place (though thank God she was absent!). Where had she gone, and why had she disappeared for so long, leaving her cubs here? Certainly it wouldn't do to be in the area when the tigress returned, but on the other hand if something dreadful had happened to her, they could hardly desert the cubs ...

One of the cubs, the one she decided she'd call Shararat – because he was by far the more mischievous of the two – now had scampered to the back of the cave, with Sunny in hot pursuit. The other one, she had christened Shaan, because there was something regal about him, even now as he lay calmly on the tattered cushions, twitching his tail, paws elegantly crossed.

'Hey, come back you! Come back!' Sunny yelled, pulling Shararat back.

'Sunny,' said Shikha feeling more and more uncomfortable as the minutes passed. 'Let's get out of here. That Sheba will kill us if she finds us here!'

'We leave them here?' he said. 'What if they fall down?'

'They've probably got better sense than that,' said Shikha not as convinced as she sounded. She looked around, and down at the Hari Pani.

'I know what,' she said slowly. 'You see that chhatri in the middle of the pool?'

Sunny nodded. 'You went swimming there,' he said.

'Yes, well, that looks like the only place down below from where we could get a view of this cave. So we'll swim out there and watch it from there. Maybe Sheba, or whoever the cubs' mother is, will return. Come on let's leave these two in the hamper and go. Pick up everything else. Quickly now!'

And so they stumbled back down the narrow ridge path, Shikha looking every which way, with increasing nervousness. Aslambhai had told her so many times, about how terribly fierce Sheba could get if she felt her cubs were in danger. They would be safe in the chhatri bang in the middle of the pool, she hoped. Sheba could swim of course, but it seemed unlikely that she would come after them, after having left her cubs for so long. God knows, they had been with them for about half an hour and she had not made an appearance – thank God for that. And Shikha knew that she had done something exceedingly foolish. They should have left the cave the moment they had found the cubs. But that was when Sunny had started talking again and she was too dazed to even think clearly. Just before the main descent began she looked over to the other side of the ridge and froze. In the deep, bamboo-shrouded gully on that side, maybe half a kilometre away, she glimpsed something fiery orange bounding swiftly through the undergrowth and the golden grass.

'Oh my God, she's coming back, she's coming back!' she whispered, and taking Sunny's hand plunged down the path at a reckless speed. They dumped their things on the pavilion steps and Shikha stepped into the cool water, where the big golden bullfrogs were still celebrating the previous night's rain. She held out her hands to Sunny.

'Come on Sunny, piggyback on me,' she said. 'Quickly now!'

He clutched her around the neck and clung to her as she set out determinedly towards her private chhatri in the middle of the water.

Shivering, they crouched there behind the lattice-work and gazed up towards the cave.

'It is Sheba!' Shikha whispered as the tigress leapt up the narrow path towards the cave, snarling in a chillingly blood-curdling manner. She had smelt them. Her snarls echoed and bounced unpleasantly off the cliff walls, rippling over them and hanging in the very air as it were, telling them exactly what she would have done to them if she had found them. If Sheba had caught them in that cave she would have ripped them to shreds, no doubt about that!

'Do you think she'll follow our scent like a bloodhound and find us?' Sunny asked in a small voice, clutching her hand, his eyes wide.

'Ah, but she'll lose the scent in the water. Look, she's reached the entrance!'

Another malevolent snarling growl followed by a roar rippled out of the cave and bounced off the rocks as Sheba discovered her cubs, crawling valiantly out of Sharifa's food hamper. Like Shikha, the tigress had had a very disturbed night too. Very early that morning, she had smelt the presence of another tiger in the area, and realized that it was Shaitan. If he found her here, with her cubs, there would be trouble. She had slipped out, and led the fellow a merry dance, calling and slipping away, calling and slipping away, further and further from the cave as he followed, getting increasingly agitated. Her luck was in, as inadvertently, she led him almost straight into Shahenshah, on patrol. The majestic tiger had leapt, snarling deep and angrily at his rival, clouted him heavily over the head and sent him tumbling. Shaitan, like all bullies had no stomach for a real fight, and fled, with a roaring Shahenshah in hot pursuit. And Sheba returned hotfoot to Hari Pani, where soon she had caught that familiar smell of those creatures that had sat and watched her on so many occasions in the past. But now she was in no mood to tolerate their company. Not in the cave where her cubs were, certainly! She charged into her den, her eyes blazing, roaring with fury, as her cubs struggled out to greet her, and immediately cooled down on seeing them. The strange smell was very powerful here, they had been here, but her cubs were unharmed. She licked them thoroughly from head to tail tip, and then, very delicately picked up the one Shikha had named Shararat in her mouth. The other one, she shushed with a call and he sank back quietly at the back of the cave.

It was time to change the nursery, and Sheba already had a replacement site ready – in the middle of a thick bamboo grove in the gully on the other side of the ridge, about two kilometres away.

'Look, Sunny, she's taking one of her cubs away. She's shifting home, I think!' Shikha whispered, feeling terrible. 'We drove her out of home and hearth!' she said sadly.

An hour later the tigress returned to collect Shaan. And then she was gone with her second cub too and the cave was deserted, except for the tattered remains of Sharifa's food hamper and the shredded cushion.

Still on their island, Shikha and Sunny watched intently and waited for half an hour after Sheba had taken Shaan.

'Okay, Sunny, she's gone!' Shikha said with relief. 'I don't think she'll come back here now.' She frowned. Now they, too, had to find a hiding place again, from their pursuers. It was almost eleven o'clock now, and thankfully there was no sign of them. 'Hmm, maybe we should just go back and claim that cave again,' Shikha said thoughtfully. 'Sheba is certainly not going to return to it. Ready for another piggyback swim Sunny?'

'Anytime, babydoll, anytime!' he said, swaggering towards the water.

Wet and shivering they went back into their cave. Quickly she changed Sunny and then stripped the wet jeans off and slipped into her denim shorts, thankful that she had had the sense to fling in a set of clothes before they had fled. And so they settled back into the cave, making it as comfortable as they could, with the bolsters and cushions that had survived the onslaught of the tiger cubs. All through that day, Shikha talked non-stop with her little brother, though by the evening, he was shooting questions at her in his usual machine-gun manner.

'Do you remember what happened that night?' she asked, deciding it was time she asked him a few questions.

'Yes,' he said. 'The car rolled over and was driving on its head! Like in the films! Man!'

'You know mama and papa have gone someplace from where they can't come back,' she said.

'Yes,' he said simply. 'Otherwise they would have come back long ago.'

'What happened toodledumps?' she asked at last. 'You just couldn't say anything?'

'I think I just forgot how to speak. I wanted to but the words were too scared to leave my mouth. They just stayed inside me. But I don't know how I remembered again!' He shrugged and rolled his eyes. 'No big deal really! These things happen!' He was over it!

'Do you like Dipti?'

He nodded. 'She's real cool! (He was fast getting back his horrible Yankee gangster mode!) But Snail Snot, ugh she's gross like a slug! She always gives us such piddly little chocolates! And she hates you!'

'And Binoy chacha?'

'He's a weirdo! Real weirdo! What are we going to do now? Are we going to live like cavemen here? Will we have to go hunting?'

'No, Sunny bunny! Sooner or later Binoy chacha is sure to

turn up here. Or Rana uncle! Then we tell them what happened. How Snail Snot and that Randhir fellow tried to kidnap you. I have the letter to prove it!'

'He's a slimeball. A real lowdown slimeball, dimplechick! Be careful of him!' He shook his head slowly.

'Yes! Sure I will!'

'Are we going to have to spend the night here?'

'It looks like it, toodledumps,' she said feeling a sudden rush of affection for him.

'I'm not a toodledumps!' he objected automatically.

'And I'm not a babydolldimplechick!' she said, grinning and kissing him.

'You are too! Won't you be scared sleeping in the cave? Suppose Sheba comes back here to sleep?'

It wasn't likely to be Sheba, but it could be any other wild animal. A hyena, sloth bear, cobra; the cave was prime property, secure and dry. Shikha frowned. They couldn't spend the night here!

'Tell you what, Sunny,' she said. 'Before it gets dark, we'll go back to the Gypsy. We can spend the night in it. And if any animal comes near us, we'll blow the horn!'

'Great idea, that'll show them! Parp parp paaaarp, gitout, vamoose!' His eyes gleamed with anticipation.

But at five thirty that evening, everything changed. Propped up against the cave wall, half asleep, and with Sunny in her lap, Shikha raised her head and listened. There it was: the distinct guttural grunt of a gear change, and then the grinding roar of an engine in low gear. Friend or foe? She raised her binoculars and trained them on the stranded Gypsy at the other side. And watched with a sinking heart as Randhir's black jeep and another lurched up by it and jolted to a halt.

Four people and a boy got out of the vehicles. Two men she

hadn't seen before, both carrying rifles, and slimeball Randhir and Snail Snot. And Ali! Ali being roughly yanked around by one of the strange men!

'They're here!' shouted one of the men, shattering the peace of Hari Pani. They had crowded around the stranded Gypsy now, pulling open its doors and looking inside. 'They must be somewhere around! They couldn't have gone far. Come on, let's search the place!'

Still managing to look saintly (how she did it was a wonder, Shikha thought), Snail Snot went down to the pavilion followed by the others, who looked around uneasily. Poor Ali's ear was still getting rough treatment at the hands of one of the men.

'I hope we haven't left anything down there,' Shikha whispered, as Sunny settled down beside her, with his own binoculars.

'We better not have!' he drawled in that hideous gangster accent, rolling his eyes. 'Or we're in deep shit babe!' He was back in form!

They watched as the men searched the pavilion and the surrounding areas, while Snail Snot sat saint-like at the edge of the stone's steps. It was beginning to get dark, and the first of the sickle-winged nightjars had already begun their experimental flights over the pool. Far in the distance, thunder rolled and rumbled, shaking the ridges and hills. The men were obviously unwilling to search the thick jungle surrounding the pool, it was getting a little too dark for comfort, and they gathered around Snail Snot for a discussion. Poor Ali was looking quite worse for wear and very tired.

'You know what I think?' Snail Snot said clearly. 'I think those children will come back to the car to spend the night!'

'Not if they see our vehicles here,' the slimeball said.

'Okay, so we drive back a little way, and park,' Bhairon said.

'They'll think we're leaving! We wait awhile, till they're fast asleep, and move in.'

'Come on, let's go! This place gives me the creeps!'

Stiff and cramped and not daring to move very much, Shikha and Sunny watched them as they huddled together and talked.

'Sunny, we've got to let Ali know that we're here!' Shikha whispered frowning. Then her face cleared. 'I know! He taught me the call of the oriole, remember?'

Sunny nodded.

'Yeah, you give that call,' he said. 'He'll cotton on! He's a cool dude!'

Self-consciously Shikha cleared her throat and cupped her hands in front of her mouth.

'Pe-olo! Pe-olo!' she fluted clearly.

Hunkered down near the water, tired and very near tears, Ali pricked up his ears. A golden oriole? Calling at this hour? When it was nearly too dark to see?

'Peeolo! Peeolo! Peeolo!'

There was a sense of urgency in the call that belonged to no real golden oriole. He'd better signal Shikha memsahib to stop, before she gave herself away completely. Casually he picked up a pebble and tossed it into the green waters of the pool, sending out ripples. And then another! One for every call.

'I told you babydoll, he's a smart dude!' Sunny said his attention caught immediately by the pebble splashes. 'He's telling us that he's heard us!'

'How do you know?' Shikha was not convinced. Ali was the sort of person who would toss pebbles in a pond just to pass the time of day, she knew.

'Uff ho, dimwit! You don't see the proper films and then ask all these silly questions.'

'Okay, babydoll, call again!'

'Anything for you toodledumps!'

'And don't call me toodledumps!'

'Peeolo!' Shikha called again.

And once again, Ali tossed a pebble high. It curved and splashed into the water, the silver green ripples fanning out once more.

'Oye, what the hell are you doing?' Bhairon marched up to the boy and yanked him to his feet. 'We're going! Come on!' The man turned to Sharma. 'Oye Sharma, have we got any rope in the jeep? We'll have to tie this bugger up!'

'There must be some! Come on let's get out of here. Then we can decide what to do with him!'

They got into their jeeps and reversed clumsily, scraping and bumping against the rocks.

'Sunny they're going!' Shikha whispered, surprised. Maybe we can spend the night in the Gypsy after all!'

'No way, no way!' Sunny shook his head decisively. Really, if she had seen any of the films he had, she would have guessed straightaway that this was a trap.

'What? What do you mean?'

'Simple! It's a stake-out! They'll just wait nearby and then sneak up to the Gypsy in the middle of the night!' He rolled his eyes. 'Then they'll walk over and bratatatatata!' He rolled his eyes and jerked like a marionette as the bullets hit home.

'Don't! You've watched too many horrible gangster films!'

'Yeah, and you can thank your stars for it!' He rolled his eyes eloquently.

In the canvas-topped jeep, Ali was squashed between Bhairon and Sharma in the front, as Bhairon drove.

'We'll have to get rid of him,' Bhairon remarked. 'He's seen too much!'

'But make it look like an accident. We can't shoot him!'

'A knock on the head, and just leave him. The animals will do the rest. No problem!'

'Stop here! This seems far enough. We can see the Gypsy from here!' Sharma said. Bhairon braked, and behind him Randhir (with Snail Snot) did the same. Ali tensed. Sharma opened the passenger door, one hand grasped firmly around Ali's bony wrist. Swiftly Ali bent down and bit him in the wrist as hard as he could.

'Aaaiiiiiiii!' Sharma howled, yanking his bleeding hand away. In one fluid movement Ali slid past him and disappeared into the darkness of the jungle as Sharma clutched his wrist, bleeding profusely. Ali had bitten deep, through to a vein.

'The bugger bit me!' Sharma shouted. His eyes widened in alarm as he saw the blood gush, then rolled up in his head as he fainted.

'Oye Sharma! Kya hua?' Bhairon, who had climbed out just as Ali had bent down and bitten Sharma, looked back inside and switched on the interior light, alarmed. It looked as if a bloodbath had taken place in the front seat (Sharma had waved his hand around spraying blood all over the place), and Sharma was half slumped out of the open door.

'Come here, come here quickly,' he shouted in panic at the other two, who had barely caught a glimpse of a shadow flitting out into the jungle as Ali fled. 'The little bugger tried to kill Sharma!'

The little bugger had by now reached Hari Pani again. Keeping well in cover, he cupped his hands around his mouth.

'Peeolo! Pi-lo-lo!' he called.

And up in their cave hideout, Shikha and Sunny grinned delightedly and exchanged high fives!

'Yess man, yess! You did it dimplechick! You sure did it!'

'Yes! Now let's get him up here pronto, shall we?'

Shikha called again, and then briefly flashed her torch, as Ali looked up towards the sound. He was up with them in a trice, dirty, dishevelled, smelling of Begum, but utterly delighted.

'Shikha memsahib! Sunny sahib!' he grinned, as Shikha gave him a hug, and Sunny swaggered up.

'About time you got here, pardner,' he drawled, shaking his hand, 'what took you so long?'

Ali's eyes widened.

'Bolta hai! He speaks!' he stuttered.

'You better believe it Ali, you better believe it!'

Shikha often wondered how they would have managed to spend that first night in the cave, without Ali. The wiry little boy obviously had done things like this before, and was perfectly at home. He collected an armful of twigs, and built a fire at the far end of the cave, near the narrow opening through which Sheba's cubs had nearly fallen. Thankfully, the smoke went straight out through the opening, and the flames could not be seen by anyone watching at Hari Pani. Shikha lit a few candles too, which made the cave seem quite cozy indeed, hoping that no one would notice their dim glow from below. Ali disappeared briefly and returned, armed with a stout stick and hunkered down near the fire: he would make sure nothing happened to his friends that night. They ate some fruit and biscuits, as the noises of the jungle night filtered in to them from outside.

The bullfrogs were in great voice, as were the shrill crickets and cicadas, and much to Shikha's horror half a dozen bats flew off suddenly from the roof of their cave. Somewhere in the ravines a tiger called and a sambhar belled in alarm. Occasionally Shikha flashed her torch around the cave to check that no snake or other nasty creature crawled in to share their food and shelter.

'Ali, do you think it is safe here?' she asked at last. 'What if a tiger or bear decides to check in for the night?'

'Then they'll have to go back! This place is full!' Sunny was categorical.

'They'll smell the fire and won't come,' Ali said. He looked curiously at the children. 'Also there is already the smell of a tiger or leopard in this cave. They might smell that and run away.'

'Oh, Ali we forgot to tell you!'

And they spent the next hour or so telling Ali about their incredible encounter with Sheba's cubs.

'Nahin ho sakta! It can't be!' he said, disbelievingly. But then he saw the tattered remnants of Sharifa's hamper, and the shredded cushion and wasn't quite so sure anymore. Then he told them his story, and about poor Begum lying in the back of the jeep.

'What? They've killed Begum?' Shikha was appalled, and soon very close to tears. How well she still remembered her first encounter with the fierce tigress – guarding her kill from those tree pies and giving her the willies with her growls and snarls. She set her jaw determinedly. 'We've got to make sure they don't escape!' she said. 'That's the least we can do for poor old Begum, now.' Ali nodded.

'They won't go anywhere today,' he said. 'They know I have seen Begum. So they want to kill me. They'll be searching for us tomorrow. We'll have to do something,' he said, and yawned. He was tired to the bone. Then he glanced outside the cave.

'Dekho!' he said, awestruck, 'jugnu! Look – fireflies!'

The bushes just outside the cave were festooned with them, crawling all over the leaves and twigs, blipping their frosty green lights. And then, suddenly a host of them came flying over, winking their little lights, and danced over the bush.

'Awesome! Just awesome!' whispered Sunny staring at them in wonder.

'Yes, Sunny! Aren't they beautiful!' Exhausted he curled up next to Shikha and put his head in her lap. He was out like a light. Ali's head too had dropped to his chest and his eyes were closed. Yawning, Shikha took Ali's stout bamboo from his limp hand, placed it next to her, and stared fascinated at the fireflies. She would keep the first watch. And then wake up Ali for his share of 'dooty'. It was going to be another long night.

19

SHARIFA ARRIVED AT SHERGARH HOUSE AT SEVEN THAT morning, alarmed and anxious. Had Shikha baby or Sunny sahib fallen ill? She had received a message at the hospital that she should go to the house as soon as possible. She had stopped at her own house on the way, to check on Ali, but as usual, the little loafer was nowhere to be seen. Probably he had gone to play with the children – at any rate she wasn't in the least bit worried about him. But worried she did get when she reached Shergarh House. For one, there were strange tyre marks all over the driveway and road, it looked like a whole lot of vehicles had come and gone from here very recently. She frowned and looked at the house. It stood, eerily silent in the gloomy grey light.

'Shikha baby? Sunny sahib?' Sharifa stared in alarm at the open door to the children's room and then rushed in. There was a bolster on the bed, but no signs of the children. She checked out the bathroom, her heart pounding, and then went into the lobby.

'Veena memsahib?' she called, looking up towards the

bedroom where she had been staying. She scuttled up the spiral staircase and entered the bedroom.

Empty. The cupboard was open and bare. The bathroom was empty – of everything. Veena memsahib had packed her bags and gone! Had she taken the children with her? But then why send a message to her telling her to come here as soon as possible? And where would she take the children? For that matter where was Ali?

She went down again and began searching the children's room. Shikha baby's knapsack was missing, as was Sunny's. The clothes spilled out of the cupboard untidily, not the way she had folded them and left them. So, they had packed hastily. Then her glance fell on the bedside table where Shikha baby had kept the photograph of her parents. It was gone! Had the children run away? But then, where was Veena memsahib? Why had she packed up and disappeared? Sharifa went back outside to take a look at the tyre tracks. She had not been married to the best tracker of Shergarh for thirty-five years, for nothing. She could read the tracks in the jungle as well as he could. First, she went to the shed and stifled a scream.

The Gypsy was gone!

She studied the tyre tracks in the damp mud. Certainly there had been one or two more vehicles apart from the Gypsy. And there was a clear set of tracks that led towards the Shergarh Tiger Reserve. She followed them until the cement gatepost, where she discovered the smashed padlock, and a clear set of tyre marks that she recognized as belonging to the Gypsy. In addition the strange tyre marks that often drove over them. Something bad had happened, and some ancient instinct told her that the children were in danger. It seemed clear that they were in the tiger reserve. She had better get back to Aslambhai and tell him. He would know what to do.

She reached the hospital at around ten o'clock and explained what she had found at Shergarh House. Alarmed, Aslambhai sat up in bed.

'But why should she go into the reserve?' he asked, bewildered. Shikha baby might swim at Hari Pani, but to disobey such a strict rule – and enter a park when it is closed – she wouldn't do that.

Unless ... unless she was forced to. Or she was frightened. Sharifa had mentioned to him how upset Shikha had been about Veena aunty and the school business. Maybe she had just run away inside to escape having to go to school. He shook his head and frowned. From what he had known of her, it didn't seem to be the sort of thing she would do. Something had scared her. Scared her so badly that she had taken Sunny and the Gypsy and fled. He nodded and looked at his anxious wife.

'Mujhe lagta hai – I feel,' he said slowly, wagging his beard. 'I think that the small tigers of Shergarh are taking refuge in their sanctuary,' he said. 'Ab do kaam kar – now do two things: one, go to the headquarters and speak to Rana sahib on the phone. They will have his number. Tell him everything you discovered. Second, check the room of that Veena memsahib in the school. She is missing too!'

'And so is Ali,' Sharifa wailed, wiping her forehead with her pallu, worry etched on her face. Aslambhai smiled and nodded.

'Don't worry about that rascal,' he said. 'He's probably with Shikha baby and Sunny sahib. Now go, and return later and tell me what happened.'

It was half past eleven by the time poor Sharifa reached the headquarters of the tiger reserve. Here they told her that the assistant field director had gone off to Shergarh town, but was expected back shortly. She waited an hour and then told the range officer that he better pick up the phone and ring Rana sahib immediately.

'But … but I can't do that!' the man said, infuriatingly. 'It is an out-of-station call and I need authorization!'

'Emergency hai – it's an emergency!' Sharifa yelled. 'Can't you see that? Those children have run away into the forest and you say you can't call!'

'Those kids are probably having a picnic,' said the range officer. 'Wait till they return and then we can shout at them. I can't disturb Rana sahib for nothing! Besides, let's wait for the assistant director to come!'

The assistant director eventually rolled up at half past two, sleepy with too much rice and beer in his belly. Sharifa was blunt.

'If you do not pick up the phone and call Rana sahib immediately, I am going to the police station to complain!' she shrilled. 'To complain that the children are missing – probably inside the reserve, and that you are not willing to do anything about it! If Aslambhai had been well he would have been inside searching for them now. Ab phone karo – now call up!'

Startled by her aggression, the assistant field director, who was a bit of an easy-going fool, shrugged his shoulders.

'Okay,' he agreed. 'But if this is a false alarm, you will have to answer!'

But it was six in the evening before contact could be made with Rana sahib, who was in Delhi, and staying with Dipti.

'Hello?' he said, frowning, and trying to understand what the faint but shrill voice at the other end was saying. 'Who is this?'

'Sharifa, sahib! Aslambhai ka Sharifa!' Sharifa shrilled.

'Sharifa? Is everything all right? Is Aslambhai all right?' Rana frowned. It would be too bad if anything had happened to Aslambhai.

'Theek hai sahib. He is all right sahib,' Sharifa said, and then dropped the bombshell. 'Shikha baby aur Sunny sahib raat se gayab hai! Shikha baby and Sunny sahib have been missing since last night! They've taken the Gypsy and gone into the reserve, it seems. That Veena memsahib is not here either. Bori-bistar layke gayab. She's taken her luggage and gone!'

'What?' Rana shouted, not believing his ears. 'What did you say?'

'Bachche gayab hai, sahib – the children have disappeared, sahib!' sobbed Sharifa, breaking down. 'They're probably in the jungle somewhere!'

'Right!' said Rana, thinking fast on his feet. 'Assistant director ko phone do – give the phone to the assistant director!'

'Hello? Hello, sir?'

It was too late. Somewhere along the way, a jagged bolt of lightning speared down and shattered a vital link in the exchange. The phone went dead.

'Oh dammit!' Rana clicked off his phone. For the next fifteen minutes he tried steadily to ring Shergarh Tiger Reserve. He frowned. What was Shikha doing in the tiger reserve when it was closed? That didn't seem to be like her. Oh, yes, he knew that she had learnt to drive on the sly – and had let that pass because he knew it could be an asset in the jungle. But she would not flagrantly disobey the laws of the park. No way. And not take her little brother with her!

'Joginder!' he shouted. 'Start packing! We're going back to Shergarh. The children have disappeared! Something has happened!'

'What? Have you informed Binoy?'

'Oh, dammit – I forgot! He's here in town! Do you know where we can contact the fool?'

'Dipti said there was a reception being organized in his

honour at the hall where his exhibition was being held, today. He's done very well, apparently.'

'The hell with his art-shart! Come on, let's go. He's going to learn something real now!'

At the hall, Binoy chacha was looking decidedly uncomfortable as he was surrounded by a gaggle of fleshy socialites, who took him by his arm and tinkled like idiot bells in his ear. Dipti stood nearby and grinned wickedly. If only the children could see this, she thought, raising her camcorder and recording the event. Their uncle was becoming a big name in art circles. Some Japanese crackpot had just bought twelve of his paintings for a vast sum of money. The press was going gaga over him. And he, poor fellow, hadn't a clue as to how to handle it all. He lit up beedi after beedi (sending off fire alarms until they turned them off), which, for some strange reason, greatly delighted the women around him (many rang their chauffeurs on their cellphones to order packets of beedis from the nearest paanwalla), and thought about his peaceful studio in Shergarh, and … Shikha's cheerful greeting as she charged in dishevelled and dusty after a day in the jungle, with the news of all the wonderful things they had seen that day. And usually, deliberately with Sunny on her hip, because she knew it annoyed Veena.

'Oye Binoy!' shouted Rana as he barged into the room, Joginder aunty panting by his side, her chins wobbling like jellies. 'Where are you?' The hubub in the room died down as everyone turned towards Rana.

Dipti looked up alarmed. What were her parents doing here? It was not their sort of scene at all. Her father had located Binoy and barged his way past the fleshy ladies, muttering 'excuse me, excuse me please!' She followed him at once, and looked at her mother's ashen face. Something was wrong.

'Binoy – I just received a message from Sharifa. The children have gone missing since last night!'

'What? What do you mean?' Binoy looked bewildered.

'It seems they have run away inside the park. They've taken the Gypsy. Did you know Shikha could drive?'

Bemused, Binoy chacha shook his head. 'No. But … but I left Veena with them.'

'Ah, yes, she's gone too! With bag and baggage, according to Sharifa. I don't like it Binoy, I don't like it! I'm leaving for Shergarh right away! If they're inside the reserve they are my responsibility!'

'Papa, if you spoke to Sharifa, did you tell them to begin searching the park?' Dipti asked. Her father shook his head.

'The phone went dead and still is. I tried all the way from your house to this place. And knowing that fool of an assistant director he won't move his butt until he has a written order.'

'Er … right,' said Binoy chacha, suddenly dazed and seeming to get the drift of things. He reeled. He had failed again! The children had run away! He had failed to give them a proper, secure home! He had failed to look after his own brother's kids! As always, he had tried taking the easy way out, and now they were gone! What good was all this painting-shainting if he couldn't even give two children a happy life?

'Binoy, are you all right? You've gone absolutely white!' Dipti said, taking his arm, and looking concerned. 'Sit down here for a minute and have a glass of water!'

'Er … yes, thank you,' he mumbled, looking gratefully at her. 'That Veena!' he mumbled. 'She seemed so concerned about them. But where has she gone? Has she taken them somewhere?' He got to his feet. 'I'm coming to Shergarh with you!'

'But this … this party?' Rana said, pointing to the people who were still coming in, including a large Japanese delegation.

'Bhaadh me jaaye – they can go to hell!' snapped Binoy chacha grimly. 'Come on!' But he still needed Dipti's steadying hand on his arm to steer him out of the hall and into the big Sumo taxi waiting in the porch. His guests stared open-mouthed, as the organizers ran behind him squeaking plaintively, 'But sir, but sir, where are you going?'

It was eight o'clock in the night.

The squall that had put out the telephone system had done far more damage than just that. It had sent many huge old trees crashing down on the roads leading out of Delhi to Shergarh – at the best of times, a twelve-hour car journey. The resulting jams were horrific, and on several occasions the cab driver said he wanted to return. It was only by threatening him that Rana kept him going. But by dawn they had only done about a hundred kilometres. There was no way they would reach Shergarh Tiger Reserve until early in the evening. Thankfully, the cab driver had understood the urgency of his passengers, and once he knew that children were involved, became more cooperative. He even agreed to take turns driving with Rana. At the back, sandwiched between her mother and Binoy, Dipti stared out at the wet ribbon of road and thought about Shikha and Sunny and Ali and the tigers of Shergarh. 'You're a sensible kid, Shikha,' she prayed. 'Just don't do anything foolish! Please, child!' She hardly realized that she was still holding on to Binoy's hand. He, it appeared, had turned completely to stone.

Their mud-spattered Sumo roared into Shergarh Tiger Reserve at three thirty that afternoon, after a hair-raising drive. The place was in a state of total confusion. Late the previous evening, a tired out Sharifa had peered into Snail Snot's room in the school. It was empty, but locked. If only her little Ali had been around, he would have found a way of getting inside. She went around the building and found the outside door to the bathroom that adjoined the room. It was unlocked. She entered and looked around. The bathroom had been used by men, she guessed judging by the shaving stuff on the shelves. She went inside the room. Empty. But there was a peculiar smell in the closed-up room. The smell of something dead and that of a strange chemical. She wrinkled up her nose and opened the cupboard. There were men's shirts hanging from the railing, so obviously Randhir and (maybe) his friends had been staying here while the woman stayed at Shergarh House. But just where was the stink coming from? Was there a dead body in the room? The children? Her heart pounding Sharifa peeked under the bed. A large gunny bag had been stuffed underneath it. She pulled it out, breathing hard. The stink was from here. Oh, please, please let it not be the children she prayed, and with trembling fingers undid the top.

And screamed!

The grimacing face of Raja looked up at her from the bag, but he had no eyes! Only an open mouth and his huge yellowing fangs!

Within hours the police were swarming all over the place, turning it upside down. The assistant field director was jumping around as though he had got a platoon of fleas in his shorts, not quite knowing what to do. The phone lines were still dead.

'Find those children, you fool!' Sharifa had screamed at him. 'They are in the reserve somewhere, they have been there for two days and you have done nothing!'

The police had sent wireless messages regarding the missing vehicles, but poaching was not exactly a high priority case with them. And they had refused point-blank to go into the reserve to look for the children. For one, there were wild animals in the jungle, and secondly, the roads would be impassable soon; what if they got stuck inside? Thirdly, no one could really be sure that the children were in the park. No one had actually seen them go in. Once they caught the poachers, they would know what had happened to the children. Poor Aslambhai raved and ranted in his bed, his blood pressure shooting up dangerously, and had to be sedated.

At around two that afternoon, the assistant field director finally gave the order that Shergarh Kila and the Chhota Mahal area be searched. The search party was still out when, much to his relief, Rana roared up and demanded to know what the hell was going on.

'Papa,' Dipti had said, halfway through their nightmare drive. 'If they are inside the reserve, Shikha will be at Hari Pani! She loved that place!'

'Right!' now shouted Rana to his assistant and losing no time at all. 'Tell those fellows to go to Hari Pani! Immediately!'

He jumped behind the wheel of his Gypsy.

'Comc on!' hc shoutcd, looking at thc bank of granitc grcy clouds looming over the horizon. 'Hurry up! We have to get there and back before it rains. The roads will be impassable then!'

Joginder aunty promptly got in beside him, and Binoy chacha and Dipti climbed in at the back.

'Not you all!' roared Rana, exasperated. 'I meant the forest guards!'

'I'm coming papa, whether you like it or not. And so are the others I think. Now get moving!' Dipti said.

Joginder aunty suddenly jumped out. 'Wait!' she yelled. 'Let me get some food and water. Those children must be starving if they are inside!'

'Papa, there is a first-aid kit in the Gypsy, isn't there?' Dipti asked, as her father banged his hands on the steering in impatience.

He nodded. 'God forbid that we need it!' he said. 'If anything has happened to Shikha and Sunny, someone is going to pay!' Then he jumped out and returned with a powerful looking rifle. 'Someone is going to pay!' he muttered. 'That lovely girl and her little brother!' He started the engine.

Four forest department Gypsys and jeeps, four motorcycles and the Canter full of forest guards (it's entire working fleet), roared through the gates of Shergarh Tiger Reserve, slithering and sliding down the slippery roads that led to Hari Pani. At the very earliest they would reach Hari Pani by six thirty that evening – just as darkness would be falling. That is if, it didn't start pouring before that, in which case they might not reach Hari Pani at all.

In any case, none of them knew whether they were already too late or not.

'What have I done?' muttered Binoy chacha, running his fingers wildly through his hair. 'What have I done? If anything has happened ...'

'Just keep your fingers crossed Binoy!' Dipti said, hanging on to dear life as the Gypsy bounced and bucked. 'And give Shikha some credit. She's a smart gutsy kid! You would have known that if you had bothered to get to know her.'

'I did know it, that's why I let her go into the jungle in the first place! I knew it was good for Sunny too. But I just hope I get another chance to know them better,' he said, shaking his head. 'She plays the piano so beautifully.'

'I think,' said Dipti softly, 'that we all need Shikha as much as she needs us.'

The convoy roared on through the darkness as over the ridge, mauve sheets of lightning flashed and thunder shook the hills.

It had been a long day for them, and was not yet over. And for the small tigers of Shergarh, hiding out in their cave, it had been a make or break day, too.

20

SHIKHA AWOKE AT ABOUT FIVE THIRTY THAT MORNING (WHILE the Ranas and Binoy chacha were battling through the jammed roads still far away from Shergarh) and blinked sleepily. Just where was she? The ground was hard and she was stiff – oh yes, this was Sheba's cave! Next to her, Sunny lay curled up tightly, and near the entrance to the cave, with his stout stick next to him, watchman Ali slumped, fast asleep like all good watchmen. She propped herself up and brushed hair out of her face as the events of the previous day flooded back. Outside, she could hear the jungle come to life: somewhere nearby a red junglefowl crowed, and grey partridges were standing on tiptoe somewhere yelling 'pateela! pateela! pateela!' She yawned and stretched, and quietly crawled to the entrance, careful not to disturb Ali. At the back of the cave, near its 'rear door' the fire had long gone out. Carefully Shikha peered through the mesh of branches and leaves that covered the mouth of the cave from prying viewers below.

Hari Pani lay in peace, a deep emerald green. The

lapwings and dabchicks were already busy getting themselves breakfast and a wild boar rootled about the muddy edges, snorting and grunting. Up in the great trees that surrounded the pool, the langurs were already feeding earnestly, occasionally driving off flocks of plump green pigeons that exploded with a clatter of wings. Shikha scanned the area with her binoculars. The Gypsy stood silently where she had left it, and there was no sign of their pursuers. Had they given up and driven off? And surely Binoy chacha would turn up today and start searching for them. Okay, Shikha, think girl! What would be the best plan for the day? She looked around, taking stock. They had a bottle of water left, two packets of biscuits and half a loaf of bread. Not bad – at least they wouldn't starve. The milk had gone bad and, wrinkling her nose in disgust, she threw it out. She glanced up at the sky – it was quite overcast and looked as if it might rain in a bit. Well, they could always catch some fresh drinking water then. There was Hari Pani too, but it would be better to leave that as a last resort. Okay, they could hunker down here for another day. But after that things would get difficult. They had Ali, of course, and he knew how to catch birds and things, but Shikha couldn't imagine herself roasting a piglet or a partridge over a fire, cavewoman style! Well, if they were really starving maybe …

But suddenly she remembered yesterday's single most significant event. With her heart back in disco mode, she went up to Sunny and shook him gently.

'Hey Sunny, wake up!' she whispered. Wake up and please, please say something. Like you did all of yesterday! Please let that switch still be on.

Sunny stirred.

'Good morning toodledumps!' she said brightly, crossing her fingers and toes.

'Mmm notatoodleumps!' he mumbled automatically opening his big black eyes. 'Dimplechick!'

A few minutes later they had a rather frugal breakfast of bread, biscuits and water. Ali, squatting on his haunches, seemed quite unsatisfied by the fare. There was so much out there in the jungle they could eat – wild berries, fruit and even grubs (some could be quite delicious!). Also, he could easily trap a few partridges and those roasted over a small fire would be divine! He'd have to get busy that day, he thought, grinning happily at the prospect. But there were other matters that had to be dealt with first.

'Ali,' Shikha suggested shortly afterwards. 'Do you think you can slip down there and check what the enemy (what else were they?) are up to? I mean, if they've gone, we can go down to Hari Pani and have a swim at least!'

He nodded. 'Abhi aata hoon – I'm just coming,' he said and vanished eel-like down the path in a trice.

The enemy in fact had spent a much worse night than the children. For one, they had not come prepared for an extended camping trip into the jungle – and all the two jeeps had yielded as far as food and drink were concerned was a packet of stale chips and two bottles of water. Secondly, the jeeps had been cramped, and the carcass of the poached chital doe (not to mention poor Begum) had begun to stink.

'Throw it out!' Sharma had said, looking green about the gills, at about eleven that night. His wrist hurt, and he was feeling nauseous.

'If we throw it out, it might attract a tiger,' Bhairon said.

'So good! We can shoot that too!'

'But we may need it for ourselves,' Bhairon pointed out. 'I don't know how long it will take for us to find that wretched little bugger!'

'I'll kill him personally if we do!' Sharma said viciously. 'When do we check out the Gypsy to see if the kids have returned to it?'

'Give them another hour. Even if they're there it would be nice if they were fast asleep. What a surprise!'

In Randhir's black jeep, Snail Snot and the slimeball were also trying to get comfortable without much success.

'Please close all the windows properly, Randhir,' Snail Snot said tearfully. 'God knows what kind of wild animals will come out at night. And the night air is unhealthy.'

'Those bloody kids!' the slimeball muttered. 'They need to be beaten! I hope they meet a tiger!'

Snail Snot sniffed. 'The things I've done for that girl,' she said. 'But really I feel sorry for the little boy. To be left all alone in the world with a sister like that! It's worse than being left with a tigress!' (Little did she realize what a compliment she had paid Shikha!)

At around midnight, Bhairon stretched clumsily and cautiously opened the door of the jeep.

'Come on, Sharma!' he whispered hoarsely, flashing his torch. 'Let's give those sleeping beauties a little surprise!'

But of course there were no sleeping beauties in the Gypsy.

'Do you mean to say, they are somewhere outside in this jungle in the middle of the night?' Snail Snot asked, looking around fearfully, and jumping as somewhere in the ravines a sambhar belled.

'Yes,' said Bhairon. 'They've probably found a hiding place nearby. Somehow I feel they won't go far from the car. We'll resume searching the place properly tomorrow.'

They went back to their vehicles, and Bhairon hefted the stinking chital carcass out of the back of the jeep. 'Let's get some sleep,' he said thickly, holding his nose.

At six they were still fast asleep when Ali crawled stealthily up to their vehicles and peeked in through the windows. He saw the carcass of the doe – already humming with bluebottles – and wrinkled up his nose. Then he went back up to the cave to report to Shikha. She was staring absently into the distance, her thoughts apparently far away, a frown on her face. Then her face cleared and she grinned.

'Ali,' she said, 'I have an idea. A rather wild idea, but if it works …' She leant forward and explained what she had in mind.

'So do you think we can pull it off?' she asked. 'Do you think it will work? It's dangerous and wild, but if it works … Do you think you can do it?'

He beamed at her. It was an idea right up his street. 'Koshish karte hain,' he said, 'we'll try!' His eyes were bright.

'Come on,' Shikha said getting up. 'Then we better get cracking. Before they wake up! Come along toodledumps we have work to do!'

'Right away! Right away!'

They slipped down the ridge path and vanished down one of the jungle paths beside which the bamboos soared. Two and a half hours later, they returned to their cave, scratched, bruised, dishevelled and sweaty. 'Let's hope it works,' Shikha said, 'now we just have to wait for the opportunity.'

Stiff and cramped, and having only dropped off to sleep in the wee hours of the morning, the 'enemy' awoke creaking and groaning at eight thirty. They shambled out of their vehicles, for a conference, irritable and hungry.

'I say, we search the area once thoroughly and then beat it,' Bhairon suggested. Frankly he'd had enough. And Sharma nodded. He was convinced he was going to get tetanus or rabies maybe and he needed to see a doctor quickly.

'First,' said the slimeball pointing to the humming carcass

of the doe. 'I think we'd better remove that from open sight. If any search party finds it here – we're done for. The tiger skin is quite safe under the gunny bags – they'll have no reason to search the jeep. Secondly, and more importantly, that boy is still on the loose. Veena says he is the grandson of one of the best trackers in the place. So it is quite likely that he can find his way to a checkpost or to the border. I think we need to find him regardless. Let's forget the other two – in any case I don't think they'll survive in this forest for another day. If they already haven't been killed by a leopard or tiger.'

'Hai!' Snail Snot wailed. 'Poor things!' She might well have said, 'serves them right!' because that's what she sounded like she meant. She imagined the dramatic tragic scene she could enact with Binoy.

'We looked everywhere! We went without food and water for two days! But the jungle had swallowed them up. I told you Binoy, I told you a thousand times – don't let them go into the forest! Now see what has happened!'

'Dimplechick, the enemy is in sight!' drawled Sunny from the cave entrance, where he had been keeping watch. 'They're down below near the swimming pool!'

Down below the search had begun. Bhairon and Sharma took one side of the pool, while the slimeball and (a very reluctant) Snail Snot took the other. They beat the bushes with sticks and branches, peered into the hollows of trees (where it would be impossible for a monkey to hide, forget about children), and looked up into the branches. While one person beat the bushes, the second stood by with a gun. All they found was an irritated cobra, which reared up and hissed, causing Sharma to shout with fright and back heavily into Bhairon, who nearly shot his head off. By the time they regained their wits, the cobra had slid into Hari Pani and disappeared.

The slimeball Randhir, who fancied himself as a tracker, kept looking for footprints, which he might have found had they not been smothered by the light drizzle that had fallen early that morning. Sweaty and tired two hours later, they regrouped again.

'Right,' said Bhairon, pointing upwards with his gun. 'Now we check those two caves up on that cliff.'

'But surely they wouldn't be so stupid!' the slimeball said. 'Caves like those are ideal hiding places for animals.'

'Then that is exactly the sort of place that Shikha would hide in,' Snail Snot said, viciously. 'Come on, you fellows.'

'Babydoll, they're coming up,' Sunny warned, and the children watched with horror as their pursuers began climbing up towards the narrow ridge path.

'I just hope they don't see this cave,' Shikha said, going pale and looking around. Ali, too, was looking alarmed. If the enemy came right up and found the cave, they'd had it. They'd be hopelessly cornered. And once he was discovered along with the others, then they would be in the same danger as he was. They would kill them too.

'Hey, Sunny, where are you going?' Shikha whispered, as Sunny crawled at top speed to the back of the cave, and began wriggling towards the opening at the far end (through which, Sheba's cubs had tried to escape). He looked back, his eyes bright.

'Just checking the back door,' he grinned.

In the event the opening (shaped rather like the eye of a needle) at the rear was easily wide enough and he had no problem getting through. Cautiously he looked around, and then whistled low and long.

'Will you look at that!' he muttered scrambling to his feet and putting his hands on his hips. He was in another small cave, the entrance to which faced the other side of the ridge. Quickly he turned around and rejoined the others, his face red with excitement.

'Dimplechick, Ali, there's another cave back there!' he said. 'We can go there. They won't be able to follow us. They're all so fat!'

Shikha got down on her hands and knees and looked at the slit. Would she be able to squeeze through? Sunny was pint-sized, Ali was an eel and could wriggle through anything, but what about her?

'Aa rahe hain – they're coming,' Ali hissed, slipping into the cave and looking scared. The enemy was in the first cave already – the one Shikha had backed out of because of its bats. The second cave was inaccessible anyway. But would they discover the third cave, higher up on the path? Would the great bush (where the fireflies had danced) be able to hide the entrance? It was too risky to assume it would.

Ali made up his mind. 'Main jaata hoon! I'm going,' he told a startled Shikha. 'I'll just dash down past them full speed and disappear. That will distract them and they'll come after me. If they find us together then they'll kill you too!'

'No way, Ali!' Shikha shook her head determinedly and grabbed him by the wrist. I've got a better idea. Do you think you can squeeze through that slit back down there?'

Ali took one peek and grinned.

'Bilkul, absolutely!' he said.

'Good, now go and take Sunny! I'll follow!'

A shout from outside caught their attention.

Tracker slimeball Randhir had spotted something!

'Look!' he yelled excitedly, pointing to a sheltered section of the path, beneath an overhang. 'A tiger's pugmarks!'

Bhairon shouldered his gun. 'Stop shouting!' he said, as Snail Snot went white as paneer. 'Do you want to wake it up?'

'The tiger's gone,' said Randhir. 'But there are children's footprints over it! And one set of barefoot ones. That blasted boy is with them! There must be another cave nearby! We've found them!'

Bhairon and Sharma, guns at the ready, stalked up the narrow ridge path, with the slimeball following, and Snail Snot huffing and puffing behind him. (This was not her sort of thing at all.)

Of course they found the cave, concealed as it was by the firefly bush.

'So that's where they're hiding!' Bhairon said, nodding with satisfaction looking around.

'We've got them!'

'Cornered them!'

'That Shikha really is a wild animal! Hiding in a cave! And her uncle thinks she's very smart!' (That of course was Snail Snot.)

'Hmm ... it means we'll have to get rid of all three of them,' Bhairon said, glancing doubtfully at Snail Snot. 'He's sure to have told them about the tiger skin.'

She nodded. 'It is a jungle after all,' she said chillingly. 'Very dangerous for little children! I told that Binoy a thousand times!' It suddenly struck her that if the children died in the reserve it would serve her purposes perfectly. One, she would have gotten rid of them for good from Shergarh House, and would enable her to gush sympathetically all over Binoy all the more, and win him over completely. And secondly, it would discredit the tiger reserve and the Ranas – maybe the authorities would shut it down (who would want to visit a tiger reserve where protected tigers ate innocent children?) and certainly they would get rid of the Ranas. Perfect. Also, she would have got her own back on that Shikha who had made trouble from the moment she had met her.

'Right,' said Randhir. 'We knock them out and dump them

in places where either the crocs or tigers will finish off the job. No shooting!'

The other two nodded.

'Uffff … I'm so fat!' groaned Shikha as she squeezed herself through the slit. On the other side, Sunny and Ali took her hands and yanked.

'Come on, you can do it!' Sunny exhorted, quite the little champion now. But it was the sound of approaching footsteps that spurred Shikha on, and with a final mighty wriggle she plopped through to the other side.

She put her fingers on her lips and tiptoed to the entrance. Well there was no way of climbing down from here – not without a rope. The rock face dropped sheer and smooth below them, for maybe a hundred and fifty feet. But the cave was big enough to easily accommodate all three of them.

'We left all our stuff back there!' Sunny whispered.

'Too bad,' Shikha whispered back. 'Now come on, let's stand together here right against the wall. If they peek through the slit they won't be able to see us.' They flattened themselves against the wall of the cave, not daring to breathe, Shikha with one eye fixed on the bats that had begun moving about uneasily on the roof.

With a clomping and thudding of boots Bhairon and Sharma barged into the first cave, guns at the ready (just in case Shikha had organized a tiger to receive them!), followed by the slimeball and Snail Snot.

'Come out you little shits!' Bhairon shouted, not believing that the cave was empty of all kids.

'They've been here!' Sharma yelled, kicking at the cushions. 'They've left their stuff behind!'

'That Shikha!' complained Snail Snot. 'Yes, this is her knapsack and that is little Sunny's.' She bent to pick it up.

'Don't touch it!' barked Sharma. 'We leave everything as it is. If we take things back and show them to their uncle, someone might suspect us. This way, we've seen nothing, we know nothing! Let the jungle keep its secret!'

'Damn kids should be somewhere nearby!' muttered Bhairon looking around wildly. 'They couldn't have gone long. They've left all their stuff.'

Sharma did a quick check outside. 'No way out of here except down the path we came up,' he said. 'They're still around here somewhere!'

The slimeball was examining the remains of Sharifa's hamper.

'What the hell happened to this?' he asked. 'And to those cushions! Looks like they've had a pillow fight here!'

'Kids!'

'Hey look!' the slimeball's voice rose excitedly. 'There's an opening back here, where a fire's been made!'

Bhairon and Sharma were down beside him in a flash.

'Do you mean to say they've escaped through that?' Bhairon asked, getting flat down and trying to peer through it.

'There is nowhere else they could have gone!'

'Can you get through it,' Snail Snot asked.

Bhairon tried. He was just a quarter of the way through when he got hopelessly jammed and began suffering from claustrophobia.

'Pull me out!' he shouted, his eyes rolling wildly. 'Pull me out! I'm stuck!'

It took a considerable effort from Sharma and the slimeball to pull him out. Quickly Bhairon went to the entrance and breathed deeply.

'Could you see anything? Snail Snot asked him. Breathing deeply Bhairon shook his head. 'There seems to be another cave back there. Either they're there, or they've escaped from the other side. We'll have to go down the ridge and over to the other side to check it out.'

Sharma, with his painful hand, had not even bothered to get down to try and squeeze through. And of course, it was completely out of the question for the slimeball (even if he was slimy, his paunch would get in the way) and Snail Snot.

'At least take another look,' Snail Snot urged, but Bhairon had had enough. He marched into the cave with his gun and shoved the barrel through the slit as far as it would go. Jammed up against the wall, Shikha watched with horror as the barrel tip thrust evilly through, pointing first straight out and then at as sharp angles as possible on either side. Instinctively she put her arms around both the little boys, jamming them against the cave wall, covering them with her own body, and whispering to Sunny and Ali to cover their ears. She put one hand over her left ear, and jammed her right ear against her shoulder to give it some cover and shut her eyes. She looked quite like a mother hen protecting her chicks.

BANG! BANG! BANG! Whing! Zing! Sweeeee!

The shots, so close and in such a constrained area, seemed ten times as loud and echoed and bounced horribly around, followed by the terrifying whining of bullets or rock shrapnel screaming past. All three children let out muffled screams, which luckily were drowned by the sound of the shots echoing around the cave and cliffs. The poor bats exploded in a flurry of panic. Acrid smoke filled the cave, but luckily dispersed immediately, sucked out through the entrance by the current of air passing through the slit.

'That should give them something to think about!' Bhairon growled viciously, getting ready to let off another salvo.

'Don't be a fool!' snapped the slimeball catching his arm.

'We can't shoot them remember? We don't even know if they're there!'

'Aiii,' Snail Snot moaned, fanning herself. She too had got the fright of her life, and the bats in the cave had expressed their own fright on her in no uncertain way.

'Wipe it off!' Sharma said, horrified by the bat shit slithering down that mighty bosom. 'It can give you leprosy!'

'What?' Snail Snot squeaked frantically. 'What?'

The enemy withdrew. In the other cave, Shikha held both Sunny and Ali tightly, tears streaming down her face. All three of them were trembling, the shots still ringing in their heads. After a short while she let them go and they stood close, their eyes glued to the opening.

Then Ali stared at Shikha in horror and pointed. 'Khoon! Blood!' he said faintly and went ashen.

Shikha looked at her bare brown arm and gasped. There was a nasty gash just below where the arm joined the shoulder and blood was streaming down. One of the bullets, or possibly a splinter of rock, had nicked her. She had been shot! She hadn't felt a thing when it had happened, but now could feel a sharp searing burning in her arm and shoulder.

'Oh my God, I've been shot!' she whispered, sitting down, not believing her eyes.

'Yeh baando – tie this!' Ali said urgently, unwrapping his headband and giving it to her. 'Doosra cave mein first aid para hai – the first-aid kit is in the other cave. We can get it when they've gone.'

Dumbly Shikha nodded, as mechanically she began doing up her arm with Ali's help, feeling her warm wet blood trickle between her fingers and the tears roll into her dimples. Steady on Shikha girl, steady on! It doesn't look too bad, there's no horrible bullet hole, it probably just grazed past you, but, but, but …

you've been *shot* girl, Shikha girl you've been shot by a gun they shoot tigers with! For God's sake you've been shot! Stop it girl, stop it this instant and get on! You can't go all to pieces now! And don't faint. Whatever else, don't roll up your eyes and faint! Don't faint! Fainting is not allowed! Fainting is forbidden! Think … think of what Sheba would do if she had been shot and injured! She wouldn't roll up her eyes and faint! She would come out roaring and slaughter the enemy. She would tear their throats out and squash that fat blimp like she was a maggot! She would not let a gash on her shoulder bother her! And she would not faint, no! Shikha shook her head to clear the woozy feeling that had begun to come over her. That's it girl, you're a real kickass chick! Come on now make Sheba proud of you!

'Okay,' she whispered at last, wiping her eyes and smiling through her tears, her face still ghostly pale, but her jaw firm. 'They've gone! It's all right now, Sunny, I'm fine!' Poor Sunny had been looking at her dazed as she had done up her arm. 'Please Sunny say something, don't let those shots turn off your talk switch!' She looked down at him. 'Are you okay toodledumps?' she whispered. He looked up.

'Dimplechick I am not a toodledumps! How many times do I have to tell you that? Are you all right? Those assholes have shooted you!' But it was a rather small teary voice.

'I'm fine, fine! Yes, I've been shot but I'm fine now! Okay, Ali, now listen. Go back in there and get that rope from the bottom of my knapsack.'

'Rassi? Rope? Why?' Ali asked puzzled. He peered over the edge. 'You want to climb down this?' he asked horrified and stepping back quickly.

'No,' Shikha said. 'We just hang the rope over the edge. If they check out the cave from the other side and see the rope they'll think we have escaped.'

Ali nodded slowly and grinned. Shikha was smart! Really smart! And what courage! Even after having been shot she could think on her feet. She had been shot and he had almost fainted!

'And Ali,' she said, her brown eyes flashing, a little colour returning to her face. 'I think it is time we took the battle to the enemy! It's time we struck back! Time to kick some ass, guys! Thank God we made our preparations! Come on, fellows, let's do it for poor old Begum and Sheba!' she said tossing her head and trying to make the world stop spinning.

Ali's grin became even wider. Shikha was his best, most courageous friend in the whole world, no doubt about that!

'Come on,' she said. 'Let's get to work.' For a second she looked sad. 'Poor old Begum,' she said. 'But it will be her revenge, in a way, I suppose! Come on, let's go get her!'

It was hell squeezing back through the opening with her injured arm, trying to prevent it from getting scraped against the rough rock face. Back in their 'home' cave she cleaned her gash with some of their precious drinking water and antiseptic, dabbed it dry and dusted it with antibiotic powder, wincing and squeezing her eyes tightly shut as the antiseptic stung. She bound it with cotton wool and gauze bandage (thank God they had brought the first-aid kit, she thought) with Ali's help. It burned and stung and hurt like hell, the pain shooting up and down her arm and shoulder, but it couldn't be helped and she just gritted her teeth, or bit her lips and shut her eyes (from which, the tears squeezed out anyway) and thought of Sheba when it got too bad. She was white as chalk by the time she had finished and dizzy, but stuck her jaw out obstinately. No fainting Shikha girl, absolutely no fainting, backbone of steel, that's the way kick-ass chick! Just sit down for a bit, pour some water over your head, breathe deeply and think ahead about what had to be done, and most of all, think about Sheba who took no shit from anyone, not even that big doofus Shahenshah who was twice her size.

At last she got to her feet, swaying slightly before steadying herself.

'Come on, guys,' she said huskily. 'Time to kick some fat ass!'

About an hour later, sweaty and tired (because they hadn't eaten anything for more than a day now) Bhairon and company trudged laboriously around to the other side of the ridge, and after much battling through bushes and scrub, located the cave entrance on the sheer ridge face. Bhairon whistled.

'Look at that! A rope! They've climbed down and gone! The girl has guts! I'll give her that!'

'But how would Sunny have climbed down?' Snail Snot asked, still peering down her bosom from time to time to check that it was free of bat shit (and leprosy).

'Knowing that girl she would have taken him on her back!' the slimeball said. 'Now what?'

'Now we get the hell out of here! God knows where they've gone! Besides they won't last out another day or so.' Sharma looked up at the darkening sky. 'It looks like rain. The roads will soon be impassable. They'll be stuck here. That's it. Now let's get out of this godforsaken place before we get stuck here too.'

'What do we tell the girl's uncle?' Snail Snot said.

'That we searched and searched for two days but found no traces of them! That probably they have been killed by wild animals! Their precious tigers!'

They were trudging their way to the jeeps, when they froze in their tracks.

'Aaaaoom! Arrooom! Aaargh!'

'Tiger!' whispered Bhairon, going pale behind his stubble and slipping his gun off his shoulder.

'Nearby!' said Sharma looking around nervously. 'In that bamboo grove!'

'It must have smelt that chital!' the slimeball whispered, bumping his paunch into Sharma's back and looking over his shoulder. 'I told you we should have got rid of it!'

'Let's get to the jeeps, please! Snail Snot pleaded tearfully. 'Aaaiie!' she squealed.

'Aaaoom! Arrooom! Aaargh!'

'The bugger seems to be following us,' Bhairon muttered, turning around and walking backwards.

'Come on, let's get to the jeeps!'

'Oye Sharma, this is a golden opportunity. If we can bag the fellow at least something will come out of this wild goose chase!'

'Aaaoom! Aargh!'

They hastened back to the jeeps and Snail Snot clambered in quickly. The three men stood outside.

'Oye Randhir, you'd better take a gun too,' said Bhairon, delving into the back of his jeep and producing an ancient double-barreled shotgun.

'Shouldn't we just wait in the jeep for it to come to the chital?' the slimeball asked, not very willing to walk back into the damn jungle.

Bhairon shook his head. 'He won't come to the carcass once he smells us. We have to intercept him on the way. Before he gets suspicious.'

'You can't leave me here alone!' Snail Snot protested tearfully. 'Randhir!'

'Just stay here and wait for us! Nothing will happen.'

The three men set off in the direction the last call had come from.

It was a narrow jungle trail that ran through a dense bamboo grove. Ideal tiger country.

Fingers on triggers, Bhairon and Sharma led abreast of each other, while the slimeball brought up the rear, looking uncomfortably over his shoulder every now and then. Tigers always attacked from the rear!

They had walked perhaps a hundred metres down the trail, without hearing anything when the tiger called again, from right ahead.

'It's there!' whispered Bhairon, indicating a dense bamboo thicket.

'Aaaaoom!' called the tiger. *'Aaaargh!'*

Their guns at the ready the men advanced, step by step. (The slimeball of course, would have preferred to be on elephant back like the maharajas of old, but thought of the story he could tell about the time he stalked a crazed child-eating tiger on foot alone in the jungle ...)

It was Sharma who spotted the tiger. He caught a glimpse of a movement just beyond two huge bamboo clumps and there it was! Its tawny coat, so beautifully camouflaged by the light and shade of the bamboo that you could lose it forever if you took your eye off it for a second.

'There!' he murmured. 'There he is!'

The tiger moved slightly again. The other two spotted it.

Three sets of barrels pointed directly at it.

Bhairon took a step to the side, to see if he could catch a glimpse of the great head. Ah, that was better – he could see an ear quite clearly now. Right ear or left ear? It seemed to be the right ear. He shifted his gunsights slightly to the left and lowered it just a fraction. Okay, right between the ears. The tiger had its back to them, and suddenly appeared to be very still. It had also stopped calling.

He squeezed the trigger.

Sharma and the slimeball fired off their shots in quick

succession, the latter giving it both barrels. None of them heard the rapid 'clickshuttukclickshuttukclickshuttuk' as Shikha, flat on her tummy on the forest floor, and well to one side from where she got a perfect angle (and this time, nowhere in the line of fire!), pressed the shutter of her faithful camera. She knew she had to get the timing right – and especially not click before the shots were fired because that would give her away; so she had waited until Bhairon had fired and then pressed the shutter button. Right beside her, straw dangling from the side of his mouth, Sunny nodded slowly, approvingly. Some sister she was! No one could pussyfoot around her!

In the bamboo clump the tiger collapsed soundlessly. No roar, no snarl, he just seemed to have fallen down and died. The forest exploded in a cacophony of alarm as birds burst out of branches and langurs shrieked hysterically and the peacocks honked dementedly. But not a peep from the tiger!

'Got him!' Bhairon muttered and stepped forward carefully. He raised his hand warning the others. 'Careful. Never get too close until you are hundred per cent sure it is dead. Otherwise you will be!'

He picked up a stone and flung it at the bamboo clump, his gun at the ready again. No angry snarl, no mad charge by a wounded animal. No movement. He relaxed.

'We got him!' he exclaimed exultantly. 'Come on, let's see what we have shot!'

They went forward. The tiger appeared to have been lying in a tiny clearing a little beyond two huge clumps of bamboo that bent low over it, as if paying homage to the great dead beast. There was just enough space for Bhairon and Sharma to stand side by side between the great clumps to view their kill. The slimeball peered over Sharma's shoulder. They stared in incomprehension at the sight in front of them.

The tiger they had shot had apparently not eaten for a long time. A very long time indeed! It appeared to have some weird disease too. It was weirdly lumpy in some parts and impossibly skinny in others. As if it had no flesh at all. No flesh and no bone. Only skin. And no eyes either. Empty eye sockets gazed up into the canopy. Eye sockets that once contained the baleful amber eyes of a tigress called Begum.

And then suddenly the forest floor appeared to come alive with snakes. Lianas and vines writhed and twisted like a den of enraged lunatic serpents, rising up from the forest floor, coiling tightly around the men's ankles, hips and arms.

Boiiing! Swish! Boinng! Swish!

'Yaaaa!'

'Haaalp!'

'What the ...?'

Suddenly Bhairon and Sharma found the very ground disappearing from under their feet. They were somersaulting topsy-turvy through the air, being smacked hard across their faces by sharp bamboo leaves. And then, dangling upside down over the forest floor, their fingertips just barely able to brush against the ground, their arms pinioned to their sides.

'Aaaaooom! Arroom! Argh!' the tiger called again, hideously close as the slimeball turned around his eyes bulging, the gun frozen in his hands.

A lithe wiry boy on the jungle path was twirling a liana round and round his head rapidly.

Swish! Swish! Swish!

Sharma brought up the gun.

'Hi uncle slimeball, I'm here!' The lilting voice of the girl seemed to come from the forest floor itself to his left. Sharma swivelled his head and the gun towards it.

Ali let fly. But alas, in his excitement he aimed too low. The rock in his sling cannoned straight into the slimeball's massive paunch and disappeared inside it.

Whooosh!

'Oooof!' The slimeball staggered backwards, his face purple, his mouth open and sat down with a bump and a gasp, the gun (which he had not reloaded) falling aside with a clatter.

Swish! Swish! Swish! Ziiiing!

This time the pebble hit home, right in the tilak spot. Slimeball's eyes rolled up and he keeled over.

'Oye!'

'Abbe!'

Bhairon's and Sharma's upside down eyes nearly popped as they tried to focus. If only they would stop swinging around like marionettes – it made Bhairon dizzy and Sharma sick. And they couldn't believe what they were seeing (upside down).

A pretty but wild-looking girl – that damn girl obviously – and a little boy had risen up from the jungle floor, the girl with a camera dangling around her neck and a bloodstained bandage on her arm, her hair full of dead leaves. She and the little boy and the little bastard they had been after, ran up to where the slimeball had fallen and were looking at him.

'Right Ali, let's have the vines and lianas,' the girl said.

The little bastard unwound lengths of vine from his waist and expertly began trussing up the unconscious slimeball.

'Okay, Ali, now the gunny bag!'

'You got it,' said the pint-size, struggling over with the gunny bag in which poor Begum's skin had been stuffed.

'Ooof, he's heavy!' Shikha groaned, as she and Ali struggled to manoeuvre the slimeball's dead weight into the big sack, feet first. Inch by inch they managed, but they were both bathed in sweat by the time they had finished. And Shikha's arm had started hurting horribly again.

'Okay, Ali, now bind up the sack!' Shikha panted. 'Leave the neck open so that his head can stick out, She stepped back and giggled as Ali finished off thc job, winding lengths of liana round and round the sack. 'He looks like some gross carpet worm!' Shikha snorted, dissolving helplessly into giggles.

And then the three children were clapping their hands and exchanging high fives and hugging each other on the narrow jungle trail.

'Ten out of ten, Ali, ten out of ten!' Shikha yelled, gleefully giving the delighted boy another thump on the back. 'You're brilliant! Just brilliant! One hundred per cent brilliant!'

'We got 'em where we want 'em, eh!' drawled the pint-sized little fellow, strutting about triumphantly and thumping his fist into his palm.

'Ali, I think we should finish the job,' Shikha said, and grinning Ali nodded. From around his waist he produced the rope they had used to fool the men at the cave entrance. The vines and lianas had already bound the men's arms to their bodies, but a little extra help with some rope would do no harm. The slimeball they had already taken care of.

'Ummmgh!' mumbled the slimeball opening his eyes groggily and staring in disbelief at the huge rhinoceros beetle crawling past his eyes. He had a rather thick skull and Ali's pebble had knocked him out but briefly. Now Ali swiftly gathered a handful of leaves and plugged his mouth with it. 'Ummffff!'

'Let us go!' Bhairon said hoarsely revolving slowly, his eyes rolling wildly as he eyed his gun, lying far away as the moon.

'No,' said Shikha sweetly. 'You've killed Begum and you tried to kill us!' She glanced at her bandaged arm. 'And you shot me,' she said, 'now it's our turn!'

'What are you going to do?'

'Leave you here, of course,' she said smiling. 'Let the animals decide what they want to do with you.'

'What?' squeaked Sharma, 'but you can't do that! There are tigers and leopards and bears here!'

'It is their jungle, uncle,' Shikha pointed out, her eyes turning frosty. 'But first I would like to take some more pictures for my journal! Now smile!' She raised the camera and clicked off a few quick shots.

'You're crazy!' Bhairon said wildly, as the slimeball's eyes nearly popped out of his head. He was going purple and the damn beetle had begun crawling over his eye.

'Have a nice day,' Shikha said pleasantly, as Ali stuffed the mouths of the other two with leaves (some of which had hairy caterpillars still on them!). He couldn't resist giving Bhairon's ear a mighty parting yank. Bhairon looked as though he would have a stroke.

'Come on fellows, let's go,' Shikha said, and the boys followed her like a pair of puppies.

'That was great,' Shikha said, 'it worked like a dream!'

Ali of course had set the traps (with Shikha's help), but they had realized that it was unlikely that they would bag more than two of the enemy at one go. So Ali had used his liana slingshot as backup. Aslambhai could put out the eye of a deer at five hundred metres, Binoy chacha had once said. His grandson had inherited his talent with the slingshot.

Shikha frowned. 'Now what do we do about Snail Snot?' she asked. She had been looking forward to a showdown with Snail Snot on a one to one basis, had she come along with the others, and was a trifle disappointed at having been robbed of her chance.

Ali shook his head. 'Darti hai – she's scared,' he said. 'She won't go anywhere! Ek, do call gaadi ke paas marte hai – we'll make one or two calls near the car! She won't budge!'

'Good,' Shikha said, suddenly weak in the knees. Her arm was hurting badly, too, and she suspected it had started bleeding again. Occasionally a wave of dizziness would hit her and she swayed as she walked. 'Hey Sunny, how are you doing toodledumps?' she asked breathlessly.

'Fine!' But she could see he was tired. She was bone weary too but, poor chap, he must be completely fagged out. Even Ali was looking a little peaky.

'Tell you what, Ali. Let's take a break. I'm just about deadbeat! You make your calls that'll keep Snail Snot snug in the car, and we'll go back to the cave for a rest. Oh shit, we should have checked those guys' pockets for their jeep keys.' She was mumbling now, fading fast she knew, and Sunny suddenly had gone quiet. 'We'll do that tomorrow. Take their jeep and drive off. I'll probably crash the jeep if I try and drive it now,' she said, talking more to herself and glancing at her arm.

They had had a hell of a day and very little food.

They stumbled out of the grove and peered towards the black jeep. No sign of Snail Snot looking out of the windows. Ali crept up and took a quick peek in. He grinned and nodded, and put his hands on his cheek. Asleep. Snail Snot was asleep.

'Aaoom!' Ali called. *'Aroooom!'* He fled like a skimming stone towards Hari Pani, where Shikha had already reached with Sunny and was dunking her head in the water to clear it of the dizziness. They looked back. No sign of any movement from the jeep. Snail Snot was dead to the world, or hopefully crouched petrified on the floor of the jeep.

'She must have taken her own sleeping tablets,' Shikha muttered. 'Come on, Ali, I don't think she'll have the guts to leave the jeep by herself. It'll be dark soon.'

'Aaaaooom! Aaaroom!' The call came from unpleasantly close by – from near their own stranded Gypsy.

The children looked at each other, startled, Ali with his mouth open wide.

'Sher!' he murmured disbelievingly. 'Sher aaya – a tiger has come! Asli sher – a real tiger,' he clarified.

'Let's get out of here!' Shikha said, 'back to our cave. We have the backup cave there even if it decides to come inside! Come on! Hurry!'

They stumbled back up the narrow ridge path and shot back into their old familiar cave. It almost felt like home. (Shikha had even propped up the photograph of her parents in one corner and the cushions and candles gave it a homely touch.)

'What a day!' Shikha muttered, panting as she collapsed on one of the surviving cushions. She opened the last packet of (chocolate, thank God!) biscuits, impatiently brushing away the ants that crawled all over it and gave Sunny and Ali most of them, saving just two for herself. They tasted divine!

A few minutes later, and revitalized almost instantly by the chocolate, Sunny was flat on his tummy keeping watch on the black jeep.

'Hey babydoll, will you get a load of this!' he said, suddenly flipping over and beckoning her with a forefinger. 'Bring your camera!'

'Umm what is it Sunny?' she asked tiredly and settled down beside him.

'Oh,' she gasped. 'It's him again! Shahenshah!'

She watched as the beautiful tiger stepped cautiously towards the carcass of the chital, looking about, as he did so, in a rather guilty manner. Jeeps he had seen plenty of times before; they didn't bother him. But whom did this nicely rotting chital belong to? He licked his chops. And he had heard a tiger calling from around here, so he had better be careful.

'Aaaaroom!' he called loudly to show who was boss. *'Aaargh!'*

Inside the black jeep, Snail Snot had stirred and her blood turned to water.

That was ... that could only be ... and where were the men?

Feeling more confident, Shahenshah stepped closer to the carcass, then changed his mind and walked straight up to the black jeep. He raised his tail high, turned his back stylishly towards it and let loose a hissing jet of spray straight through the open window.

Just as Snail Snot raised her pale pasty face above the rim to take a peek at what was going on outside, her mouth falling open with fright. She got the jet stream straight in her face, as powerful as if from a fire hose, but far more pungent.

'AAAiieeeee!' she shrieked and spluttered and fell back in a dead faint.

Poor Shahenshah bolted as if he had been shot! With one mighty bound he was back in the forest, racing away. Mighty macho man had got the fright of his life!

Clickshuttukclickshuttukclickshuttukclickshuttuk! Shikha kept her finger pressed firmly on the shutter button and tried desperately to keep her hysterical giggles at bay. She knew it was a bit too dark but just had to try. It was too good to miss! Talk about poetic justice! At last she put down the camera and gave herself up to her hysterical giggling.

She was dead tired now, ready to collapse, and weak with hunger, pain and loss of blood. But she knew there was one more thing she had to do. Wearily she rose to her feet and took her torch.

'Okay buster, cover me!' she drawled at Sunny. 'I'm going down to have a showdown with Snail Snot.' Sunny nodded slowly.

'Yeah, you do that dimplechick. She has it coming!'

Shikha walked down a little way, and stopped. If she was going to do this, she might as well do it properly, she thought. She went back to the cave.

'Toodledumps, come on. We're going to do this together. That'll show her! You come too Ali – I'll need you!'

With Ali following, they made their way down and cautiously up to where the black jeep was parked.

'Okay, Sunny,' Shikha whispered, picking him up with an effort, groaning as she tried to protect her injured arm. 'Ooof you are getting too heavy for this!'

He was about to protest, but really was very tired and it always felt so nice to be carried. She took a step forward and knocked softly on the window of the black jeep, flashing her torch inside.

Pale as vomit, her hair bedraggled, Snail Snot's petrified face slowly came up from the floor. Her eyes grew round with horror and she looked as if she were about to scream again, but the wild girl staring at her from outside shook her head and put her fingers on her lips. And with one finger indicated that she lower the window. On her hip, jutting out at that vulgar angle as always (with her midriff peeking out shamelessly), was the little boy she had wanted to take away last night. Slowly Snail Snot lowered the window and peered out fearfully.

'Hello, Veena aunty,' Shikha said pleasantly, hitching up the little boy firmly. 'I want to ask you a question. Did Binoy chacha know that you had planned to kidnap Sunny? Now please answer truthfully. I have the letter you see, and Shahenshah might come back'. She grinned wickedly. 'You see he's my boyfriend now – I'm sorry if he was rude, but that's just his way. Now tell me, did Binoy chacha know? ' The little boy in her lap grinned and nodded.

The woman scrabbled about a bit and opened her purse. She took out the letter and saw Sunny's grotesque drawing (rather like Binoy chacha's work!) of her being eaten by a tiger. 'Aiiii' she wailed, putting a plump hand on her bosom, and then looked up at the wild children outside. She shook her head. 'No,' she whispered. 'Binoy didn't know anything. Shikha beti, where are the others and what are you going to do?'

'Nothing,' Shikha said tiredly. 'The others we have taken care of; don't worry about them! But I want you to stay inside this jeep and not move. I've told Shahenshah to keep an eye on it and he's pretty upset that you scared him by screaming. You hurt his ego, you see, and no macho tiger likes that very much! Shaitan will be laughing at him.'

'Mm … macho tiger? He's a macho tiger? Your boyfriend is a macho tiger? You have a tiger boyfriend called Shaitan?'

Shikha nodded. 'He's just one of them,' she said and turned to the darkness behind her.

'Right, Shahenshah pumpkin, tell her what you think and what you will do if she so much as puts a foot outside that jeep, kittycat!'

'Sh … Sh … Shahenshah pump … pumpkin?' Snail Snot stammered, bewildered. 'Kittycat?'

'Aaaaooom! Aaarooom! Aaargh!' roared Ali from the dark, but looked around nervously, hoping that the real Shahenshah had fled far away!

Snail Snot clutched her hair and moaned. 'Hai! Hai! Hai! You have bewitched a tiger!'

'Goodnight aunty!' Shikha said pleasantly. 'Come on Sunny, let's go!' She turned on her heel, and with Sunny still clinging on to her, disappeared into the gathering darkness.

A few minutes later, back in their cave, all three of the children were droopy with sleep. It was six thirty in the evening, and the mauve twilight was deepening. The rain had stayed away, but it was damp and threatening. But Sunny was restless, still hyper from chocolate biscuits on a very empty stomach. At seven he arose and looked outside. The fireflies were back on the bush outside, hordes of them. He looked at his sister, stretched out on the cave floor, dead to the world, her face ghostly pale, breathing softly. He grinned and nodded. He would do it. It would make her look so funny.

At seven thirty Ali rubbed his eyes and yawned. He saw Sunny flit in and out of the cave and his eyes widened. He grinned. Good idea Sunny boy. He got up and putting his fingers on his lips began helping the little boy at what he was doing. Then he stiffened and Sunny looked up sharply. They could hear engines. Several of them, labouring and grunting their way up the final slope overlooking Hari Pani.

Sunny slithered to the firefly bush and peered through his binoculars, back in his favourite position. Beams of light lit up the rim of the ridge where they had left the Gypsy and near where the other two jeeps were parked. Then a Gypsy with blazing lights breasted the rim and jolted to a halt. It had a red light on its roof, and blue light on its nose. Two motorcycles skidded to a halt next to it.

'About time they got here pardner!' Sunny muttered to Ali standing up. The cops always turned up when everything was over. Well, not the cops in this case but anyway … More jeeps and a Canter had arrived and men were spilling out of them like peas from a packet.

Suddenly Hari Pani seemed to be full of people. And Ali grinned with relief. This time he would not have to duck out of sight of Rana sahib. And anyway there were so many others with him. Jogi memsahib and Dipti memsahib and Binoy sahib.

'Chalo,' he whispered taking Sunny's hand. 'Let's go down! Wake Shikha up!'

Sunny shook his head slowly. 'Better not disturb her,' he said solemnly. 'She's like a cobra when you wake her up! Maybe Rana uncle or Binoy chacha can pick her up and carry her down.' Shikha could be awfully crabby if woken up suddenly.

But they sent a couple of rocks clattering down the path as they stumbled down in the semi-darkness and that woke up Shikha. In the jungle, she slept lightly.

'Sunny?' Shikha said sleepily, raising herself on an elbow. Then alarmed by no answer, she got up and heard the voices of the people below at Hari Pani.

Down at Hari Pani Rana was breathing fire and brimstone. The woman they had found in the black jeep appeared to be absolutely bonkers; she was stinking of tiger piss and screeching hysterically about a tiger who was Shikha's boyfriend and that had apparently devoured three men and had made a dreadful pass at her on the specific instructions of the girl.

'A tiger made a pass at you, madam?' Rana shouted, not believing his ears and terribly derailed by thinking how that might have happened. 'No, no madam, he has made a piss at you definitely yes, that I can believe, but … but no tiger would make a pass at you! How he made a piss on you beats me too!' He shook his head wonderingly. And then got back on track:

'Madam, where are the children?' he shouted at her to no avail, holding his nose.

'Sahib, this chital has been shot!' one of the guards said, momentarily distracting him again.

Binoy chacha and Dipti had already searched the Gypsy.

'There's nothing inside it.' Dipti told her father.

'Sahib, yeh dekho – sahib look at this!' said another guard, who had been searching the second jeep thoroughly. 'Sher ka daant – a tiger's tooth!' Indeed it was, one of poor Begum's big killing canines that had fallen out when Shikha and Ali had stuffed her into the gunny bag and dragged her off, while the enemy had gone off to check the second entrance to their cave hideout.

Snail Snot was still screeching hysterically. 'Get me out of here! Get me out of this horrible jungle!' she screamed. 'Kill all the tigers in the world! Burn that girl who bewitches tigers! Only then will we be safe!'

'But … but Veena what happened here?' Binoy chacha stammered, almost beside himself with anxiety and completely bewildered. 'And where are the children? Did a tiger get them?'

'I wish one had! I hope so! Especially that Shikha! Do you know she's been roaming around the jungles with tigers as her boyfriends? That's what she's been doing all these months here! They come to her when she calls them! She's bewitched them! She's evil!' she shouted, shaking a fist.

Poor Binoy chacha looked as though he had been shot and had to sit down rather suddenly!

Dipti took him by the arm and led him away.

'Come away Binoy dear, she's not well,' she murmured.

'Arre dekho!' one of the guards suddenly shouted pointing towards the ridge path.

Swaggering down it, a twig dangling from the corner of his mouth like a cheroot, flashing SOS on Shikha's torch, Sunny came down the mountain to meet the cavalry, as it were, with Ali smiling uncertainly behind him.

'Abbe dekho! Udhar dekho! Hari Pani ki rajkumari! Look! Look there! The princess of Hari Pani!' the forest guard said again, lowering his voice in awe now.

A girl was making her way uncertainly down the path a little way behind the two little boys, weaving slightly from side to side.

A slim, very dishevelled girl in denim shorts and a blouse. In her hair, which cascaded wildly around her shoulders, she wore living emeralds. Hundreds of them, winking on and off like lights. And floating around her head, were more emeralds, shimmering and winking like a halo that had come alive.

Sunny had passed the time in the cave by catching the fireflies on the bush (the female ones, waiting for their mates) and letting them loose in his sister's hair while she slept. Assisted very ably by Ali. When Shikha stumbled down the path after the boys, still half-asleep, unaware of the fireflies in her hair, the male fireflies wafting over the bush watched in horror as their mates sort of waltzed off down the path. They followed, winking their frosty green lights desperately around her head.

'Shikha!' Dipti whispered too, stunned even to be relieved. 'Binoy look! She's got fireflies in her hair! Hundreds of them!' She rubbed her eyes in disbelief. And Binoy chacha looked, frozen with astonishment and wonder. He had never seen anything so beautiful in his life.

Beautiful or not, there was no getting away for Dipti from the little figure that came charging straight at her and nearly knocked her off her feet.

Sunny!

'Bachche!' Joginder aunty shrilled as she caught up with the rest, huffing and puffing. Dipti hugged Sunny hard and lifted him up, kissed him, put him down and he raced towards Joginder aunty, to be enclosed into another huge embrace. Ali stood shyly at a little distance and smiled, and missed Sharifa and Aslambhai.

Shikha suddenly seemed to come awake.

'Dipti?' she said questioningly. 'Am I dreaming or is that you? And Binoy chacha!'

'Of course it is babydolldimplechick!' yelled Sunny. 'Can't you see dumbo?'

Dipti smiled. 'And child, am I dreaming or do you always wear emeralds in your hair when you're here?'

'What?' asked Shikha bemused. She ran her fingers through her hair, and looked at the fireflies in her hand in astonishment.

'How did they get into my hair?' she asked automatically. Her faced cleared. 'Oh yes, toodledumps, do you know anything about this?'

'You look like a spacegirl!' he chortled. 'Which planet are you from?'

Suddenly to her immense surprise she found herself being hugged by, of all people, Binoy chacha.

'Are you all right my dear? Are you all right my dear?' he repeated again and again, stroking her hair and dropping the fireflies out of it like confetti. 'Thank God you're all safe! Thank God you're all safe!'

'Shikha, child, but Sunny's talking!' Dipti said, taking her into her arms.

Shikha grinned happily. 'Yes, Dipti! He found Sheba's cubs and was playing with them and just began talking again!' She looked at Dipti's incredulous face. 'It's a long story and I am very tired,' she said, her heart flying high. But Dipti had spotted the rank bloodstained bandage around Shikha's arm. 'What's this?' she demanded. 'Shikha, are you hurt?'

'A bit,' Shikha admitted, suddenly realizing how stiff and painful her arm was. 'They tried to shoot us in the cave,' she murmured, the tiredness coming back.

'Ah Shikha my dear, even here you look so lovely!' Mr Rana boomed, striding up with the old familiar twinkle in his eye and as if nothing out of the ordinary had happened, but hugely, hugely relieved. 'I always knew you'd be able to look after yourself and Sunny! And that rascal of course!' he added glancing at Ali.

'Papa, they shot her!' Dipti said in a choked, shocked voice. 'They shot her! They shot a child!'

'It's okay, Dipti. It's just a gash. I put some stuff on it from the Gypsy's first-aid kit!'

'What? Let me see that! Jogi come here – get the first aid out of the car!'

'Uncle, we couldn't have managed without Ali.' Shikha said wincing as Joginder aunty gently unwrapped her sodden bandage, her expression like Sheba's when she had returned to her cubs. 'He's the one who saved us. He trapped them in the jungle! God I'm so tired. Have you guys brought anything to eat? We're starving!'

There were shouts from the forest guards nearby and Mr Rana stomped off to see what the noise was about. He returned a few minutes later and looked at Shikha with that old sardonic expression of his. 'Ah, my dear, I suppose you wouldn't know anything about two fat stinking poachers we just found hanging upside down in the forest down that path, with guns scattered around them, another trussed up inside a gunny bag and a tiger skin that has been shot through the back of its head?' he asked.

Shikha grinned and shook her head. 'I think you better ask Ali about that,' she said. 'That's his area of expertise!' She giggled. 'But Dipti, that Shahenshah was very rude,' she went on. 'He squirted straight into Snail Snot's face! I photographed the whole thing but I hope it wasn't too dark!'

'And you my dear, are at the very end of your tether!' Dipti said, handing her over to Binoy chacha who literally had to hold her up. She went and put her arms around Ali.

'Thank you very much Ali, you have saved their lives. I

know they wouldn't have made it without you!' she said, hugging him hard and kissing him. 'Well at least not hanging two men upside down and stuffing another in a gunny bag like that,' she added grinning. 'Where did you learn to do such things? Come on kids, let's get back!'

'Umm ... all our things, the camera and stuff they're in the cave up there, ' Shikha mumbled pointing vaguely in the direction of the cliff, weaving drunkenly a bit and then leaning against Binoy chacha for support. 'Where the fireflies are.'

'Come on, come on, we'd better hurry!' Mr Rana yelled. 'If it starts pouring we'll be stuck here for three months and God knows how many more will end up hanging upside down!'

But Joginder aunty was not quite ready to go as yet. She strode up to where Bhairon, Sharma, the slimeball and Snail Snot stood, the men still bound by liana and flanked by several forest guards, her face like thunder.

'Which one of you had the courage to shoot at an unarmed child?' she demanded ominously. Without waiting for an answer she took a step forward, and raised a powerful arm.

The four slaps echoed like gunshots in the forest, causing the peacocks to honk in alarm and Mr Rana to jump and spin around.

'Jogi, enough!' he said. 'Come on, we'd better go!'

'I think we should leave them here! Joginder aunty muttered, still fuming. 'We'll pick them up after the rains have gone! See how they rot in the forest! Shoot at a child they will!'

'Don't worry Jogi, they're in very big trouble. Now come on!'

None of the children knew very much about the journey back. Sunny had passed out in Joginder aunty's lap. Shikha, happy between Binoy chacha and Dipti, just leaned over on to Binoy chacha's chest and was out, well not quite like a light because there were still a few stray fireflies winking in her hair.

And Ali found himself jammed willy-nilly next to Rana sahib in the front.

'Ah Ali,' Rana sahib said, patting his head kindly. 'Beta, you must teach me how to make those traps! Wonderful contraptions they are! Hmm … a family secret eh?'

'Neend aa rahi hai – I'm feeling sleepy!' Ali muttered and keeled over into the big man's lap.

21

SHIKHA SQUIRMED AND WRIGGLED DELICIOUSLY IN HER BED. Slowly she opened her eyes, and for a second wondered where she was. In that cave again? No. It seemed more like the big old four-poster bed at Shergarh House. She looked out at the now familiar view, but it was gone. Rain streamed down the windows, and curtains of water wafted lazily across her line of sight, completely obscuring her usual view of Shergarh Kila and its ridge. The monsoon had broken. But where was Sunny? He wasn't next to her. She blinked and looked around sleepily.

Dipti was sitting in the tea planter's chair, with Binoy chacha standing behind her.

'Good morning, Shikha!' Dipti said, smiling, and reached forward to kiss her. To her immense surprise, Binoy chacha did the same. 'You've slept for one and a half nights and a day. How are you feeling, sweetie? And Happy Birthday, child!'

'Ha … happy birthday? It's my birthday?' She was blank.

'Child, you must be the only fifteen year old to have forgotten her own birthday! Of course it is your birthday!'

'Where's Sunny?' she asked sitting up, and wincing at her stiff arm. 'And how … how did I get here? I don't remember anything!'

'Sunny's playing with Ali. He's already been out in the rain twice! Of course you don't remember anything. You just passed out with exhaustion. Binoy chacha had to carry you here. Sharifa threw a fit when she saw the state you were in and insisted on cleaning you up before putting you to bed. We had the doctor come yesterday and look at your arm. He even gave you a tetanus shot and you didn't stir! Now how do you feel child?'

'The arm still hurts a bit,' Shikha admitted. 'But I'm fine otherwise. Er … what happened to Snail … er … Veena aunty and the others?' She shuddered as she remembered those horrible glinting barrels poking through the cave entrance.

'They've been taken away. Snail Snot is obviously not quite okay in the head. Don't worry about them. Now come on, and open your presents, sweetheart!'

'Hi sleepyhead!' Sunny came charging in and cannoned straight into her.

'Hi toodledumps!' she shot back.

'Notatoodledumps!' he said. He bulged his eyes. 'So there dimplechick!'

'Okay toodledumps,' she grinned. 'And I'm not a dimplechick! Sheesh!'

'Ooof, you babydolls are all alike!' he said witheringly and disappeared.

A large gift-wrapped box was lying at her place in the dining room, with a card that said: 'Happy Birthday, Shikha dear. Lots of Love, Dipti and Binoy chacha'.

'Open it,' Dipti said, as Sunny gazed at it, his eyes large as soup plates.

Inside a gold and black box, beautifully packed, lay the

most stunning camera she had ever seen, with a fabulous zoom lens glinting blue and mauve.

'Wow!' she breathed. 'But it must have been so expensive!'

'You deserve it,' Dipti said. 'And since Binoy has done so well in his exhibition, we thought why not?' She glanced at Sunny, who had suddenly gone quiet.

'Ah, yes, Sunny bunny and this is for you,' Dipti said and produced another little box like a magician.

It was a smaller camera for him and he was just thrilled to bits.

'Er … Shikha,' Dipti went on, colouring faintly. 'I … er … we have something to tell you!'

'What?' asked Shikha, looking at her puzzled. Binoy chacha was gazing at the ceiling fan again.

'Er … Binoy chacha and I have decided to get married,' Dipti said.

'What? But … but …,' suddenly she remembered the lovely laughing portrait she had seen in Binoy chacha's studio – the only happy painting in the whole place, according to her.

'So what do you think?' asked Dipti, taking Binoy chacha's hand.

'I think … I think you should see the painting he's done of you,' Shikha said, grinning cheekily. 'He's hidden it in his studio, facing the wall!'

'What? Binoy?' Dipti was looking decidedly alarmed.

'No, no, no!' Shikha added hastily, going crimson. 'Don't worry, it's not one of those … those nangu-pangu things,' she said hardly daring to look at her uncle. 'It's very nice,' she finished lamely.

'I should hope so!'

'Er … when are you going to get married?' Shikha asked, desperate to get off the subject of paintings.

'Soon,' said Dipti firmly. 'The sooner he has someone to look after his life the better,' she said. 'Before he gets hold of people like that woman!' She looked at Shikha and grinned. 'Child, this will mean more changes for you and Sunny,' she said.

'What do you mean?' Shikha asked suddenly alarmed. Not the Paradise Valley Boarding School, please! Not any boarding school! Not yet!

'Don't worry, sweetheart. For the present, nothing will change. I just thought that during the monsoon, you and Sunny might like to come back to Delhi with us for a sort of holiday. You can meet up with your old friends and catch up with things.'

'But what about school?' Shikha asked faintly.

'You'll go back to school only when both of you are ready to,' Dipti said. 'Not before! You've had one hell of a time, child, for the last so many months. You need time to recover for yourself – you haven't done that fully as yet, you've been completely engrossed in looking after Sunny and keeping that female at bay. Now that Sunny seems to be getting okay in leaps and bounds, you will too.'

'So ... so after the rains we come back here?' Shikha barely dared to ask the question. Dipti nodded.

'If that's what you want! You will always have your work with the tigers here ...'

'I know,' Shikha said softly. 'Without them I would have gone crazy!' She looked at Dipti. 'They ... Sheba and Shahenshah and even Shaitan, they took my mind off all the horrible things that had happened but let me get used to them also bit by bit so they didn't hurt so much. And they helped me fight that Snail Snot too! Every time I had a fight with her (she glanced briefly at her uncle too!) I used to think of Sheba snarling at us when we got too close, saying "that's it kids, enough is enough not a step closer", and it helped me do the same! I thought about her after I'd got shot and of how she would have behaved if she had been shot and wounded while protecting Shaan and Shararat! It was the only thing that kept me from fainting!' She glanced at Dipti again. 'So that means that Sunny, Aslambhai, Ali and I can go into the tiger reserve just as we used to?'

'Yes, of course! But Shikha, in the long term this is how we thought things might work out,' Dipti went on. 'You and Sunny will go back to school in Delhi. I know you have lost a couple of years, but you have learnt a lot more here than you would ever had in school. Naturally, you'll live with us – in my house in Delhi, while Binoy will come and go from here. He's become quite a big-shot artist now, so will have to come to Delhi quite regularly, whether he likes it or not, and because we'll be there. During the holidays, of course we all come here. Now how does that sound?'

'Great!' Shikha said, her eyes shining. 'Just great! Mama and papa would be so happy if they knew.'

'Who knows, Shikha dear, maybe they do!'

Well, eventually that is how things worked out. Shikha and Sunny spent another whole year at Shergarh (well almost), having a wonderful time watching Sheba bring up Shararat and Shaan. Shikha's pictures of the cubs put any doubts to rest about whether the children had actually played with and fed the cubs or had imagined the whole thing. Those pictures made them instant stars with the forest department staff because they knew that no one, ever, had played with such young wild tiger cubs before in the temporary absence of their mother! Mr Rana had pursed his lips and said nothing, yet again the kids had had a mighty narrow escape, and Shikha's explanation that she was too overwhelmed by Sunny's recovery at that moment to have properly realized the danger they had been in just had to be accepted. The only thing that Shikha admitted (a little regretfully!) that she might have imagined, were the sightings of 'her' rajkumar and Badshah on the battlements of Shergarh Kila. (Though she did recall that she had seen him for the first time *before* Sharifa had told her the story about him, so that still puzzles her from time to time.) She never saw them again, and thought that it was probably a trick her mind had played on her to lessen her stress. (Sharifa still teases her about him, though.) Her pictures of the gang shooting at poor Begum's skin also went a long way in getting long jail terms for the slimeball, Bhairon and Sharma. That, and of course the bullet wound in her arm (which made it an 'attempt to murder' charge), the scar of which she is immensely proud of; there was no doubt that the shot had been fired from Bhairon's gun, the shells had been found in the cave and matched his unspent ammunition. Snail Snot never recovered her mental balance after having been squirted by Shahenshah. She had tried her best to get the children out of Shergarh House permanently, so that she could cozy up with Binoy chacha, and had suggested to her slimeball cousin brother that killing off tigers at Shergarh would be one way of discrediting the place – and the Ranas. (And he and his friends could make a fortune selling the skins and bones and other parts of the tigers.) If all, or most of its tigers could be killed, then what was the point of having a tiger reserve in the first place? Later, when the kids had disappeared inside the reserve, it had suddenly struck her that if they died inside the park, ostensibly at the hands (or rather teeth) of tigers, both her objectives would have been achieved. The children would be out of the way, and the park (and Ranas) thoroughly discredited. Who in the world would want a national park or tiger reserve where two tragically orphaned children had been eaten by the animals? There was another bonus too, which she realized when she found out how much money the children had inherited from their parents: if they died, it would all come to Binoy chacha, and with her in control of Binoy chacha, it would really all be hers. The villagers, whom she had tried to instigate to 'invade' the reserve, had been appalled by her attempt to kidnap Sunny. They had given up their agitation immediately; Shikha's care of and fierce devotion to her orphaned baby brother had become the stuff of legend in the village, thanks mainly to Sharifa's storytelling skills, backed by Aslambhai's highly embellished tales of how she had protected Sunny from danger and how she seemingly had some intangible relationship with tigresses as fierce as Sheba, who let her play with her cubs, and tigers as great as Shahenshah whom she had ordered to teach Snail Snot a lesson! Like, long ago, the relationship that the young tragic rajkumar had with his tiger Badshah ... 'She is the new princess of Shergarh, make no mistake about that,' he said, wagging his sunbird beard. Today, if Shikha goes into Shergarh village she is besieged by both the women and men and has no choice but to sit down and spend some time with them (much to Sunny's disgust) drinking lassi, and passing the time of day, something she quite enjoys doing.

The missing tigress Queen Victoria eventually showed up with four cubs in tow, and is another family whose fortunes Shikha is eagerly following. Her first love, however, will always remain Sheba.

Aslambhai recovered completely, and still lets Shikha drive the Gypsy in the reserve, which she does quite openly now and Mr Rana happily lets it pass. Ali has been devoured by Mr Rana, so to speak, and is being trained to be a forest guard. (Not that there is much for him to learn about jungle lore.)

Mr Rana and Jogi aunty have resigned themselves to the fact that Dipti has married a rather unconventional (but basically good) person, and have also realized that with her firm handling and affectionate nature (and love for the children) things would work out fine. They had always known that something was in the offing, so it really came as no great surprise.

Binoy chacha remains much the same, absent-minded, whimsical and not very talkative, but far more visibly affectionate than he used to be. He has set aside a small part of his studio for Sunny, and often they both emerge from it looking as if they have been painting each other rather than on canvases. And he loves to sit out on the verandah and listen to Shikha playing her 'scatterbrained birdwing jazz' on her piano, which Dipti calls, 'goosebump jazz'. (If painting could be converted straight into music that's what it would sound like.)

Sunny has recovered completely and talks (nonsense most of the time, according to Shikha) nineteen to the dozen. He's still not quite out of his American gangster movie phase, and still calls Shikha 'babydolldimplechick' (or the other way around) in public much too loudly, much to her annoyance. He is still a little embarrassed by his long 'period of silence and terror' as Shikha calls it; she remembers it with a shudder; he with a diffident shrug of his shoulders. He absolutely adores Jogi aunty who spoils him rotten at every opportunity. There is no doubt in anyone's mind that Shikha's care and the tigers of Shergarh were responsible for his miraculous recovery.

Dipti and Shikha remain thick as thieves. 'You,' Shikha told her once, 'are quite hopeless as a wicked aunt! Now had Binoy chacha married Snail Snot ...,' and dissolved into giggles.

'And you, Shikha sweetheart, remain as always, an enfant terrible!' Dipti said. 'Snail Snot! How did you think of such a name? And please remember to pick up all your and Sunny's swimming stuff from Hari Pani the next time you go there. I found this bright yellow inflatable tiger floating in the water! Papa will throw a fit if he finds out!'

Of course both Shikha and Sunny still miss their parents a lot but in a sort of sad-happy way, not a sad-unhappy way. And now Dipti and Binoy chacha are always there to cheer them up. (As are Shaan and Shararat.)

Ready for her first day back at her old school after an absence of two years, Shikha couldn't help feeling dreadfully nervous.

'I feel awful,' she told Dipti, 'I'm two years behind all my old friends. They might treat me as though I'd failed! Like a junior!'

Actually, the principal had changed during this period and the new one had wanted Shikha to drop yet another year, which would have put her three years behind.

'She's been away for so long, I think she needs to repeat a year,' she told Dipti. Silently Dipti passed over the three thick volumes that made up Shikha's tiger journal.

'Mrs Khanna,' she pointed out in her most flinty voice. 'In those two years, Shikha has learnt more than most kids in this school will learn in their entire time here and maybe the rest of their lives, and I am not discrediting you or the teachers here. Well, I'm not going to say any more, except spare some time to go through these. You'll know what I mean.'

Next day a rather ashamed looking Mrs Khanna handed back the journal. 'I'm sorry,' she said. 'I had no idea! I would give the girl a double promotion, but she has to sit for her boards. You're right. She need not worry about anything. Ever.' She stared at Dipti. 'I didn't sleep the whole night!' she added.

Now Dipti looked at Shikha and smiled. 'If they ever make you feel like that, or you just feel like that, think of Shergarh,' she said. 'Of how you stood there with Sunny behind you as Shahenshah walked past you. Of how you refused to give an inch to Snail Snot. Of those two days you spent inside, with Sunny and Ali, protecting them from those horrible men. Of how you tried to make sure that they would not be shot, and how you outwitted them. You know Shikha, not even Ali would have made it without you! You gave him the confidence to carry out your mad plan, even after you had been shot. There are not many adults who could have carried on the way you did, while carrying a gunshot wound in their arm! Think of Sheba and of why you like her so much even if she can be so terrifying. You know, you are really like her a lot. Just think of all these things and then put your "senior" friends in your place. How many of them would have come out with the flying colours the way you did?'

But the best was yet to come. In the holidays, children from Shikha's school visited Shergarh, and amongst them were some of Shikha's 'senior' friends, one or two of whom (especially Sunaina) had been rather snooty with her. They shut up quickly when Shikha drove them around (but nowhere near Hari Pani of course, which was private) in the Gypsy, awed by her knowledge and familiarity with the place and its tigers. And later at Shergarh House she showed them the pictures of herself and Sunny playing with Sheba's cubs (who they had just seen frolicking in the grasslands, great big handsome louts now, but still very much mama's boys!).

'Wow!' said Rini.

'They're so cute!' gushed Sunaina. 'I would love to have a tiger cub as a pet!'

'Shikha are they wild? It looks like a cave – their den!' Ms Nikita was frowning. She knew a thing or two about tigers (thanks mainly to Shikha). 'They look like wild cubs!'

'That,' said Shikha pointing, 'is Shararat, and the other one is Shaan! They're Sheba's cubs – the ones we saw fooling around this morning. And of course Shahenshah's cubs too!'

'The ones we saw this morning? Those huge tigers?' Sunaina had gone a little pale.

'But ... but where was Sheba at the time? Surely she wouldn't let you close to her cubs?'

'Oh,' said Shikha her face absolutely deadpan, her brown eyes deadly serious. 'Actually Sheba and Shahenshah had gone off hunting and asked us to babysit the cubs,' she said, watching Sunaina's horrified face. 'And they rewarded us well too,' she added keeping a straight face. 'You know that woman that had been bugging us and who tried to kidnap Sunny and send us to boarding school? Well this is what Shahenshah did to her when I told him! If you don't believe me just ask the people in Shergarh village!'

And she produced the photograph (rather dark but clear enough) of Shahenshah giving it to Snail Snot full in the face.

'So you see,' Shikha went on relentlessly and staring at Sunaina in that peculiar intense manner she had learnt from Sheba, 'Sunny and I have good protection here!'

'You said it babydoll!' Sunny said, swaggering into the room. 'Should I call Shahenshah on his cell?' He picked up his toy cellphone lying on the bed and punched a few numbers.

'Hey Shahenshah, you big doofus! How you doin' man? Babydolldimplechick here wants to call in a favour!'